Financing Regional Growth and the Inter-American Development Bank

The crisis of the current global financial order is challenging us to critically reflect on how this order has been driven, and the development outcomes produced by its central political and economic actors. There is a great deal of academic knowledge about the role of the international financial institutions, powerful states and capital markets in international development, but there is little understanding of how regional dynamics and regional institutions influence global governance and developing countries.

This book offers an independent and grounded investigation concerning the political economic role of Regional Development Banks through a study of the world's leading Regional Development Bank, the Inter-American Development Bank (IDB). The book examines the political economy of the IDB and its role in regional and national development during the neoliberalisation processes of the 1990s. In particular, the investigations explore the IDB's power in regional and national development – via its technical, political and financial interventions – to frame policy alternatives, absorb opposition forces, support specific coalition forces and justify a particular direction of development, all in order to legitimise specific political economic projects directed by market-led pro-reform coalitions aligned with global financial forces and financial development guidelines.

This book will be relevant to scholars and professionals interested in the international and regional political economy of development financing.

Ernesto Vivares is Research Professor in Political Economy and Research Methods, and Head of the International Relations programme at FLACSO Ecuador. He holds a PhD in International Relations from the University of Sheffield, and his research focuses upon the political economy of South American regionalism, development and conflict.

Routledge Studies in Development Economics

Financing Regional Growth and the Inter-American Development Bank

The case of Argentina

Ernesto Vivares

Routledge
Taylor & Francis Group

LONDON AND NEW YORK

First published 2013
by Routledge
2 Park Square, Milton Park, Abingdon, Oxon OX14 4RN

Simultaneously published in the USA and Canada
by Routledge
711 Third Avenue, New York, NY 10017

Routledge is an imprint of the Taylor & Francis Group, an informa business

© 2013 Ernesto Vivares

British Library Cataloguing in Publication Data
A catalogue record for this book is available from the British Library

Library of Congress Cataloging in Publication Data
Vivares, Ernesto.
Financing regional growth and the Inter-American Development Bank: the Argentine case in the 1990s / Ernesto Vivares.
pages cm
Includes bibliographical references and index.
1. Economic development—Argentina. 2. Argentina—Economic policy—20th century. 3. Financial institutions, International—Argentina.
4. Inter-American Development Bank. 5. Globalization—Argentina. I. Title.
HD82.V568 2013
332.1′538098209049–dc23
2012039542

ISBN: 978-0-415-66065-5 (hbk)
ISBN: 978-0-203-07392-6 (ebk)

Typeset in Times New Roman
by Book Now Ltd, London

Printed and bound in the United States of America by Publishers Graphics, LLC on sustainably sourced paper.

Contents

Illustrations

Tables

Figures

Summary

This book is an in-depth study of a central piece of the international financial architecture, the Regional Development Banks (RDBs), via an investigation of the Inter-American Development Bank (IDB) and its financially oriented role of development in South America and Argentina in the 1990s. Furthermore, it examines how the complex relation between the regional development finance and the international financial architecture come to frame the distribution of power and perils of development during the stage of global neoliberalisation of the region. To do that, the book explores the genesis, process and results of the IDB's interventions and role in the regional and Argentine context of neoliberal transformation in the 1990s through two case studies that reveal the complex political economic nature of these regional actors. First, the debt swap for the privatisation of electricity public utilities considered one of the icons of the convertibility regime–IDB–IFIs partnership; second, the bank's role in the decline of the neoliberalisation process via its interventions in the privatisation of social security and role in the international financial support to the Argentine governments during the crisis of 2001.

Applying a critical International Political Economy (IPE) approach, the book traces the dynamics of the Latin American political economy of development financing, situating the IDB's development mission and role within the framework of globalisation, regionalism and multilateralism. The investigation examines the structural forces shaping the nature of the IDB and its role and powers in the region throughout the period of the internationalisation of production and globalisation of development financing. And to show the IDB's changing development mandate, attention is drawn in particular to its interventions in the region in relation to its hemispheric, regional and global commitments, revealing the dynamics of its technical, financial and political capabilities.

Turning specifically to the case studies of the IDB's role in the consolidation and decline of the convertibility regime, the book examines the impact on development of what we call the power-balance legitimisation. That is, the RDB's development capacity – via its technical, political and financial interventions – to frame policy alternatives and to justify a particular direction of development, to legitimise a specific political economic project and to favour certain types of pro-reform support coalitions aligned with particular financial development guidelines.

Finally, the book aims to show the dynamic role of the IDB within the regional and domestic political economy, providing evidence concerning the exhaustion of the IDB's historical mandate as a result of a dominant financial focus of development challenging this historical institution to re-find its development mission in the region.

Acknowledgements

As the world is increasingly crossed by crisis and transformations, the questions concerning region, finance and development are, these days, increasingly converging in the academic and political debate as a complex central and growing area of importance that redefines all what we used to understand by 'development'. There lies the focus of this book, the changing political economic nature of development within a world and regional order, and the power and nature of a phenomenon that has received little academic study – regional development banking.

The book finds most of its origin in my doctoral work, accumulating plenty of debts with a large number of colleges, friends and family. First, I wish to express my gratitude to Jean Grugel, Tony Payne, Tony Heron, Georgina Waylen, John Smith, Rob Collins, and Sarah Cooke from the Department of Politics at the University of Sheffield, UK. I finished my early research with the experienced guidance of Jean and the timely advice of Tony Payne. Since then, Tony has been of invaluable support, personally and intellectually. To all the people at the Inter-American Development Bank who voluntarily provided information for this investigation I extend my most sincere gratitude and respect. Finally, this book is dedicated to all my colleges and in particular my students at the program of IIRR in FLACSO Ecuador.

I have also benefited greatly from the encouragement of my family. In particular I would like to thank Susana Vivares, my eternal support and friend, Maria Carreras, Ernesto Vivares, Elena and Valeria, all of whom have constantly kept me afloat during all these years. Finally, I want to thank Cheryl Martens and my sons Genaro Vivares and Ayel Vivares – to whom I owe everything. Throughout this process, they have made major sacrifices in order to enable me to go ahead with my work.

Ernesto Vivares

Abbreviations

AFJP	Private Pension Funds Administrators
ANSeS	National Administration of Social Security
AyEE	Water and Electrical Energy
BCIE	Central Bank for Economic Integration
CABEI	Development Bank of the Caribbean
CACM	Central American Common Market
CAF	Andean Development Corporation
CAMESA	Whole Electricity Market Management Company
CCGT	Combined-cycle gas turbine
CEPAL	Economic Commission for Latin America and Caribbean
CEU	Central Execution Unit
CGE	General Confederation of Business
CGT	General Confederation of Work
CPPs	Provincial Retirement Funds
CTA	Central of Argentine Workers
EAI	Enterprise for the Americas Initiative
EIA	Energy Information Administration. Official Energy Statistics from the US Government
ENRE	National Energy Regulator
ERP	People's Revolutionary Army
ESOP	Employee Share Ownership Program
FAR	Peronist Army Force
FDI	Foreign Direct Investment
FIEL	Foundation of Latin American Economic Investigations
FSF	Financial Stability Forum
FTAA	Free Trade Area of Americas
GATT	General Agreement on Tariffs and Trade
GDP	General Development Product
GEC	Guyana Electricity Company
G-7	Group of Seven
HRF	Human Resource Facility
IAPI	Argentine Institute for Change
IBRD	International Bank for Reconstruction and Development

ICSID	International Centre for Settlement of Investment Disputes
IDB	Inter-American Development Bank
IFIs	International Financial Institutions
IIC	Inter-American Investment Corporation
IMF	International Monetary Fund
INTAL	Institute for the Integration of Latin America and the Caribbean
IPE	International Political Economy
ISI	Import Substitution Industrialisation
JP	Justice Party
LAC	Latin American and the Caribbean
LAFTA	Latin America Free Trade Association
LFN	Latin American Financial Network
MDBs	Multilateral Development Banks
Mercosur	Southern Common Market
MIF	Multilateral Investment Fund
MIGA	Multilateral Investment Guarantee Agency
MIT	Massachusetts Institute of Technology
NAFTA	North American Free Trade Agreement
NGO	Non-Governmental Organisation
NICs	Newly Industrialising Countries
OAS	Organization of American States
OECD	Organisation for Economic Co-operation and Development
OVE	Office of Evaluation and Oversight, Inter-American Development Bank
PBL	Policy-Based Loans
PSD	Private Sector Department
RDB	Regional Development Bank
SAP	Structural Adjustment Programmes
SDD	Sustainable Development Department
SEF	Small Enterprise Facility
SEGBA	Electrical Services of the Great Buenos Aires
SGRs	Second Generation of Reforms
SPTF	Social Progress Trust Fund
TCF	Technical Cooperation Facility
UIA	Argentine Industrial Union
UK	United Kingdom
UN	United Nations
UNCTAD	United Nations Conference on Trade and Development
UNDP	United Nations Development Program
US, USA	United States of America
WB	World Bank
WTO	World Trade Organization

Introduction

About the book

This book is a contribution to the understanding of the political economy of regional financial architecture of development in its complex relation with both the international financial order and actors as well as the national configuration of forces and opposing projects of development. More explicitly, it concerns the nature of powers, developmental role and perils of Regional Development Banks' market-oriented function of development by the blind adoption in the 1990s of the economistic fallacy. Thus, the most basic question of this investigation is how an RDB working in tandem with the major international financial institutions and national government came to nurture and mismanage the most important financial and political crises of the last decades? To answer this, the investigation focuses on the Inter-American Development Bank's role in the rise, consolidation and decline of the Argentine process of its historical process of neoliberalisation in the 1990s. Throughout the work the central assumption is that neither the international economic integration nor the national development can be organised around market and financial-oriented understanding of development.

The research today is relevant for three particular reasons. First is that given the similarities in the policies followed in the European Union between international and regional development banking to address national financial crises, it might help to critically reflect upon the prospects of the market-oriented and fiscal austerity solutions pursued. The second reason is that, given its empirical scope, it can provide us with useful insights concerning the political economy of the rise, consolidation and decline of regional banking institutions along with diverse development perspectives and the extent to which these bodies are determined by the world financial order or by regional tendencies. The third reason is because the research is addressed towards understanding the political economy of the power of development finance, political capabilities and the complex international–regional–domestic nature, it will help in comprehending the role and tensions between the international, regional and domestic in development banking.

To achieve that, the study applies critical political economy of development based on the works of Karl Polanyi (1975), Robert Cox (1981), Anthony Payne (2005; Payne and Phillips 2010), Bjorn Hettne (Hettne and Söderbaum 1999) and

Fredrick Söderbaum (2003), as well as the contributions of Stephanie Griffith-Jones (1988), Roy Culpeper (1993), Francisco Sagasti (2002), Mario Frenkel (1998), Eduardo Basualdo (2003), Morten Bøås and Desmond McNeill (2004), among others. It is critical in the sense that it stands apart from the prevailing international and regional political economic orders of development and asks how these orders rise, consolidate and decline. In that sense, the approach concerns change and how the axis and dynamic between the international, regional and national, to an important extent, shapes options and paths of development. It is political economy since it addresses them both not as separate dimensions but as expressions of political projects of configurations of forces that define the distribution of power and define the balance of development. Finally, it is centred on development as the academic factor able to transcend area studies and rigid discipline that is unable to deliver responses in a time of crisis, transformation and global change.

Empirically, this investigation focuses on the developmental challenges, changes and tensions at the basis of the Inter-American Development Bank's market-oriented development mandate and interventions in the 1990s. It does that by exploring the case of the IDB's changing role in the process of consolidation and the decline of the convertibility regime in Argentina. As all RDBs can only be understood within the geographical and institutional contexts in which they exist, this investigation is framed within a thorough study of the regional political economy of Latin America in the context of the Americas.

Created within the framework of the major world institutions of the post-1945 system, the liberal economic explanation holds that RDBs were instituted to foster development by mediating the transfer of capital from surplus countries to nations facing shortages of capital (Griffith-Jones 1988; Meltzer Report 2000). RDBs thus represent one of the most important innovations associated with the experiment of cooperative development in the period of state capitalism and have been key actors in the financing of development during the subsequent period of global market capitalism. The realist version says that the IDB was the developmental outcome of the regional elites and governments' quest for hemispheric political and financial integration with the USA in the context of the rise of the Pax Americana and the Cold War. RDBs were strategic players in the Cold War and, at the same time, promoters of developmentalism in the 1960s and 1970s and leaders in the regional promotion of neoliberal globalisation and pro-market reforms in the 1990s.

In a few decades, these scarcely studied regional institutions jumped from being small and unknown regional agencies of cooperation into sophisticated regional multilateral banks, widening their powers and functions and exceeding, in some cases, the World Bank's financial lending to the regions. This expansion in power, however, did not come without its own perils, and as RDBs enthusiastically embraced the neoliberal credo of development in the 1990s, they themselves became a polemical and key issue of debate within the field of International Political Economy (IPE). Five decades after their creation, while the major international financial institutions (IFIs) are lagging behind efforts to deal with the consequences of neoliberal globalisation and states are increasingly engaging in building-up regional responses, RDBs face the challenge of adjusting their development mandates to new realities as they are increasingly subject to the dynamics and tensions between globalisation, regionalism and multilateralism.

Regional Development Banks

Regional Development Banks are usually understood under a particular economic perspective as international financial intermediaries whose corporate governance includes both borrowing developing countries and donor developed countries. They were created to mobilise resources to foster sustainable financing of development, initially from countries with capital surplus and, in the past two decades, from private capital markets to 'developing' countries. They make loans to countries on more favourable conditions than markets, and they provide technical assistance and advice for economic and social development (Bezanson *et al.* 2000). The multilateral capacity of these institutions is assumed to be based on two major elements (Rodrik 1995). First is the quality of information they produce and use, deriving from continuous monitoring of government policies in recipient countries, providing them with the knowledge and expertise to address any issue related to financing and the path of development in developing countries. Second is their degree of autonomy from the governments that own them, whereby their political economic nature is assumed to remain politically uncontaminated by the interests of borrower countries and intergovernment links.

Today, RDB institutions provide long-term concessional loans at below market rates of interest and with long repayment periods, guaranteed to enhance private investment, and finance for technical assistance and capacity-building in borrowing countries. They fund their long-term operations via borrowing in the international capital markets, while concessional loans are funded through contributions by non-borrower members ('replenishments') and from the RDBs' net income. Given the participation of developed countries in their structures of governance, RDBs enjoy the status of preferred creditor in relation to private lenders, whereby they are financially shielded against any financial contingency in borrower countries such as financial crisis or default on sovereign debt. This is a key advantage, allowing RDBs to enjoy high or 'AAA' credit ratings from bond-rating agencies and to raise funds on favourable terms in international capital markets (Bezanson *et al.* 2000).

The three major world RDBs are the African Development Bank (AfDB), the Asian Development Bank (AsD), and the Inter-American Development Bank (IDB). Each RDB comprises a cluster of affiliated agencies with financial and technical functions which boost its regional powers. At the core of each cluster is a non-concessional lending facility to channel the Banks' ordinary capital, along with concessional lending windows, similar to the International Development Association (IDA). The Banks' ordinary capital is composed of contributions of member countries, and, depending on the charter of each Bank, this is the window used by the international community to channel financial resources among eligible countries according to their performance and adherence to multilateral guidelines (Culpeper 1993). As a result, RDBs are subject to the delicate balancing act between acting as bank and financial intermediary, and meeting the development needs of developing regions and countries, the very reason of its development function (Bezanson *et al.* 2000: 6).

The idea to create the first RDB was conceived in Latin America, aimed at improving Latin American development via hemispheric cooperation with the United States' sphere of influence through the creation of the IDB. Following its creation, multilateral financial assistance grew faster than bilateral aid, its share increasing from about 25 per cent in 1970 to about 35 per cent in 1980. However, the debt crisis of the early and mid-1980s radically shifted and expanded yet further the role of RDBs in development. As a result, they were subordinated operationally to the IMF and World Bank's guidelines and surveillance, and their policies were redefined in line with structural adjustment programmes. Pro-market reform rather than infrastructure for development became the credo and precondition for developing regions' access to external financing. Hence, RDBs came to play a significant role in pushing borrowing countries towards domestic openness and state withdrawal from the economy. As a result, by the early 1990s, almost 50 per cent of total financing to development in developing regions had taken the form of multilateral development finance directed toward structural reforms (Bezanson *et al.* 2000). The dominant explanation is that it was the logical response to the economic wisdom after the failure of developmentalist and crony capitalism. The critical political economic explanation might be that, at some point between the 1980s and 1990s, the world order pushed the world economy into something similar to what Polanyi (1977) named the 'economistic fallacy': a misconception where development is equated with markets and money, and labour and land are commoditised.

The IPE of RDBs

The comprehension of RDBs is among the most important strands of development thinking, which for the past two decades have dominated and contended at international level about the meaning of the development and the role of markets and states. They dominate the political environment of multilateral institutions, in particular in Washington and are sustained and reproduced by a complex network of state, academic and private institutions aligned with each strand of development thinking and political direction. They were particularly influential at the international level in the 1990s and though their influence since then has declined, they still dominate the comprehension of RDBs and their development function, in the form of markets. One of the central problems with these specific economic perspectives is that they subordinate the comprehension of development to a supposed universal and ahistorical scientific interpretation of economics and finance. And in doing so, they tend to both obscure the complex political economy of RDBs, and reproduce and subordinate their varied roles to top-down, market-led or polity-led, technical and ahistorical understandings of development.

A central epistemological issue with these two approaches is that they leave out the contexts within which RDBs exist and by which their development missions are shaped, namely the historical structure of the world and regional orders. The problem with this is that in economic and political terms we are pushed to accept two top-down and apparently different interpretations of world economy and development. The first idea is that powerful states are the leading force behind globalisation and that global market expansion is the driving historical force (Sally 2000; Meltzer 2001, 2002; Vasquez 2003; DeLong 2004). The second interpretation is that market-led globalisation increases the impact of market failures on national economies, by which the stability of the international economic order demands an update and deep reform of the old Bretton Woods system and its major financial institutions including RDBs.

In this regard, important issues here are the approaches underlying the interpretation of the development effectiveness of RDBs, something traditionally addressed in a partisan fashion, in a zero-sum debate, either from what in this investigation are grouped under the generic category of markets, or polity-oriented global approaches to development. The intention with these two categories is not to put these approaches and their scholarship into boxes but to use them as ideal types to identify those elements that by a constructive dialogue with critical thinking may enrich our understanding of the challenges and perils of development. The two concepts pretend neither to dissolve into one structural idea the richness and varieties contained in mainstream approaches nor to downplay their important contributions to development debates. Instead, they pursue a double purpose, on the one hand, to facilitate a theoretical engagement between orthodox and heterodox perspectives, and on the other, to understand their political character in terms of power relations in a development context and the outcomes of development.

For market-driven development supporters, private financial institutions, corporations and individuals in the industrial countries now supply the largest part of capital flows to the developing world, and so today these institutions are largely ineffective (Meltzer 2001: 1). IFIs and RDBs lending to governments with access to capital markets is unnecessary, distorting market efficiency and keeping developing nations permanently in debt to the IMF and RDBs. The increasing overlap in the functions of all these institutions demands structural changes, and RDBs should restrict their activities to those areas where the private sector shows no interest (Meltzer Report 2000: 3).

On the other hand, for polity-led global development supporters, the RDBs represent an international system that must be reformed and their functions expanded rather than reduced. RDBs played a delicate balance among 'their three main functions: a) financial resource mobilization; b) capacity building, institutional development and knowledge brokering; and c) providing regional and global public goods' (Bezanson *et al.* 2000: 69). RDBs have always experienced tensions between their financing and development roles, exacerbated by the addition of the public good function, producing, particularly in times of crisis, 'trade-offs between pursuing one or another function at the expense of the others' (ibid.). They are provided strategically with an independent rationale and a less politicised identity that permit them to efficiently monitor government policies in borrower countries and exercise conditions to promote changes in government policies.

These elements make RDBs optimal actors, allowing them to act as a catalyst for private capital flows, since they legitimise national political economic projects in the eyes of capital markets (Rodrik 1995; Sagasti 2002; Ratha 2001).

Briefly, these approaches have three theoretical limitations. First, they overemphasise the multilateral character and agency role of inter-state organisations governing the international economy and do not account for international and regional political economic changes impacting on RDBs' development mission. They presume that a specific form and functioning of the capitalist market economy is universal and that social agents act within a system of 'rationally deducible behavioural laws' (Cox 1992: 495). Second, they presume the supremacy of the economy over other dimensions of development. For instance, the measure of development effectiveness of RDBs is always given as the economic and financial benefit and expansion of the private sector rather than the development of society as a whole. The economistic fallacy closes with the idea that the economy is an independent social dimension governed by its own rules and detached from civil society and separate from the state. This concept is central, as it leads to the technical presumption about the necessary tradeoffs of development between incentives for growth and social adjustment costs. Third, since these approaches consider the RDBs as autonomous from state lenders and borrowers, these do not inform the political character of the RDBs' development mission and their political economic role.

Therefore, since some mainstream perspectives bear in themselves significant limitations to understanding the RDBs' complex nature, the central aim of this book is to contribute to the empirically grounded research programme of the discipline of IPE, via critical and integral study of the RDBs' changing nature and development mission. Accordingly, a more integral and critical perspective will have to deal with three analytical issues regarding development narrowly addressed by these perspectives. The first is the agency/structure dilemma or power/authority dichotomy, which in mainstream perspectives is usually magnified through an overemphasis on either agency or the decision-making process of state and elite power in shaping the agenda of development. The second is the analytical divorce between economics and politics in which the RDBs' interrelated character and role are dissolved and separate from the states that own them. The third is the empiricist separation between the international and domestic, and the impossibility of integrating the regional dynamics of development, which have led mainstream approaches to see RDBs as an internationally and multilaterally top-down phenomenon rather than one that is regionally and socially determined.

The Americas and the IDB

As an institutional actor in regional development financing, the nature of an RDB is determined by a function that unfolds in the interface and middle point between regional and international financial architecture. The riddle is that even though regions define the central features of RDBs, it is the power of the international financial architecture which set their range of options, level of dependency or autonomy of the international financial architecture. In other words, different balance of power between both spheres can define different orientations and developmental role of RDBs. It necessarily follows then that an RDB can act either as a direct arm of the international or regional political financial architecture.

World orders or forms of international political authority and regional development banking are interrelated concepts in which the latter is subordinated to the former, since it provides the context of its existence. In the same way, the notion of regional forms of political authority provides the context where the international and domestic meet (Cox 1992: 494). It necessarily follows that the comprehension of the political economic nature and development mission of the RDBs is possible only with reference to a particular region and historical moment; in our case, the Americas as the contextual region of the world's leading RDB, the IDB, in a time of globalisation.

Since the 1970s, as declining US hegemony and world economic recession impacted upon international development, new forms of global political authority and regionalist projects began to emerge. The regionalist free-trade-based projects in North America, Europe and Asia soon began to take shape and became the point of intellectual reference of the RDBs' new market-oriented role. The case of the Americas is particularly important, as the USA has been the dominant power within the hemisphere ever since the end of the nineteenth century and the most important member of the IDB. Historically, the USA has been important beyond security issues but also in many strategic areas of development, as it has been the most important partner in trade and investment for the region for more than a century. As many scholars conclude, the political economy of development and identity of Latin America 'has for much of the twentieth century [been] framed in opposition [and in relation] to the United States' (Gamble and Payne 1996: 253).

The concept is central, since the major regional multilateral institutions in Latin America were created under the political umbrella, support and participation of the USA. Perhaps this is not more patent than in the IDB, in which the USA, at the time of its creation, held 40 per cent of the voting power, and Latin American countries 50 per cent of the total. However, despite the apparent authority of Latin American governments within the IDB's governance, the influence of the USA in the IDB's development mission and role was so important that for most of the time the IDB oriented its institutional actions towards US hemispheric concerns (Tussie 1995). Many scholars have argued in favour of the strategic control of the IDB by the Latin American countries (Tussie 1995; Culpeper 1999; Griffith-Jones 2002b; Birdsall 2003). However, notwithstanding their voting power, rarely in history have these countries voted together or even jointly opposed any US initiative.

All the RDBs appear to be structurally determined by the form of capitalist dominant and political economy of development dominant in their particular region. The IDB shares this common feature; however, it is unique as it operates under the umbrella and regional dominant position of the USA, which is also its major shareholder, and its epistemic communities its major source of ideas. As the RDB for Latin America, the evolution of the IDB has been tied to the hemispheric history of regional development and its varied political orders. In a few decades, what seemed an agency of development cooperation has become the major official source of financial, technical and intellectual resources for the region.

The key according to Enrique Iglesias (2004) is the 'sense of ownership and trust' that the structure of the IDB's corporate governance endows based on the majority vote of its borrower member countries (BMCs). However, it is also the complex network of consensus generation tied to this structure of governance that has permitted it to enjoy access and direct dialogue with all kinds of domestic actors and to participate in strategic state initiatives in the region (Tussie 1995: 116; Griffith-Jones 2002b; Iglesias 2004: 84). If the nature of power is social, the IDB is one the best historical and regional examples at hand.

Up to the early 1980s, the IDB established for itself a reputation as the 'water and sanitation bank', because it was the major provider of external funding for infrastructure for development, mainly US official resources. However, in the 1980s Latin America entered into its most severe, longest and deepest crisis of development, experiencing the IDB's loss of influence in the region and the need to re-invent itself in relation to the new challenges of development. The very existence of the Bank was questioned, and internally and externally it was pushed to shift away from its traditional developmentalist approach to support debt swaps for reforms within the guidelines of structural adjustment programmes. In a few years, the IDB became the world's leading Regional Development Bank, assuming an active and significant role in reforms led by Pinochet's dictatorship in Chile, Sanchez Lozada in Bolivia, Collor de Mello in Brazil, Fujimori in Peru, and Menem in Argentina.

The IDB undoubtedly represents an inseparable part and pillar of the history of the development of the Americas and its regional financial architecture. As regionalist tendencies have been taking centre stage in development, understanding the complex nature and interventions of RDBs has increasingly become more important for academic and policy purposes. This book stands for the idea that a new IPE of development is certainly a basic condition or initial step for exploring the rise, consolidation and decline of these unique institutions and their role in development in the light of new historical and regional configurations of power. In this study, the term 'new' IPE of RDBs is used in two different but complementary ways. First, it refers to both the body of theoretical literature that will be used to frame this investigation, and the model of analysis and theoretical framework underpinning the study of the empirical aspects of the investigation. Second, it applies to the empirical aspects of the IDB's development mission and role in the Americas. From this perspective, the term works as a dynamic approach informing the international and regional political configuration within which the IDB operates. In accordance with these two usages of the term 'new' IPE, the aims of this study were: How can we grasp the political economic nature of IDB and what are the main capabilities defining their development role in different regional political configurations? Are the IDB's development mission and role defined by political, technical or financial elements?

Case studies

Of all the interventions in development by the IDB during the stage of the globalisation of development financing in the region, there are two which illustrate their development capabilities and have officially been recognised more than any other. The first of these interventions is the Bank's political economic role in the consolidation of the Argentine convertibility regime up to 1995. In this case study, the book explores the IDB's legitimising role in the inseparable processes of the debt swap for privatisations of public utilities (perceived as the end of state capitalism) and the consolidation of the market-oriented model of globalisation in the country. The second is the IDB's complex role in the decline of the convertibility regime. In this case, the investigation examines the Bank's legitimising role in the processes of privatisation of social security and its financial and political support during the period of decline of the convertibility regime in Argentina.

The first case study, debt swap for privatisations, which in particular takes as its example the privatisation of electric energy public utilities, represents a key element in the comprehension of the political economic nature of this regional body. The case is relevant for three reasons. First, because it represents the most dynamic period of IFI–government partnership and policy coordination, providing a useful window for comprehending the political economic dynamics of the IDB's development function in times of international–domestic complementarity and coordinated implementation of strategies of development. The period is marked by the debt–equity swap for the globalisation or internationalisation of public utilities via privatisation of chief public utilities as a way to reorient the country's financing of development. Second, the study of this case informs us about the necessary conditions accompanying the IDB's effective exercise of its development mandate, the outcomes of its interventions and the capabilities and sources used by the institutions at technical, financial and political levels.

In this regard, the analysis shows the qualitative and active role performed by the IDB through the adaptation, framing, justification and legitimisation of these pro-market reforms and defence of the political economic project of liberalisation in Argentina, the convertibility regime. Third, at the time – and for some even today – the Argentine electricity privatisation constituted one of the most substantial and successful pro-market reforms ever undertaken in this sector at regional level within democratic settings. It is a historical case study as the IDB participated in a coordinated fashion with the World Bank, within the framework of the Washington Consensus. Strikingly and beyond the initial success, what was at first a formula to deal with problems of country financing of development, a decade later became the centre of the national debate and dispute concerning the restrictions of the market model and foreign investment capacity to foster further infrastructural development.

The second case study focuses on a period of confusion concerning the IDB's role in the structural reforms promoted, the increasing dominance of finance in its development mandate and how it came to overshadow its political and technical commitments at the domestic level. This is central, since the Bank came to play more and more a political role in the period 1996–2001 as tensions began to mount between the government and the major IFIs and the convertibility regime began to decline. The period has been defined officially by the Bank as a stage in which programming entered into a period of confusion with no other alternative but to provide liquidity to the sustaining of the convertibility regime. Accordingly, the study reveals the shift in the agency structure of the IDB's development function, from a legitimising role in the consolidation of the political economic project of the convertibility regime towards inconsistent and sometimes contradictory interventions aimed at supporting its financial and political survival. The case is also relevant as the process shows the split of the IDB's political economic capabilities into their main dimensions as a result of the growing tensions between the international and domestic tendencies. The fact is expressed in the increasing contrast between the Bank's interventions addressed towards the promotion, support and legitimisation of structural reforms, and the domestic challenges of development and the political stability necessary and locally demanded for the survival of the convertibility regime. As these elements pulled in different directions, it seems they might have generated an inconsistency between the Bank's actions and its development mission in the country, aggravating the internal tensions between the IDB as a bank and as an agency of development.

Given the new function of promoting neoliberal global integration, defined for and adopted by the IDB within the global financial order, the institution became a regional official bank with wide powers to frame policy alternatives, justify and legitimise macroeconomic reforms addressed to the globalisation of public utilities, and defend the convertibility regime. Therefore, this investigation inquires: What roles did the IDB play at the financial, technical and political levels in the consolidation and decline of the Argentine convertibility regime? And, who was affected by the IDB's exercise of its development powers, and how? As tension and differences between global and domestic interests grew throughout the convertibility regime's period of decline, how and to what extent did the IDB exercise its development function in financial, technical and political terms?

At the interface of these sets of questions lies the particular issue which this study sought to investigate further: To what extent are the RDBs' political economic nature and role in development configured and reconfigured by globalisation, regionalism and multilateralism? The work is concerned with the political economic process by which regional development bodies may rise, consolidate and decline, and expand or diminish in their development capabilities, either bridging or increasing the tensions between global and domestic tendencies.

Book outline

The book comprises six main chapters and a conclusion. Chapter 1 outlines the basic concepts of the investigation through a review of the existing political economy literature and sets out a particular interpretation of what the thesis means by 'new IPE of regional financial institutions' in the context of Latin America.

Based on a critical review of the main stages of the Latin American development, Chapter 2 lays out the general framework for understanding regional financial institutions in the light of political economy. The chapter identifies the major changes and regional structural processes behind the rise and configuration of the IDB's role in regional development since its creation up to the 1990s. Central to this chapter is the framing of the development of the IDB within the structure and agency of the Latin American political economy of development, and the identification of its regional structural and agency factors.

Chapter 3 explores and defines the main structural factors and agency processes whereby, in the 1990s, the IDB became the world's leading Regional Development Bank, almost matching the size of development aid given by the World Bank in the region. The analysis pays special attention to the changes in the IDB's agency capacities as it became subordinated in its policies to the guidelines defined by the major IFIs. The chapter highlights how this fact has been at the centre of the growing tensions and contradictions between the IDB's original development mandate and regional policy outcomes of the reforms promoted in the region under the aegis of the hegemonic neoliberal economic approach of development. The chapter concludes by stressing the importance of two key stages of the Bank's role and interventions in the region before and after 1995.

Chapter 4 moves on to a critical review of the Argentine political economy within the framework of regional and international development. Particular attention is given to the identification of the main political economic stages and events accompanying the rise, consolidation and decline of the convertibility regime. The chapter focuses on examining the agency and structure of the liberalisation process led by the Argentine government–IDB–IFIs partnership, and how these defined the IDB's changing role and interventions. Hence, three political economic events and processes are highlighted as being at the root of the convertibility regime's consolidation and decline. The first is the globalisation of country financing of development centred on the privatisation of public utilities. Another is the erratic social reforms and policies implemented to limit the financial problems of the regime and social consequences of the reforms. Finally, there is the process of rupture of the government–IFIs partnership and international–domestic businesses alliances as the contradictions of the model grew defining the exhaustion of the convertibility regime.

On the basis of the central stages identified in Chapter 4, Chapter 5 attempts to grasp the IDB's role in the consolidation of the convertibility regime in the 1990s. It focuses on the case of the successful privatisation of electric energy utilities within the framework of the strategy of global economic integration led by the government–IDB–IFIs partnership. The case explores and demonstrates the Bank's ability to justify, defend and legitimise the convertibility regime as a political economic project, through interventions in a coordinated fashion with the major IFIs and the government. The Bank's role was defined by its ability to adapt to global tendencies and economic guidelines, framing policy alternatives, justifying, legitimising and defending the Argentine political economic strategy of reforms, in line with the exigencies of global financial governance.

Chapter 6 explores the changes in the development mission and shift in the IDB's role after the mid-1990s, that is, from a legitimising role towards an inconsistent and contradictory role in development. The chapter examines the Bank's interventions in Argentina throughout the period of the convertibility regime's decline between 1995 and 2001. The stage is relevant as it has officially been evaluated by the Bank as a period of confusion and inconsistencies in the IDB's mandate, role and interventions in the country. Accordingly, the chapter traces the causes of these inconsistencies in the political economic tensions produced by the strategy pursued for financing development, the fragmentation of the liberalisation coalition and the growing distance between IFIs and the government given their different stakes. In particular, it highlights the political and versatile nature of the IDB's interventions and roles when faced with opposite interests. Notably, this stage featured the splitting up of the Bank's interventions in the economy and social affairs, and the politicisation of its role entailed by its support for the regime. This process, in addition, shows the contradiction between the IDB as a bank aiming at global economic integration and the IDB as a technical agency targeting development challenges of the country.

Finally, the book ends with a concluding chapter which aims to bring together the different strands of the investigation. It begins with a summary of the research findings and the general contribution that this thesis has made to the study of Regional Development Banks' political economy. The second part attempts to readdress the theoretical aspects focused on in Chapter 1 on the basis of the research findings outlined above. The chapter ends by considering those matters relating to the political nature of the Bank derived from the investigation which may serve as the basis for future research.

1   The political economy of Regional Development Banks

Introduction

This chapter critically reviews the dominant perspectives and their limitations in political economy that inform the understanding of RDBs and briefly introduces a core set of ideas and concepts associated with what has been termed critical IPE. It is argued here that some of these leading views, given their specific economic and political assumptions, tend to yield top-down, market-driven or ahistorical interpretations of development with a narrow focus on economic, agential and domestic factors. These assumptions bias the interpretation of development within the framework of globalisation and regionalism by taking for granted the divorce between the international and the domestic, the political and the economic and the rational efficiency of multilateral institutions upon borrower members. The ideological construct is a positivist discourse wherein politics and economics, and the international and the domestic emerge as separate domains defined by different rationalities, impeding deeper comprehension of the political economic nature of regional financial architecture and RDBs' developmental role.

As they tend to present only one side of the coin, the chapter contends that such interpretations provide an inadequate basis for addressing the central questions of this book. Instead, it proposes to turn to the rich field of ideas of the new IPE, with the aim of finding in this critical, eclectic and open-ended approach the necessary elements to address our particular research concerns. More specifically, the analysis engages with the historical materialist approach of Robert Cox and his method of 'historical structures'. The objective of this chapter, therefore, is to differentiate the conceptual framework of this investigation from the dominant perspectives, by introducing and outlining key debates and concepts – globalisation, the state, hegemony, regionalism, and international and regional financial architecture.

The chapter is accordingly divided into three main sections. The first identifies and analyses the dominant approaches to RDBs, with a particular focus on their underlying assumptions regarding globalisation, regionalism, development and finance. The second is directed towards 'new IPE', as an alternative way of conceptualising the historical and social dimensions of the relation between globalisation and regionalism, and development and finance within which the political economy of RDBs can be understood. The third is devoted to the more specific task of identifying and examining the ways in which regionalism is represented in the light of the dynamics of globalisation–regionalisation, and constitutes, therefore, a more robust framework within which to interpret the nature, role and policies of the IDB as an RDB. Finally, a short conclusion summarises the major findings of this analysis.

Regional Development Banks in political economy

The role and impact that RDBs have on development is part of the growing and lively debate in South America about regionalism, the relation with a changing world order and the failure of IFIs' development role and interventions in the last two decades. Today there are few doubts about the power and influence of RDBs; what is at stake, however, are both their orientations of development and regional commitments rather than international ties. Strikingly, the regional and international debate concerning RDBs is still dominated, to an important extent, by two discernible political economic perspectives present at official and academic level. In contrast, the subject has remained largely unexplored from the perspective of critical IPE, which can offer an optimal basis for the critical exploration of the development mission of these institutions in the light of the historical structures of power of globalisation and regionalism.

Briefly, mainstream views are organised around two major political economic perspectives in relation to the RDBs' role and accompanying specific political projects of development (Bøås and McNeill 2004). For realists, given the origin of the resources they command, the RDBs emerge controlled by donor countries, in particular the USA. RDBs represent an extension of the influence and power of industrialised countries in different regions to promote neoliberal ideas and gain market trade and financial markets, absorbing any new counter-hegemonic ideas against their stake. States are the leading force behind globalisation but growing free global markets are the driving positive and historical force (Meltzer 2002; Vasquez 2003). In the second perspective, institutional liberalism, RDBs are understood and defined by their necessarily consensual and technocratic character as part of a system unfolding in world of increasing interdependence and cooperation. They are positive catalysers of development of a technical nature that offers to countries the objective chance to reduce risk deriving from globalisation and reinforce the view of regional projects as market-driven development, in particular in terms of trade and finance. Its advocators hold that the expertise and technical superiority of RDBs puts them in optimal conditions at regional and national level to promote development and collective goods (Arestis 1992; Wyplosz 1999; Sagasti *et al.* 2001; Birdsall and Rojas-Suarez 2004).

Remarkably, these perspectives share chief elements, although, at the same time, they promote different agendas of development, related more to different strategic means than to the final development objectives pursued. These interpretations of RDBs in political economy share a common rationalist/positivist epistemology marked by two elements. They focus on agency issues of development, and rest on the assumption that institutional development must be subordinated to premises of free trade and finances that demand disciplining of domestic politics (Söderbaum and Shaw 2003; Hobson and Ramesh 2002). Both the neorealist/neoliberal perspective and the new multilateral global perspective take the world and the political order as given, and usually as good, and provide guidance to correct or solve specific problems in the light of a systemic, ahistorical, and either evolutionary or cyclical universal perspective of reality (Hobson and Seabrooke 2006). Briefly, they are mostly concerned with the efficacy, legitimacy and functionality of RDBs in relation to their development projects, usually with rationality of programming.

However, in the late 1980s and 1990s, these rationalist/problem-solving approaches moved closer together as a result of the growing importance of globalisation and regions in development, causing them to compete for influence within multilateral institutions given their increasing role in regional and national development. In a nutshell, the neoliberal perspective came to advocate global market-oriented development as a way to promote capitalist expansion, while the new multilateral perspective envisaged a sort of global polity-oriented development, strengthening and increasing the role of existing multilateral institutions (Payne 2000).

Significantly, the locus of these problem-solving and competing interpretations of development could lie in two major international bodies, the United Nations system and the Bretton Woods institutions, although these two options of development could be found struggling within the same international and regional bodies as in the case of the IDB as well as governments. Paradoxically, both discourses were characterised by economic determinism, featuring the dominance of finance over social forces in development, but with central differences. The Bretton Woods paradigm relies on the tenets of market governance, while the United Nations approach emphasises inter-state cooperation and market regulation to orient or lead development (Payne 2000; Gamble and Payne 2003).

It is possible to say, therefore, that to a significant extent the political economic understanding of the RDBs' development mission is defined by these two mainstream approaches – global market-oriented and global polity-oriented development – whose central interpretations, concerning the nature of globalisation, development, states and the financing of development, now deserve our attention.

The global market-oriented development perspective

The advocates of global market-oriented development and governance share the assumption that history and development are the result of free market forces in which states and politics are subordinated to the way in which the economy is organised (Gamble 2003). Overall, they consider RDBs to be obstacles that distort the natural unfolding of global market forces, generating more political bureaucracies and uneven development. Their intervention in regional and domestic development distort the natural dynamics of global market forces and generate negative incentives for countries to implement structural reforms necessary for access to external financing of development. This approach can be found in the Americas in the works of leading economists such as Edwards (2000), Caballero (2000; Caballero and Dornbusch 2002), Dornbusch (1996, 1999; Dornbusch and Edwards 1991), Schwartz (1998), Meltzer (1998, 2001, 2002), DeLong (2004), Yeager (2001), Schuler (2002), Hanke (2002) and Vasquez (2003). In addition, it exerts its influence through powerful think-tanks such as the CATO and Hoover Institutions. In Argentina this approach is represented by the works of Murphy *et al.* (2003), Llach (1997) and the FIEL institute and CEMA University.

The latter group approach globalisation as a new epoch of human history, the arrival of a new era in human affairs, in which states no longer have control over their economic policy-making sovereignty (Held *et al.* 1999). Globalisation represents for them primarily an economic phenomenon through which the state will be gradually replaced by non-political forms of economic interdependence (ibid.). The state form is constrained by the way in which global markets work, pushing them to leave development and its financing in the hands of market forces (Gamble 2003: 54).

Partisans of market-oriented development claim that regionalism is primarily a regional concentration of states, setting market rules that foster free trade and finance (Edwards 1998; Vasquez 2003). Here regionalism is comprehended as a unilateral process of trade and financial liberalisation, 'liberalism from below' led by states, and the sum of states as a region. That is the case of countries such as Chile and Argentina which 'have gone ahead under their steam, largely without the need for external' multilateral pressure (Sally 2000: 3). Countries have shown an increasing capacity to individually access capital markets to finance development, whereby the RDBs' development mission has been reduced to and refocused on providing modestly technical support and focused expertise. RDBs constitute a system of minor multilateral regional bodies subordinate to the major IFIs, whose development function is to promote technical coordination and assistance for market development and global liberalisation, preparing countries for gaining access to external financing (Meltzer Report 2000).

However, in the post-Bretton Woods era, the role of RDBs in the financing of development has been marginalised; official lending, bail-outs and misuse of financial intermediation have increased moral hazard and accentuated financial crises (Vasquez 1999). In point of fact, countries in Latin America – e.g. Chile, Mexico, Colombia, Argentina – as a result of the harmful effects of the use and abuse of multilateral lending for decades, have come to undertake economic restructuring independently of multilateral institutions and avoid distorting the natural functioning of markets (ibid.). Against the global polity-oriented tenet that changes come from above, advocators of this perspective contend that the world economy has evolved through changes coming from the national level, particularly in Latin America.

For neoliberals the level of capital market integration shows that the world is more globalised than ever, making obsolete the use of taxes and multilateral sources to finance development (Meltzer Report 2000). The task today is, therefore, to maximise capital mobility as it improves production and growth, absorbing the capital and labour released by inefficient sectors, in what is a particular adaptation of the Ricardian theory of comparative advantage to the modern global economy (Gray 1998). Global financial integration demands the consolidation of free global financial markets rather than reform obsolete multilateral institutions, a process that bears some social costs, although only temporarily (Balassa 1980).

There, the development of global capital markets is thus imperative for the financing of development in Latin America; if there is a role for RDBs, it is to promote this development (Hartwell 2001). Government intervention produces weak 'domestic economic fundamentals' – fiscal discipline, open outwardly oriented trade regimes, and the absence of sound financial systems (Glick *et al.* 2001). Financial crises, in essence, constitute self-fulfilling currency crises generated both by government macroeconomic mismanagement through a mix of pegged exchange rates, a weak banking sector, and market distortions and/or crony capitalism (Krueger 2002). The pro-market answer to financial crises stresses the need for floating exchange rates, independent central banks, the management of the macro economy and low fiscal deficits (DeLong 2004; Hartwell 2001; Dornbusch 1996, 1999).

Supporters of this perspective assume that in a world of perfectly integrated financial markets, the financing of development need not depend on national savings, since countries may complement these by borrowing from capital markets (Walter 2002). Global market-led governance became the dominant development credo in the early 1990s, particularly in terms of the financing of development, justifying the long process of structural adjustment under the guidelines of the so-called 'Washington Consensus'. The global market-oriented approach came to define the central elements characterising the development mission of RDBs: (1) reliance on capital markets as a source of financing (Meltzer Report 2000); (2) global financial integration through trade and financial openness (Vasquez 2003); and (3) structural domestic adjustment, through openness in trade and finance, to international conditions, privatisation of public utilities and pension systems, and flexible labour markets (Balassa 1980: 1–2; Levine and Zervos 1996).

The global polity-led development perspective

This study gathers together, under the broad category of 'global polity-oriented development', the wider range of theories and discourses that on the basis of economic assumptions understand RDBs and the relations between global, regional finance and development as something subject to the development of a global or international polity. In general, this category gathers the most important and organised tradition of thinking of development economics with presence in international institutions, which has opposed and contested neoliberal thinking. They have played a chief role in identifying the weakness and risks associated with market-oriented development and unregulated capital flows. In addition, their scholars have produced a whole set of important concepts such as the need to make IFIs and transnational actors accountable to civil society, environment, gender and energy for development among other issues, stressing the political and systemic nature of the global economy.

Their advocates share with the 'global market-oriented development' perspective a preoccupation with the stability of the international economy rather than with uneven development and inequality, issues which they address only tangentially. They approach the political economy of the RDBs' development mission as the evolution of institutions, rules and regimes, in which changing discourses of global financial governance and the growing capacity of global governance IFIs and networks shape their roles and policies. RDBs represent part of the international financial system, playing an undeniably positive role in promoting development and global economic integration.

Accordingly, the international financial system represents a public good, one which has to be delivered by states; otherwise, free trade and finance without global public goods will lead to the revival of protectionism, isolationism and eventually to war (Wyplosz 1999; Sagasti *et al.* 2001; Griffith-Jones 2002a, b). In the economy, most of their tenets continue to be inspired by or derived from John Maynard Keynes's *General Theory of Employment, Interest and Money* (1936). They hold a dominant position, mainly in the UN system and in particular in the United Nations Development Program (UNDP), with a significant influence in the IDB.

Supporters of global polity-oriented development assume that globalisation is bringing into existence a Post-Westphalian order in which the state is being redefined (McGrew 1997). This is because the increasing interdependence of state and societies pushes states, gradually, to rely more and more on international cooperation. This in turn, brings about a polyarchic, decentralised and pluralist world order, in which the increasing institutionalisation of the world is the product of the necessity for cooperation rather than the exercise of hegemonic power.

The global economy constitutes a historical process that rests on free trade and capital mobility governed by uncertainty of actors given the absence of conditions of full information. Expectations thus have a significant and unavoidable impact on economic events, whereby economic and political institutions play the significant role of reducing uncertainties and risks, being of 'paramount importance in shaping economic events' (Arestis 1992: 89). Global finance is a reflection of the national economies and of the relations between them; in other words, the sum of countries' balance of payment deficits and surpluses, as Keynes conceived it (Griffith-Jones 1984). The main issues in international finance are concentrated upon the definition of the levels of deficit that countries are allowed to sustain, and the organisation of financial intermediation between capital surplus countries and those demanding financial resources for development, which require external official assistance.

Financial crises are the consequence of mismatches between the development of the global economy and the development of the global polity (Gamble 2001) due to changes in the composition and predominance of different kinds of capital flows – e.g. from FDI to institutional investors in the 1990s (Kaminsky and Reinhart 1999, 2000; Kaminsky *et al.* 2001). As a result, these changes have made it necessary to redefine the international financial architecture through a new set of rules promoting 'prudential regulation', which demands major levels of state cooperation and agreement in order to avert future crises (Eatwell 1996: 2; Goldstein and Turner 1996; Stiglitz 2002). For supporters of this perspective, the main instrumental link between international finance and national economies lies in the exchange rate mechanism regulating the relation between national currencies, whereby financial crises are primary exchange rate crises (Cox 1996a; Diaz-Bonilla and Schamis 2001).

Within these perspectives, financial crises are associated to the policing of nominal exchange rates, triggering speculative behaviour on the part of the international private sector (Kaminsky and Reinhart 1999; Kaminsky *et al.* 2001). From this are derived the concepts of financial contagion and sudden outflows of capital from developing countries, stimulated by macro conditions such as fixed exchange rates, public indebtedness and overvalued currencies (Eatwell 1996; Eatwell and Taylor 1999). This approach claims that sound banking regulation and supervision – the regulated openness of capital accounts, free trade, and labour market flexibilisation – are keys to sustaining the financing of development in this path of growth (Stiglitz 2002; Ffrench-Davis 2002; FitzGerald 2002; Culpeper 1999; Griffith-Jones 1988, 2002a; Rojas-Suarez 2005).

Followers of this perspective claim that development requires major levels of engineering from above and growing state cooperation to guarantee the stability of international finance, a chief condition for the stability of capital flows between suppliers – countries or capital markets – and country demanders of capital (Culpeper 1999; Ocampo 2000: 533). Accordingly, the external financing of development is not only desirable but also indispensable if the development of depressed regions is to be accelerated, a Keynesian tenet that became a credo for economists bounded to the CEPAL, Economic Commission for Latin America and the Caribbean (ECLAC).

For proponents of an institutionally regulated global order, 'regionalism' refers to the idea that 'agreements among countries within regions can be a step toward greater integration into a global trading and financial system'. Regionalism is therefore 'a strategy to speed the development of regional and domestic institutions, and thus generate faster and steadier growth' through trade liberalisation, mostly based on geographical – comparative – advantages (Birdsall and Rojas-Suarez 2004: 1; Gurria and Volcker 2001). Within this perspective, neoliberal institutionalists argue that 'regionalism thrives in the policy spaces left by multilateralism but at the same time when these lacunae are too many or too wide these tensions are then re-played in the multilateral sphere' (Tussie 2003: 100). Regionalism, therefore, provides substance for multilateralism reinforcing RDBs' development mission as countries benefit through better opportunities for market access. Global capital markets are far from perfect, and therefore RDBs have to contribute an important developmental role and expertise for facilitating access to capital markets by developing countries and favouring regional trade integration (Gurria and Volcker 2001).

RDBs play a significant role in this regard, since they are efficient regional financial mediators in transferring capital from the North to the South. They are endowed with the political advantage of influencing the directions of development and reforms in their member states. Furthermore, they are the chief financial institutions at a regional level, and have been almost the only lenders and source of financing of development to countries in times of financial crises and social turbulence (Gurria and Volcker 2001; Culpeper 1993, 1999). However, RDBs are not so much regional bodies as components and parts of global financial governance; their primary mission is to promote the integration of countries into the global economy.

Advocates of this perspective approach RDBs by focusing upon their agency of their development function, measured by the internal rationality of their programmes and the financial efficiency with which these institutions execute their development mandates (Rodrik 1995). RDBs are regarded primarily as technical institutions driven by a mandate to promote development in the regions where they make loans.

The advantage of RDBs lies in their expertise, which is based, in the first place, on the information that stems from external continuous monitoring of government policies in recipient countries, and second, on their autonomy from governments, which ensure they remain uncontaminated, domestically or internationally, by sectional interests (Rodrik 1995). RDBs are primary lending institutions and even though they operate as a bank, charging some interest on their loans, they are non-profit institutions based on the participation in their governance of their borrowing member countries and their donors, which guarantee their politically and ideologically uncontaminated nature.

Hence the legitimacy of RDBs derives from their consensual character, from international acknowledgement of their technical expertise, and capacity to access domestic actors and processes. Accordingly, RDBs' interventions have historically generated a positive impact on the financing of development by encouraging private flows and private sector support for country members (Culpeper 1999). RDBs are endowed with the advantage of being able to exercise conditionality (lending that is conditional on changes in government policies), while at the same time guaranteeing multilateral support for development financing in order to counteract volatility in global financial markets (Sagasti *et al.* 2001; Dasgupta and Ratha 2000; Ratha 2001).

New International Political Economy

The two sets of perspectives outlined above assume a world that is interconnected according to economically determined facts about globalisation, regionalism, states, development and change. Unquestionably, these perspectives have become common and conventional interpretations of IFIs and RDBs, offering sometimes a static and self-proclaimed universal view of development. They appear as natural or legitimate although they are informed by a hidden political bias based on the idea that change comes only from above or markets, through the actions of powerful elites acting either through states, or by the actions of state-created international regimes/institutions (Murphy and Tooze 1991a, c; Gamble and Payne 1996; Hobson and Seabrooke 2006). The analytical problem with these perspectives is that they turn the analysis of the internal efficiency and rationality of multilateral strategies and programmes into the central way to understand the IFIs' political economy, development intervention and role. These assessments in turn emerge subordinate to the unquestioned assumption that multilateral institutions have universal and immutable mandates of development nurtured only by their own rational and technical expertise. The final outcome and sometimes the problem, is that in approaching the domestic they run the risk of producing self-fulfilling interpretations of their perspectives rather than reflecting the reality. That can be the case, for instance, of fiscal deficit, contingent liabilities, monetary expansion, inflation and flexibilisation of labour market. Here are to be found the limitations of these approaches to critically focus upon IFIs' interventions in domestic development.

Academic analyses and critiques of the limitations of these mainstream development perspectives have been widely and systematically elaborated for several decades in seeking a more fruitful dialogue about the problems of development (Strange 1970, 1971; Cox 1987; Murphy and Tooze 1991b; Higgott 1994; Gamble and Payne 1996; Underhill 2000; Foley 2003). Dissatisfaction with the largely unquestioning positivism and functionalism of these perspectives was what pushed scholars from a wide variety of backgrounds to put the rationalist/positivist model of production of knowledge in perspective and favour the openness of a new field within international relations, the new IPE. Overall, its scholars assume the absence of unitary reflectivist research programmes as a necessary condition for preserving an open academic field defined by the pluralism of its research agendas and methods, rather than reducing them to a single and dominant mode of production of knowledge.

Among all the diversity of these heterodox perspectives, a different approach was developed by Robert Cox. Briefly, Cox's main contributions are twofold: to have shown the political character of IPE knowledge, and above all, to have defined an approach in which the dynamics of social forces precede the world dynamics of development. Understanding the political economic nature of our historical time has been a central Coxian concern in new IPE. In this regard, this version of new IPE defines itself in relation to a whole – the world order – which defines its ontology in relation to a mode of thinking – historical structures – which defines the mode and methodology of its production of knowledge about reality.

The Coxian approach is based on the distinction between two types of theories or two modes of production of knowledge in social sciences. The first is the problem-solving theory, which focuses more on responding effectively to pressing problems of the present. This emphasises how to deal with particular problems within the existing order of things and the aim of the theory is to make this reality work better by 'dealing with particular sources of trouble' (Cox 1981: 88). Problem-solving theory 'takes the world as it finds it, with the prevailing social and power relationships and institutions into which they are organised as the given framework for action' (ibid.). Overall, problem-solving theory usually presents itself as ahistorical in its approach, positivist and rational-deductive in its method, and functionalist in its explanatory model of analysis.

The second mode of thought is 'critical theory', which addresses change and transformation in historical perspective, identifying the sources of contradiction, conflict, and crises that allow change to be sorted into different patterns (Sinclair 1996). Accordingly, 'critical theory ... stands apart from the prevailing order of the world and asks how that order came about' (Cox 1996a: 88). It addresses the particular in relation to the whole – e.g. institutions in relation to the structure of a historical order – 'rather than to separate parts', leading to the construction of a larger picture anchored in the pattern of historical change (ibid.: 89). Critical theory is thus a theory of history, a theory of the material history based on the historical mode of thought following the tradition established by the contributions of Ferrero, Vico and Polanyi. Four chief elements of the new IPE inform the approach embraced by this investigation: the method focusing on historical structures, the debate on the state, and the role of international institutions within the world order and regionalism.

Historical structures

New IPE rests on a historical, critical and flexible methodological approach that can be integrated, to some extent, with rationalist/problem-solving approaches to development. For that, the chief concepts and assumptions here sued concerning the relation between international finance and development are analytical derivations, carefully adopted, of both critical and problem-solving works from wide range of scholars.

The notion of historical structures focuses on the historical material and ideological character of the making of world orders by historical blocs through the production of different hegemonic and non-hegemonic structures, and outcomes of development. Here, power emerges from social processes, and the world is represented as a pattern of interacting social forces functioning on different levels. At the base of social forces are the historical structures, which represent configurations of forces – material capabilities, ideas and institutions – which interact reciprocally to reproduce a particular social and political order as well as its institutions (Cox 1981).

This configuration of forces does not determine actions, although it does impose constraints and create opportunities (Gamble and Payne 1996). Thus historical structures refer both to material constraints and to the collective, inter-subjective social meaning that sustains, reproduces or challenges a particular social order (Cox 1981). They represent persistent social practices, produced and transformed by collective human activity, in which people are not only their bearers but their creators (Gamble and Payne 1996: 8). These are persistent patterns of human activity produced by collective responses to specific common problems, which become congealed in practices, institutions and intersubjective meanings for a significant group of people, to whom these constitute the objective and truthful world (Cox and Sinclair 1996: 515).

The dynamics of historical structures take place across three interrelated levels. At the first level are the social relations of production and its configuration, which constitute the undeniable base that produces social forces in the form of classes and social movements – e.g. feminism, ecologism. Social relations of production 'covers the production and reproduction of knowledge, social relations, morals and institutions that are prerequisites to the reproduction of social forces in the form of classes that are the most important actors' (Cox 1989: 39). Each particular production relation gives rise to particular social forces and collective identities in a historical bloc or coalition, which becomes the bases of power within and across nation states and within a specific world historical order (Cox 1987: 4).

The second sphere of activity is the forms of state which are related to the particular configuration of social forces in a given historical time. Forms of state are historical constructions shaped by historical blocs, which represent the core structure of the state–civil society complex. A historical bloc or coalition integrates various different classes and collective identities, expressing particular historical social configurations, and reflecting, as a whole, the 'unison of economic and political aims', intellectual and moral unity (Gramsci 1971: 181–182). Different forms of state express, therefore, different historical blocs, which in themselves constitute structures that bind together structure and superstructure, subjective and objective elements in the foundations of different social orders and path of development.

The third sphere of activity is world orders, including the relative stability of successive and different world orders, and any conflicts occurring during the rise, apogee and decline of different hegemonies (Cox 1981: 102–104). The concept of the world order in this approach indicates 'a structure which may only have a limited duration in time and which does not have the inevitable equilibrium connotation of system' (Gamble and Payne 1996: 9). To put it simply, order 'is used in the sense of the way things usually happen' (Cox 1981: 152); order is expressed in the common sense of a time and place.

The dynamics and flexibility of this approach permit us to describe world orders in terms of either social forces or configurations of state power. Social forces do not exist exclusively within states, but may overflow national frontiers, whereby world structures can be represented as social forces 'just as they can be described as configurations of state power' (Cox 1981: 105). The political economic perspective explains world power in terms of emergence from social processes, and the features of world orders comprise different types of configurations of material capabilities, ideas and institutions.

In this sense, the power and outcomes of development of social forces and its different configurations crystallise in the form of hegemony. That is,

> a coherent conjunction or fit between a configuration of material power, the prevalent collective image of the world order (including certain norms) and a set of institutions which administer the order with a certain semblance of universality (that is, not just as the overt instrument of particular state's dominance).
>
> (Ibid.: 103)

Hegemony

Any interpretation of the concept of hegemony must apply the realm of social forces shaped by production relations as a framework, on the assumption that 'ideas and material conditions are always bound together mutually influencing one another and not reducible one to the other' (Cox 1987: 7). In this sense hegemony is more than the dominance of a single world power, it is

> dominance of a particular kind where the dominant state creates an order based ideologically on a broad measure of consent, functioning according to general principles that in fact ensure the continuing supremacy of the leading state or states and leading social classes but at the same time offer some measure or prospect of satisfaction to the less powerful.

> (Ibid.)

Dominance is essentially negotiation. It can exist without hegemony but hegemony is one form of dominance that brings together coercive and consensual elements of power. Hegemony represents a dynamic and balanced perspective between ideologies and objective elements of power central to the maintenance of a world order. Power is conceived as a centaur, part man, part beast, deploying different elements according to the needs of the order. New IPE approaches adopt these conceptions and are strongly committed to historical research seeking to understand the dilemmas of the present by reference to the changes of the past (Gamble and Payne 1996: 10).

The starting point for understanding hegemony is a study of the two world orders that have had a major impact on our era, the Pax Britannica and the Pax Americana. The emergence of the liberal world order or the Pax Britannica founded the liberal state and expanded the norms of liberal economics (free trade, free movement of capital and persons) in the world, providing a universalistic ideology expressing its interests, indifferent to the situation of peripheral countries. In this period there were no formal international institutions of world order, and the administering and regulating of liberal order was done by the City of London on its own, with British sea power as the potential enforcer (Gamble and Payne 1996: 10).

However, at the end of nineteenth century this world order began to decline and the liberal state was challenged by the incorporation of the new industrial labour forces of capitalism. Economic expansion demanded more state action in terms of market regulation and welfare policy, complemented with policies of protectionism and access to new markets and colonies. Germany and the United States overtook the supremacy of Britain and even though some international institutions, such as the League of Nations, come into being after the First World War these were not enough to sustain a new hegemony, as this order collapsed into rivalry between regional power blocs. The process ended with the US triumph in the Second World War (Cox 1981: 105).

The new configuration of power, the Pax Americana, was more rigid, taking the form of state and transatlantic alliances handing on US power, created to contain the expansion of the Soviet Union. The new hegemony was marked by two processes. The first was the reassertion of liberal economics ideas across Western Europe and the inclusion and subordination of the vast majority of new emerging states of the Third World. The second was the containment of the major alternative world order under the leadership of the Soviet Union (Gamble and Payne

1996: 11). The Pax Americana was preceded by an unprecedented period of institutionalisation generating the major international institutions. Since the Great Depression and the rise of Keynesian doctrines, which blurred the separation between economics and politics, the national economic management of domestic economies became legitimate and necessary, as did the multilateralisation of the management of the international economy (Cox 1981: 105). Another central feature of the Pax Americana was the freeing of trade between national economies and the convertibility of Western currencies with the US dollar, in parallel to 'the development of national security states in the West' (Gamble and Payne 1996: 11).

Of the two kinds of world order mentioned, the hegemony of the Pax Americana by large rested in great measure on consent and negotiations of power among states except for those under the Soviet Union's influence. The new hegemony provided enough benefits to the associate and subordinate states in order to gain their consent, although submission became thin, and either mixed or replaced by force, at the periphery. The principles of the Pax Americana were the free movement of goods, capital and technology and reasonable predictable levels of exchange rates similar to the Pax Britannica but more institutionalised. The new international institutions were mainly oriented towards reconciling domestic social pressures with the needs of expansion of the world economy, employing state functions as part of a process of internationalisation of the state. International institutions became mechanisms for supervising the national adaptation of international norms and made financial and technical assistance conditional upon evidence of domestic application of the new political guidelines of development (Gamble and Payne 1996: 11).

The golden years of the Pax Americana and the new international order that emerged from this were marked by the reconstruction of the liberal international economic order and the development of the national security states in the West, a readiness to absorb or coerce any peripheral regime opposing the hegemony. The Keynesian style of development laid down the basis of the ideology of the Cold War. In this regard, the Truman Doctrine became an inseparable element of the Marshall Plan, promoting either the destabilisation of radical Third-World regimes or the support of those regimes aligned with the hegemony (ibid.: 11).

The crisis of the Vietnam War marked the start of the Pax Americana's declining impact on the entire West, as this negatively affected US provision of the financing of development. The USA began to transmit inflation internationally, and profit levels dropped, pushing governments and corporations for further action to cover their levels of incomes, driving up raw material prices. Within this context, the dollar shifted from top-currency to negotiated-currency status, bringing about the USA's loss of international control of the financing of development and the diffusion of power within the global political economy. However, the hegemonic reaction to reassert US authority came about in the 1980s, when the USA attempted to regain control of the order 'by means of the political economy of Reaganism' (ibid.: 13).

Its purpose was to defeat and eradicate Third-World nationalism and regain the hegemonic role that once had enjoyed in the world order. Its project was based on the twin prospectuses of militarism and monetarism, outsourcing its world military machine and imposing the neoliberal credo within multilateral financial institutions as international rule of development. However, Reaganism did not completely succeed in reasserting its authority in a world order which had substantially changed. There were internal failures such as trading and expenditure deficits, but above all the neoconservative project failed to deal with a rather different and more complex international scenario.

The economies of Europe and Japan were steadily growing and stronger than in the preceding decades. Even though the US economy was the major international supplier of capital for development, the Newly Industrialising Countries (NICs), Europe and Japan were also exporting capital and less dependent on US flows. It was a new non-hegemonic world order in which US power was still unquestionable, in particular in the military terrain and to an important extent in the economy, although the USA was no longer powerful enough 'to shape on its own the rules of a consensual hegemonic order' (ibid.: 14).

The 1970s and 1980s marked the rise of new world order in which no single state or group of state was able to control it or rule development. Instead, promoted by the Reaganism, the vacuum left was soon occupied by the actors managing the key and multilevels of a genuine global economy. That is 'the unofficial and official transnational and international network of state and corporate representatives and intellectuals who work towards the formulation of a policy consensus for a global capitalism as a *nebuleuse*' (Cox and Schechter 2002: 33). The new spirit of the ideas ruling the world has been clearly summarised by Leys (1996b: 42) stating 'it is hardly too much to say that by the end of the 1980s the only development policy that was officially approved was not having one – leaving it to the market to allocate resources, not the state'. Within the new non-hegemonic world order, there was now a multilevel exercise of power in which the state had come to be constrained by global forces and in particular, by the international power of mobile capital and the IFIs promoting it. The new global order constrained state development strategies but at the same time enabled them, depending on the orientation of the domestic configurations of social forces after two decades of change (Weiss 2003a).

Returning to our main point, the critical review of history shows that historically, all the forms of hegemony were nation-based developments, overflowing national boundaries to become internationally expansive phenomena, accompanied by different levels of institutionalisation of power and norms. One of the lessons derived from this is the impact of the hegemony on peripheral countries in a more passive way. The effect of this process comes as a more or less direct reflection 'of international developments which transmit their ideological currents to the periphery' (Cox and Sinclair 1996: 134). This is a particular phenomenon of change internationally and domestically addressed, which constitutes one of the central characteristics of the global order under globalisation (I. Taylor 2001, 2005). The impact of hegemony on the periphery or semi-periphery in a passive way is an important idea for this investigation since it is relevant to understanding the interplay in the international, regional and domestic dynamics of change of power in the global political economy and uneven development. These concepts are analysed below.

It is clear that hegemony cannot be reduced to the dominant means of production but refers to the amalgam of ideas and material conditions expressed by historical blocs under a hegemonic social class. A historical bloc comprises the integration and articulation of different class interests and forms of identity within a specific alliance of forces in which the interests of a part are presented as the interests of the whole. Given its social character, a historical bloc is a relationship constantly constructed, contested and negotiated and 'is never a static reflection of an alliance of social class forces' (Morton 2007: 97). Hegemony is, therefore, a social, economic and political structure and is expressed in norms, institutions and mechanisms which lay down the rules of behaviour which support a particular mode of production (Cox 1987). In this sense, international organisations are one of the mechanisms for expressing the norms of the world hegemony.

Hegemonies and historical processes are dialectic and can be shaped either by structural and superstructural processes, as in the case of the Pax Americana and the 'internationalisation of production' that accompanied it, or by the 'internationalisation of the state' preceding the neoliberal financial globalisation (Cox 1987: 109). The concept is not determinist and the influence assigned in the analysis to agency and structure, or economics, politics and culture, may vary according to specific processes. Briefly, the central element is hegemony's social basis. The only problem with Cox's understanding of hegemony, however, is the difficulty of fully separating analytically all the different elements that constitute it in different structures of power.

To solve the problem, hegemony can be conceived as being composed of separable and interrelated elements of power located in the security, production, financial and ideological structures of the global political economy, as suggested by Susan Strange (Gamble and Payne 1996: 9). However, to refer to hegemony, power and authority demands clarification of the concept of state, which we do next.

The state

The academic interpretation of the concept of the state is central to an understanding of the dynamics of the world order that defines the context within which international institutions and RDBs exist and function. An exploration of this is vital for this investigation, as it establishes both the state–society and the international–domestic relationships. In IPE it is possible to see two dominant models of the state, a realist and a pluralist model, associated respectively with the contributions of Max Weber and Emilie Durkheim (Palumbo and Scott 2003).

The influences of Machiavelli's and Hobbes's political realism are quite clear in Weber, who retains elements of a materialist methodology divorced from its original political programme. His conception of the state recognises it as an expression of rationalised collective will, identifies the material basis of its power and its role in the formation of the nation, and describes the manner of its institutionalisation. In Durkheim, in contrast, the influence of both French and German political theory is the distinctive feature. Here, the state is, in essence, a deliberative organ of political societies and the guardian of their *collective conscience* or collective morality. These concepts are the foundation for two dominant ideas in mainstream IPE: the natural international state of anarchy, and the sovereign equality of states. They facilitate the management of conflict and cooperation among states and they regulate the mandates of international organisations. However, they obscure the hierarchical relations of power between states and other actors in the world order and in particular the social nature of change, conflict and development.

In this investigation, the state is understood in historical terms as the development of political authorities 'arising in different times and places in the context of different influences' (Cox and Schechter 2002: 32). Here, the notion of the state refers to the state–society complex, an inseparable composite unit, 'the institutions of authoritative rule in relation to the balance of social forces that can sustain or undermine them' (ibid.: 32). The state is thus the product of a social relation, through which capitalist order and hegemony are expressed and constructed (Cox 1981). External and internal tendencies are mediated with relative autonomy, ensuring the functioning of the capitalist state benefiting the hegemonic classes or groups (Poulantzas 1975). Historical blocs or coalitions precede the rise of world orders, and historical blocs are national phenomena that cannot exist without the hegemony of a social class exercising its domination through the control, legitimisation, and propagation of a hegemonic style of development (Cox 1981: 168; 174).

Once hegemony has been consolidated domestically it may expand beyond national borders by expanding its particular mode of social relations of production and, today, internationalising the state (Gamble and Payne 1996: 171; Cox 1987: 149–150). The tendency towards the internationalisation of the state is never complete, according to Cox, since it produces 'counter-tendencies by domestic social groups that have been disadvantaged or excluded in the new domestic realignments', and counter-tendencies may reverse the internationalising tendency (Cox 1987: 253). Cox adapts the Gramscian concept of passive revolution to represent an abortive or incomplete transformation of society within the world order that can take different forms:

> One is change induced in a society by an external force that attracts internal support from some elements, but does not overcome the opposition of the other entrenched forces ... [Others can take] the form of a stalled war of position strategy which is strong enough to provoke opposition, but not strong enough to overcome it. Furthermore, a strategy on the part of dominant power gradually to coop elements of the opposition forces – a strategy known in Italian politics as *transformismo* – is another form of passive revolution.
>
> (Cox and Schechter 2002: 106)

'Passive way', 'passive revolution' or 'revolution from above' refer to the processes and relationships shaping and shaped by interscalar articulation between international and domestic directing a change. That is, a process of change through state intervention addressed to the expansion of capital over labour with the inclusion of dominant groups within the hegemony of a political order, co-opting, absorbing and fragmenting civil society and labour opposition groups (Cox and Schechter 2002: 106; L. Taylor 2001, 2004).

Briefly, the concept of passive revolution refers to the way in which state powers have been increasingly adjusted to the prerogatives of the global political economy through three processes. The first is inter-state consensus formation within a common ideological framework, as advocated by IFIs. The second is hierarchical and structured participation. The third is the process through which internal structures of the state are adjusted so that each state can transform this global consensus into national policy and practice, what is termed *transformismo* (ibid.: 254). The last of these is a central concept for understanding the international–domestic dynamics of development under globalisation and in particular that of RDBs.

International institutions

The notion of *transformismo* as the foremost hegemonic form of the global order at the peak of neoliberal globalisation does not locate political power in either the international or the domestic realm, but in both, as it assumes that the international–domestic relationship is institutionally and socially mediated. The international order, the institutions mediating the international–domestic relationship, and the state not juxtaposing but integrating, whether harmoniously or in conflict – all are elements of an inseparable complex (Underhill 2000; Cox and Schechter 2002; Weiss 2003b). The essence of this complex, under *transformismo*, is that even though external forces seek to impose specific guidelines of development in their own interests, there is room enough at domestic level to resist or contest them, which in turn depends on the balance of social forces within the state (Cox and Schechter 2002). *Transformismo*, as a concept derived from the theory of passive revolution, refers to the multiscalar articulation, the agency and structure of the international and national in the social, political and economic dimensions of development.

Given the nature of *transformismo*, globalisation within the present global order represents an intergoverned domestic–international process, which can assume different forms and present different balances of powers between the external and domestic terrains. This governed interdependence inherent to *transformismo* defines different power relations through diverse forms of cooperation or conflict between economic and political alliances or partnerships (Weiss 2003b: 308). Accordingly, domestic structures can assume passivity or not, be transformational or not, be co-opted by external forces or not, with states being able to make use of similar transformative capacities according their hierarchical position within the management of global order and their relationship with international and regional institutions.

The intergoverned domestic–international process of global integration, at the political level, is anchored in the IFI–state relation, wherein the IFIs were themselves created by states; and which, independent of their greater or lesser autonomy, remain tied to the political structures and agency that created them and sustains them. The IMF and the WB in their relationships with the USA and Europe, and their known models of governance are a clear expression of this.

The institutional character of the IFI–state relationship provides a power-distributional effect to any intergoverned process of globalisation (Thelen 1999: 392–396, cited by Weiss 2003b: 23). This is a central political economic element of the IFIs' role which favours the interests of specific actors or coalitions. This is because the arrangements and outcomes of these IFI–state relations foster, justify and legitimise, by and large, specific political economic projects in line with the guidelines of the management of the global economy. In other words, the IFI–state complex provides domestic actors with a power balance and legitimisation effect on development and this is the central political economic nature of the IFIs' role.

The management of the global order is a central concern in new IPE as it defines the structural conditions for development. According to Cox, the management of global capitalism

> is a multilevel process, determined at the national level by the balance of social forces within states, at the transnational level by an evolving ideology (neo-liberalism) produced by business schools, journalists and other intellectuals, at the international level by those institutions that develop officially endorsed policy guidelines, and again at the national level by the translating of these guidelines into concrete measures of national fiscal and monetary policy.
>
> (Cox and Schechter 2002: 33)

This multilevel process is defined by the internationalisation of the state, referred to by Cox as:

> The unofficial and official transnational and international network of state and corporate representatives and intellectuals who work towards the formulation of a policy consensus for global capitalism as nebuleuse ... The world economic agencies function as part of ... the nebuleuse that tries to generate a consensus for the management of global capitalism among governmental and corporate powers in which the United Nations takes a subordinate but compliant place.
>
> (Ibid.: 33, 39)

Accordingly, IFIs are an important instrument through which the values of global hegemony are articulated, framing and thereby circumscribing the actions of domestic and international actors (Cox 1992: 178–179). As a result, the central function of IFIs is the justification and defence of a particular political economic project, materially and ideologically promoting specific values and intervening in domestic development. International institutions are 'legitimising agents of the hegemonic order from which they arise and act as the embodiment of the central norms around which this order is constructed'. They are 'sustained by global norms and institutional procedures that act to establish behavioural rules for governments' (Taylor 2001: 10). Hence, in intervening in development, IFIs are able to co-opt national elites on the periphery and assimilate opposing (counter-hegemonic) positions.

The achievement of the IFIs' hegemonic role is dependent on their success on the broader ideological and policy field of development. Thus, the structural capabilities of IFIs are defined by their capacity to frame policy alternatives, assimilate opposing positions, justify and defend a particular political economic project, and legitimise those transformations along the guidelines of development set by the management of the global economy. Within this approach to the IFIs' development role, framing constitutes perhaps one of its most distinctive political economic capabilities, since its exercise limits the power of ideas that can potentially harm capitalist expansion. The process of framing is mainly technocratic and takes place through the political strategy of depoliticisation, economisation and operationalisation of ideas and guidelines of development. In this depoliticisation, ideas are detached or decontaminated from any political dimension; in the economisation, the remaining ideas are anchored to and justified by neoliberal assumptions; and finally, in the operationalisation, they are translated into policies and programmes addressed to domestic development (Bøås and McNeill 2004). A central example in this regard is the IFIs' guidelines and policies on privatisations promoted in their country programmes.

Globalisation

As the central role of IFIs is to generate consensus and promote the expansion of a particular form of organisation of the global economy, they predicate an understanding of what development is and how it may be achieved within globalisation. The starting point is a particular understanding of what globalisation is, for the mainstream an 'inevitable' contemporary process based on the universalisation of market economy with scant room for any state involvement in the economy. There the state is and must be reduced to a minimal indirect institutional regulator. The execution of this role is based on what Karl Polanyi (1975) called the 'economistic fallacy' through 'the institutional separation of society into an economic and political sphere'. This propounds a highly problematic understanding of globalisation, of the dynamics of development, and – the subject of this investigation – of the RDBs' development mission.

For new IPE scholars, instead, globalisation is a 'long historical process characterised by contradictions, shaped by conjunctures and contested by increasingly aware and hostile political forces' (Payne 2004: 10). In contrast to mainstream approaches, globalisation in new IPE does not posit any predetermined future or format of development, whether global market-led or global polity-led. This long-term historical process is a transformative force, shaking societies, economies, and institutions of governance and world order, dissolving the limits between the international and the domestic, in an endless game whose outcome remains uncertain

(Giddens 1996; Mann 1997; Held *et al*. 1999). Globalisation imposes new constraints, but rather than closing down development it opens up a new range of important options of development (Payne 2004).

At the heart of globalisation is the increasingly global character of production and finance, turning the economy into the matrix of change. Global production is able to use territorial differences to maximise reductions in costs, taxes, regulation-avoidance, and control over labour. Production is subordinated to the way finance works, and global finance has reached the point where it has become almost a 'virtually unregulated 24-hour-a-day network', whose collective decision-making 'is centred in world cities rather than states – New York, Tokyo, London, Paris, Frankfurt' (Cox 2000: 27). The rise of a global economy, based on growing capital mobility, has pushed states to strategically reorganise their fiscal, industrial and welfare policies. That is because a passive stance and indiscriminate openness threaten state control of development, particularly impacting on its financing of instrumental policy areas such as capital accounts, exchange rates, monetary policy, fiscal policy and public welfare spending (Diaz-Bonilla and Schamis 2001; Weiss 2003b; Hobson 2003; Swank 2003).

Globalisation, consequently, seems to be recasting the pattern of global social stratification, weaving together the conditions and praxis of the upper and middle classes from different countries. These incipient class hierarchies tend to be global with a regional character rather than domestic, reflecting the accentuation of social polarisation between rich and poor between and within societies (Castells 1996; Wallerstein 1993; Cox 2000). In turn, the global process of social re-stratification is re-engineering power in a confluence of authority, national and international, over what occurs within a country (Held *et al*. 1999).

Because of global economic and social tendencies, the historical form of the state is deeply reorganised, accompanying the changing hegemony through the process of the internationalisation of the state. In this regard, weak states initially tend to respond passively to the impact of the changes, which adjust national economies to the dynamics of an under-regulated global economy. Nonetheless, since hegemony is also present primarily in the form of asymmetric bargaining processes in trade, finance and labour markets, the internationalisation of weak or peripheral states may turn in a second phase to the mediation or repression of social actors to contain conflict (Cox and Schechter 2002).

Another important element is that the top levels of capital and the intelligentsia have a propensity to take an active role in reducing the contradictions between the external and the internal. In particular, they play a key role conducive to a redefinition of state policy that guarantees state control over vital areas of development and in particular over the orientation and organisation of its financing. Thus, the limits of the sustainability of the internationalisation and mediation of the state are domestic, since a shift in development strategy is only viable with the emergence of new historical blocs. However, as the global economy and especially global finance impose new constraints upon state strategies, it also enables them in their policy making. Briefly, changes establish new global and regional scenarios whose positive or negative features vary in relation to the wide range of probable relationships between domestic configurations of social forces and global structures within the intergoverned process accompanying the strategy of global integration.

Regionalism, multilateralism and RDBs

Regionalism and multilateralism

There is a broad academic consensus that the changes beginning in the 1970s up to the end of the Cold War brought a different world order into being. One of its features has been the growing importance of maintaining a balance in terms of power and anchoring of development between world order and national states, which is regionalism. The issue has been mainly voiced by two contending positions within mainstream approaches regarding how to understand the emergence of regionalist projects.

Some observers consider the development of regions to be a threat to the global economy, as the world divides into three broad regions – Europe, the Americas and Asia Pacific – leading slowly towards trade wars that may develop into 'real wars'. This is justified by the tenet that in the post-US hegemonic order, the world will degenerate into conflict with regions and civilisations as the main actors (Huntington 1993). In a world of a few large blocs, the monopoly of power of each unit will tempt them to shift the terms of trade in their favour, a tendency that could only be minimised by a world of many small trading blocs (Krugman 1991).

The other approach holds that regionalism is a positive tendency, as long as its reason and ultimate objective be trade and liberalisation (Birdsall and Rojas-Suarez 2004). In this view, regionalism occurs naturally as a result of the development of private markets, in a progressive convergence of economic and social parameters between localities and regions, increasing interdependence (Devlin and Castro 2004). Since multilateral trade liberalisation is slow and uncertain, countries tend to opt for regional trade liberalisation through regional trade agreements (RTAs), in a convergence of regionalisation and multilateralism (Bergsten 1997; Tussie 2003). As a result, the focus of the debate here has been usually whether regionalisation is leading to a more polarised or a more cooperative world economy and world order within which the RDBs' development mission must be understood.

Partisans of market-oriented development claim that regionalism is primarily a regional concentration of states, setting market rules that foster free trade and finance (Edwards 1998; Vasquez 2003). Here regionalism is a unilateral process of trade and financial liberalisation, a 'liberalism from below' led by states, wherein countries such as Chile and Argentina 'have gone ahead under their steam, largely without the need for external' multilateral pressure (Sally 2000: 3). Countries have shown an increasing capacity to individually access capital markets to finance development, whereby the RDBs' development mission has been reduced to and refocused on providing technical support and focused expertise to support that. RDBs constitute a system of minor multilateral regional bodies subordinate to the major IFIs, whose development function is to promote technical coordination and assistance for market development and global liberalisation, preparing countries for gaining access to external financing (Meltzer Report 2000).

On the other hand, for proponents of a regulated global order through multilateral rule, 'regionalism' refers to the idea that 'agreements among countries within regions can be a step toward greater integration into a global trading and financial system'. Regionalism is therefore 'a strategy to speed the development of regional and domestic institutions, and thus generate faster and steadier growth' through trade liberalisation, mostly based on geographical – comparative – advantages (Birdsall and Rojas-Suarez 2004: 1; Gurria and Volcker 2001). Within this perspective, neoliberal institutionalists argue that 'regionalism thrives in the policy spaces left by multilateralism but at the same time when these lacunae are too many or too wide these tensions are then re-played in the multilateral sphere' (Tussie 2003: 100). Regionalism, therefore, provides substance for multilateralism reinforcing RDBs' development mission as countries benefit through better opportunities for market access. Global capital markets are far from perfect, and therefore RDBs have to contribute an important developmental role and expertise for facilitating access to capital markets by developing countries and favouring regional trade integration (Gurria and Volcker 2001).

Briefly, mainstream approaches share two central elements that frame the understanding of and define the RDBs' development mission: first, the assumption that RDBs constitute part of the global system of management of development. They mediate, positively or negatively, between global capital markets, international organisations of development, and developing and less developed countries. They have common, universal and unchangeable development mandates understood within specific approaches. Second, that all debate about development within globalisation revolves mainly around how far regionalisation can go without increased free trade and finance (Devlin and Castro 2004: 77).

Since regionalisation is associated with the trend towards globalisation, and regionalism with the political construction in the 1990s of the new neoliberal hegemony, it is important to characterise both. For some scholars, regionalisation thus refers to those processes which are deepening the integration of particular regions, and which can be traced, at the first stage of analysis, to changes in the flow of trade, FDI and migration (Stalling 1992; Hirst and Thompson 1996). This is exemplified by Latin America, with growing intra-regional trade and FDI, especially in the 1990s (CEPAL 2000).

Nonetheless, these increasing economic exchanges exhibit an uneven pattern, integrating some places and sectors while marginalising others. The other impact is the increasing presence of core areas which act as powerful magnets, dragging 'areas and societies into their orbit', generating new forms of stratification (Payne 2004: 20–21). The irregular impact of regionalisation and the emergence of new patterns of stratification within regions have been the issues addressed by regionalist projects. Therefore, globalisation and regionalisation are defining the importance of 'new regionalism' as a response to some of the key elements of the post-Cold War agenda of liberalised trade (Grugel 1999: 11).

Contrasting with mainstream perspectives, new IPE approaches regionalism in the whole context of changing hegemony and the rise of the neoliberal world order, transcending the traditional dispute between unilateral or multilateral views on regionalism. As a result of world changes, driven by hegemony, the global order is increasingly characterised by aggressive trade competition, in which negotiations between powers determine outcomes. Different authors agree that this represents coexistence between regionalisation and tendencies towards globalisation (Held *et al.* 1999). At the root of this there is an increasing convergence between multilateralism and regionalism, most notoriously in the 1990s in what has come to be called the 'new regionalism' (Hettne and Inotai 1994; Fawcett and Hurrel 1995; Gamble and Payne 1996; Stalling 1992, 1997b).

Two significant positions can be identified normatively within new IPE regarding the relationships between globalisation/regionalisation and multilateralism. In the first place, there are those who are more enthusiastic about the regional phenomena. In these, following Polanyi's ideas, regionalism represents the 'return of the political' through intervention in development as a result of the dialectics of market expansion and actions at political level in defence of society (Hettne 2003). Here, new regionalism forms part of a global transformation that includes the participation of a variety of non-state actors invisible to state-centric approaches. Accordingly, it is necessary to make a central distinction between formal regions and the real regions. Formal regions are defined by the membership of the dominant formal regional organisations and inter-state frameworks; these are subordinated to the major regional configurations – i.e. European Union, North America and Asian Pacific (Hettne and Inotai 1994; Hettne 2003; Hettne and Söderbaum 1999). However, the concept of formal region does not inform other realities outside the state whereby in order to gain the integral substance and general directions of regions, the formal must be related to the de facto, informal or real region. The notion of a real region seeks to grasp what is beyond the state as the main regionalising actors focusing on the multitude of other actors such as informal sector, social movements, social networks, civil societies and the varied civil associations at different levels of the regional social life (Hettne and Söderbaum 1999).

Other scholars consider today's regionalism to be open regionalism, a manifestation of economic globalisation and prevailing forms of hegemony, wherein distinct models of capitalism are shaping regions – Asian, European, Anglo-American models – through free-trade strategies led by policy-making elites in the core states (Gamble and Payne 2003: 52). Within this framework, the key question is to what extent state–society complexes are building state-led existing regionalism and if that is from below or from above (Gamble and Payne 1996, 2003; Payne 2004). They are critical of existing regionalist tendencies, exploring the extent to which state-driven regional projects are mitigating the negative effects of globalisation and free market capitalism. Accordingly, they claim the need to give closer examination to the different instances of intra-regional politics of development, and to embrace the formal and informal dimensions of regionalisation and regionalism, taking into account the substantial differences between regional projects, state–society complexes and development strategies.

Beyond the enthusiasm and pessimism of new IPE scholars towards regionalist tendencies, they share the idea that the study of the relations between national and regional strategies of development and multilateral organisations still demands more efforts (Payne 2004). Actually, extant investigation in the field shows the existence of a striking range of different relations and impacts in developments, which vary according to the position of regions and states within global and regional orders.

However, if the formally organised regions are defined by the dominant formal regional organisations and inter-state frameworks, and if they present substantial differences between regions, then the structural conditions shaping RDBs are necessarily different. The regional presence and participation of the USA in the Inter-American Development Bank is not the same as the impact of the European countries in the European Development Bank. In fact, even though RDBs function under the global guidelines set by the major IFIs and industrialised states, structurally they diverge, since they are shaped by different RDB–state configurations and state–society complexes in each region.

This is a key element of any conceptual framework attempting to apprehend the political economic nature of RDBs in their historical and geographical context, for two reasons. First, because this permits us to perceive the different mixes and balances of ideas and forces, something that obviously changes from one RDB to another. Second, the areas of development addressed by the RDBs vary between regions, as do their institutional structures and their instruments of intervention, let alone their structure of institutional governance. Briefly, this element is vital to grasping the power dimension of the RDBs' development mission. As Cox states:

> [I]nstitutions reflect the power relations prevailing at the point of origin and tend, at least initially, to encourage collective images consistent with these power relations ... Institutions are particular amalgams of ideas and material power which in turn influence the development of ideas and material capabilities.
>
> (1987: 19)

Therefore, even though RDBs represent a system subordinated to guidelines of other major international actors and hegemonic states, this explains only one side of the coin, their agency of its developmental mission. To apprehend their structure or dynamics of change and evaluate their role in development in middle and long term, we need something else. It is necessary, to begin with, to identify the structural elements or central changes shaping their internal balance of power and in particular their particular regional political economic dynamics of development. For this investigation, these structural elements include the Americas as a region, in particular the Latin American historical identity, and the configuration and sphere of action of the Inter-American Development Bank.

The first characteristic that makes the Americas different from other regions is the presence of the USA within the hemisphere, where regional configurations have been historically related to the changing forms of US authority (Grugel

1999). Regionalism in Latin America has been a way to mitigate the unilateral influence of the US hegemony, although South American regionalism transcends, to some extent, the relatively recent phenomenon of 'neoliberal regionalism' (Grugel 2001). Since the 1930s, the USA has led the region, with its power exercised more through coercion than consent in the Latin American area referred to as the United States' 'backyard' (Gamble and Payne 2003: 52).

The declining US financial power and the shift of its stance towards Latin America at the end of the 1980s– with the launching of Bush's Enterprise for the Americas, and the establishment of the North American Free Trade Agreement (NAFTA) in 1994 – represented a major structural change. A transformation contested this a decade later with a regional shift to a new regional reconfiguration and entrenchment of its political economy of development, now known as new South American Regionalism (Bonilla and Long 2010). The shift redefined the hemisphere and in particular the historical identity of 'the Latin-American' through the creation of new regionalist free-trade-led projects based on neoliberal guidelines of globalisation and development. A milestone in this process was the disconnection from Latin America of Mexico and its final integration into the Northern American bloc, turning Latin American regionalism increasingly into a South American affair.

Something similar was observed by Varas (1992), for whom the processes in motion in the 1990s constituted the end of Latin America as a coherent unit and the emergence of a depressed Andean subregion, an embryonic Brazilian– Argentine axis, and countries such as Chile looking for individual options in terms of trade diversification. According to new IPE scholars, the Argentina–Brazil axis has increasingly become central in the Southern Cone, with the creation of Mercosur (Mercado Common del Sur – Southern Common Market) as a new arena of support for the return of democracies (Grugel 1999).

The second characteristic is that the new subregions had been configured as regional responses to liberalised trade. It has reflected the adoption by states of external strategies to improve their global market position protecting powerful domestic actors from the pressures of globalisation (Kuwayama 1993, 1999; CEPAL 1994; Bulmer-Thomas 2001). Therefore, this 'open regionalism' has been shaped by an extensive liberalisation of intraregional markets. Briefly, this consisted of a strategy of international economic opening, underpinned by multilateral agreements, addressed at promoting the assumed virtuous formula of financing development based on state cooperation, enlargement and access to new markets and domestic adjustment through macroeconomic reform and privatisation of public utilities (Kuwayama 1999: 9).

Towards a new IPE of RDBs

In IPE, the understanding of RDBs within the context of the relationships between globalisation, regionalism and multilateralism is certainly elusive. This is for three major reasons. The first is because RDBs present themselves as consensual and technocratic entities of development banking, autonomous from governments and endowed with the advantage to exercise policy conditionalities upon borrower members. Another is the fact that RDBs are tied to the state structures that give them origin, and fund them, whereby they do not seem so independent. The final element is that, in cases such as the IDB, their corporate governance lies in the hands of borrowing members, giving the impression that they have the power to define to some extent their development role. For these reasons, any new IPE approach about RDBs must deal with and integrate these perspectives to inform the agency and structural dynamics of these institutions and their development role.

One way to grasp the political economic nature of RDBs within the new IPE approach is by focusing on the exercise of hegemonic power and the changing world order. RDBs play a vital role in hegemony, ensuring the continuance of a particular political economic project by the mediating, consensus-forming and legitimising functions that they perform. It is through framing, negotiating, setting conditions and assimilating opposing domestic positions that they build consensus for the management of the regional economies among governmental and corporate powers. Historical complex configurations of states, international organisations, economic actors and specific forms of knowledge exercise power and frame the development mission of these regional bodies within specific regional contexts marked by historical configurations of social forces and epistemic communities.

As institutions, RDBs reflect the power relations prevailing within their scenarios and dominant values; they seem also to be agency spaces wherein the global is domestically contested and built. They play complex and varied roles according to their region, which are defined by the particular amalgam of material and ideological resources which far overflow their own institutional boundaries, through political, technical and financial channels, instruments, and regional networks accessing domestic areas and actors.

Three dimensions of the RDBs' development role reflect the complex political economic nature of these regional bodies of development: the political, technical and financial dimensions that are traceable in their organisational mandates, constitutions, programmes and outcomes. These three dimensions are interrelated and complementary and, depending on the RDBs' interventions, they occupy a major or minor role. The political dimension comprises their relationships with the major IFIs, and lender and borrower members, allowing them to participate directly in intergoverned strategies of global integration adopted by countries. The technical dimension is defined by the central consensual devices anchored in epistemic communities through which RDBs play their hegemonic consensual role, depoliticising specific ideas of development, and operationalising them into rules, procedures and programmes. The financial dimension encompasses their capacity both to channel official and private resources to support a political economic project, and to provide access to capital markets through assessing creditworthiness and officially endorsing country strategies and policies.

At the top of the RDBs lies their complex corporate governance – given the participation of country lenders and borrowers in their structure of decision making, which has been widely regarded as their chief strategic advantage (Griffith-Jones

2002b; Sagasti 2002; Birdsall 2003). RDBs' corporate governance exhibits a dual political economic nature or an integrated interdependence within their corporate governance defined by both the RDB–IFI relationship and the relationship between RDBs and member states. These complex relationships endow RDBs with two central advantages. The first is their AAA credit risk rating, provided by the participation in their governance of industrialised states, without which these institutions could neither survive nor access capital markets and transfer capital to borrower members at low cost. However, this element ties and limits their role and interventions in recipient countries to orientations defined by donor states. The second is their sense of ownership in borrower member countries as a result of borrower-country participation in their corporate governance. This, in turn, delineates a central characteristic of RDBs' development role, namely the capability to favour the creation of complex regional or international alliances, and legitimise the particular balance of social forces or coalitions sustaining the domestic political economic project of member countries. These elements mean that the RDBs' development function can be effective only to the extent that policies and programmes are functional for the development strategies of borrower member countries within the framework and expansion of capitalist style of their lenders (i.e. Chile).

The presence of developing and less developed countries within RDBs' corporate governance is perhaps more evident than in any other multilateral organisation. It provides these institutions, even though structurally limited, with room enough to strengthen and pursue regional political commitments with their members. As a result, RDBs are not simply agents of hegemony but can, at particular stages of history, enter into a conflict between their regional political commitments and their global ones, to the extent that this does not put their own survival at risk, as Chapter 6 will show.

The mix within these regional bodies of both the IFI–RDBs and RDBs–borrower members endows these institutions with their final central characteristic and capability: the power to intervene in domestic areas by strengthening the co-opting and assimilating powers of national elites and resisting opponents of mainstream development. This represents the major social feature of RDBs, which in social terms extends to vast regional social networks, integrating their elites into a broader technical, depoliticised and economised consensus. The RDBs' ideological function has the power both to frame policy alternatives and to absorb regional political and intellectual elites while providing strategic access to domestic areas and actors of development.

Technically, RDBs have historically proved to be technical and consensual institutions with the power to institutionalise social action, crucially through framing development policy alternatives, presenting them in 'the sense of the way things usually happen' with a central role played by ideas (Cox 1989). Given the presence of core regional countries and borrowers, RDBs are influenced also by the orientations shaped by the constellation of power of their own regions, institutionalising particular ideas of development 'through the exercise of hegemony' and 'through the adoption of shared ideas and agreements concerning collective images' (Bøås and McNeill 2004: 6). This dimension of RDBs is indissolubly bound to their political nature and explains why they are social constructs and battlefields for opposed ideas contesting each other through technocratic means (ibid.).

Within this function and process, there are three interrelated forces at work, distorting, adapting and framing ideas of development: the market-led and the polity-led global approaches, and the economic technocratic nexus. Independent of the variety of distortions in ideas, they have in common their political strategies of depoliticisation, economisation, and operationalisation of these approaches to development policy. Perhaps the strongest of this is the strategy of depoliticisation, a process within which ideas 'are drained of any overt political content, even if they are not wholly drained of their power', making critical appraisal of multilateral policies particularly difficult since they conceal what they stand for (Bøås and McNeill 2004: 6). On the other hand, economisation, common to competing approaches of development, represents the technical subordination of ideas to mainstream economic interpretations to development. Finally, operationalisation reflects the institutional process through which RDBs use technocratic means to produce depoliticisation and economisation, further hiding the beneficiaries of their policies and programmes (ibid.).

Finally, the most debated dimension of RDBs is their financial dimension as banks and their financial role within development (Rodrik 1995; Sagasti and Alcalde 1999; Meltzer Report 2000; Ratha 2001; Birdsall and Rojas-Suarez 2004). The political economic nature of the RDBs' financial role is indissolubly bound and determined by the sources and transformational character of the world order. The nature of its role is facilitated by, among others, international financial institutions and financial actors. Therefore, to focus the analysis about their development effectiveness only on finance per se, or the quantitative size of RDBs' financial instruments, definitely narrows our understanding of their development function. In fact, the political economy of RDBs' development function materialises through two additional political strategies: depoliticisation and economisation. These strategies are key components and operate throughout the whole process of creation of consensus, diagnostic of development issues, design of measures and instrumentation of RDBs' programmes combining financial, technical and political resources, incentives and compensations.

The real dimension of the RDBs' financial function lies in the power-balancing impact of the development role of these institutions. That is, the extent to which the RDBs' financial interventions support, consolidate or sustain a particular political economic project, promoting different forms of cooperation and alliances between businesses and ruling elites and offering privileged access to domestic projects financed by these banks. Finance is vital to the intergoverned process of global integration, a fact that leads RDBs generally to favour and promote country access to external financing on the basis of country accomplishment of international standards.

RDBs work within the set of standard procedures, rules, and guidelines of the international development finance structures, defined by the major IFIs, the IMF and the World Bank and the industrialised states. The role of this official framework of development financing is to legitimise the participation of borrowing and investing countries within the RDBs, providing banks with the power to impose conditions upon borrowing members. However, the exercise of this regulatory power is dependent on the member country's power inside the regional institutions; bigger countries tend to be freer of constraining conditions than small member states. In addition, working within and tying themselves to the official framework of development financing furnishes RDBs with access to the official financial resources of the major IFIs and industrialised states, reinforcing the dual character of the structural relations and powers of these regional agents. The contentious issue here is the function of and in particular the use of financial adjustment instruments that contribute more to the survival and growth of these institutions than to their country recipients.

Summarising, the political economic character of RDBs and their development mandate is determined by the interrelation of their political, technical and financial roles, combined into an amalgam of ideological and material capabilities. These elements are at the very foundation of RDBs' capabilities to adopt and transform ideas in pro-market discourse, to frame policy alternatives, and to legitimise and support specific political economic projects. As a result, RDBs exert a power-balancing and legitimising effect upon regional and domestic social forces through their intergoverned process of global integration.

Conclusion

This chapter has introduced a new IPE approach for the appraisal of the political and economic character and the changing development role and policies of RDBs within the framework of globalisation, regionalism and multilateralism in development. It has posed, for subsequent chapters, the task of examining the relation and influence of the IDB's role and policies in the processes of liberalisation reforms in Argentina in the 1990s. The chapter began with the identification of those dominant academic and political theories and discourses which have, during the past three decades, attempted to comprehend the political economic nature of RDBs and their missions. In doing so, the work has recognised two main sets of discourses: the market-led and the polity-led approaches to globalisation and development.

A number of weaknesses or deficiencies within these perspectives have been noted regarding the interpretations of interconnections between finance and the production of welfare in development under globalisation, deficiencies which limit their utility as tools for the understanding of the political economy of the RDBs. These limitations have been identified by extracting the conceptions underlying their approaches to globalisation, international finance, development and the state, and the role of RDBs within these. Among the most important weaknesses which have been identified are their reliance on a predefined view of globalisation and the world order, a narrow and economistic understanding of development, and an over-reliance on the virtues of external development financing. Another point which has been stressed has been the divorce between the international and domestic spheres.

In contrast, a new IPE approach and method has been introduced, integrating those approaches into a whole picture of development, within which the political economy of IDB can be read. The chapter has briefly presented the main issues in the historical debate on the interconnections between international finance, development and the state in order to introduce this new IPE approach. It has been argued that the new IPE perspective grasps the weakness of dominant approaches and enriches some of their virtues by defining an integral framework of development that is able to apprehend the changing political economic nature and policies of RDBs.

In the process, the first step has been to define the ontological and epistemological scope of the new IPE approach based on the distinction between a 'critical theory' versus a 'problem-solving theory'. This was followed by outlining the method of historical structures to introduce three key concepts that inform our approach – state, international institutions and globalisation. The second step moves on to consider the relationships between regionalism, multilateralism and RDBs to define the more focused conceptual framework required for the central inquiries of this investigation.

There it was argued that the political economic nature of an RDB and its development mission must necessarily integrate and find meaning with reference to a particular region and political economic structure. Accordingly, it established a frame of reference to grasp these, following the guidelines suggested by Robert Cox and other scholars in new IPE. Consequently, two concepts were introduced which frame RDBs and their development mission: the intergoverned international–domestic interdependence and the power-balancing capability and legitimising effect of RDBs' development interventions. Given the aims of this investigation, the analysis took a further step towards establishing the complex political economic nature of RDBs through the interrelations of three dimensions which define in turn the structure of their development roles: the political, technical and financial dimensions. It now remains to trace the regional political economic dynamics that have determined the constitutions of our case study, the Inter-American Development Bank, and the way these have shaped its mandates across different stages of development.

2 Towards a new political economy view of the Inter-American Development Bank

Introduction

It has become commonplace in economics and politics, when appraising the economic and political misfortunes and achievements of Latin American governments and regional institutions such as the IDB, to refer to global economic changes pre- and post-Great Depression. Longing for a return to the golden age of 'liberal international trade', neoliberals identify the period – and in particular the 1940s onwards – as the origin of the major historical economic and political distortions in the region. According to neoliberals, populist and developmentalist projects neglected the principle of comparative advantage in favour of inefficient import substitution policies pursued by populist governments (Platt 1985). In contrast, new international liberals approach this period – and in particular 1929 – as a 'critical historical point', a time of changes and innovations, marked by the demise of the primary-export model and the creation of major international and regional financial institutions, including the IDB (Thorp 2000: 1). Briefly, as shown in Chapter 1, both views bear in themselves important limitations which affect their ability to apprehend the political economic nature of the IDB. What is more, their disregard for the political economic dynamics between international and domestic politics and economics renders them limited in their ability to account for shifts in the roles and policies of regional financial institutions.

Following the theoretical concepts and methodology defined in Chapter 1, this chapter deploys a new IPE approach to analyse the IDB in the light of the political economy of the Americas, with particular attention to South America. It argues that the political economy shaping the IDB's role may find a framework of clearer explanation in the long run through the concepts of the internationalisation of production, the internationalisation of the state, and the globalisation of finance instead of an analysis pointing out the achievements and challenges of each IDB administration. It contends that the inception, take-off, and evolution of the IDB's role and lending policies reflect the complex sequence of political economic stages that have occurred since the decline of British hegemony, which is the rise, consolidation and decline of US hegemony, and the rise of globalisation in the region.

The first of the four main sections analyses the first stage, highlighting the main processes shaping the organisation of the financing of development, as well as the role played by the IDB in the evolution of the Pan American Union into the Inter-American system. This process, fuelled by the internationalisation of production, defined the context within which the original design and inception of the IDB took place. The second section explores the changes in the IDB's role in the period between the launching of the Alliance for Progress in 1961 and the decline of (and reaction to) US hegemony in the region, culminating in financial crises in the 1980s. The third section is devoted to the analysis of the period characterised by US hegemonic decline and the hemispheric reaction to the reassertion of US political and economic control over the region through dictatorships – a period of crisis, transition and change spanning the decades of the 1970s and 1980s. The fourth section analyses the great South American transformation of the 1990s, placing special attention upon the IDB's shift towards neoliberal strategies of development, along the lines of the Washington Consensus, and on the new form of regional governance: state-led new or 'open' regionalism. The chapter finishes with a short conclusion summarising the main conclusions regarding the IDB's role in development within the New Political Economy of the Americas.

Between the Pan American Union and the Inter-American system

The political and economic developments in the Americas between the 1920s and 1940s were marked by the rise of domestic-based industrialisation processes in South America and the particular configurations of social forces accompanying them. Notably, these processes were responses to international isolation and shocks, and by the emergency of the first forms of corporatist welfare state addressed at alleviating the social outcomes of decades of export-led development. Overall, by the 1930s, the new hemispheric processes had displaced the traditional regional ruling elites eager to participate, under US leadership, in the creation of new hemispheric institutions. Hemispherically, this period witnessed the rise of the US-sponsored Pan American Union and the creation of major regional institutions such as the Organisation of American States (1947) and the Economic Commission for Latin America and the Caribbean (ECLA/CEPAL), reflecting the USA's capacity to maintain, shape, and demonstrate control over hemispheric processes (Payne 1996).

The 1929 Great Depression and World War II represented a turning point in the history of Latin America. Overall, the international shocks left the region isolated from world trade, which produced a sharp decline in strategies of export-led development. In weakening the liberal order, this process stimulated an unanticipated process of rapid recovery and growth based on domestic-dependent import-substituted industrialisation (ISI) bound with the rise of heterogeneous configurations of social forces. The process was a reaction, and in that sense, it took the form of an unplanned industrialisation shaping and shaped by key facts. These were a growing sense of nationalism, the widening of the role of the state, and the rise of new social phenomena, such as massive urban expansion stimulated by the emergence of industrial workers, and by rural and European migration (Halperin Donghi 1993: 247–248; Diaz Alejandro 2000: 18).

Free from the pressures of international markets, the embryonic process of industrialisation was oriented towards domestic consumption, growing under state protection and financed through the transfer of resources from primary export sectors. Overall, the domestic-dependent ISI processes shaped a complex economic and political landscape of popular movements, military groups, oligarchic landowners and intellectual elites, some favouring and others opposed to the economic and social form of industrial autonomous capitalism emerging in the Southern Cone (Halperin Donghi 1993).

In the larger Latin American countries at least, by the 1940s, national industrialisation had become an alternative for development, counteracted only by those working for a return to the older classical model. In order to strengthen social cohesion within this new order, the backers of industrialisation took measures in favour of the new pattern of growth, broadening urban employment, and developing the first functions of the welfare state in the region. Under the umbrella of the 'national popular state', the Latin American state was reshaped in most of the region's countries, reflecting an alliance between domestic-based industrial groups, nationalist military elites and urban movements led by industrial workers.

Notwithstanding the significance of this accelerated industrialisation, by 1945 Latin American economies continued to be mostly dependent on primary exports (Thorp 1985; Bulmer-Thomas 2003). Furthermore, instead of targeting the industrial take-off during the 1940s, Latin American governments used reserves accumulated during wartime to nationalise foreign-owned debt, finance public services and import manufactured goods for the emergent middle classes. Far from promoting an open industrial sector, governments instead attempted, by managing tariff barriers and nominal exchange rates, to protect an embryonic and domestic-oriented industrial sector, as a way to defend the interests of urban consumers, and increase workers' share in national income and pro-reform coalitions (Weaver 2000: 127–144; Diaz Alejandro 2000).

As World War II ended, the United States turned its attention back – to some extent – to the region, nurturing from the 1950s the growth of an externally dependent industrial sector through its traditional support to US corporations. As the US hegemony consolidated, the internationalisation of production became the major source of financing for development in the region, shifting anchoring the organisation of development to the use of external FDI as the main source of finance. In less than a decade, the new externally dependent industrial sectors expanded into the region, providing goods and services to newly well-off people, serving the top of the social pyramid with textiles, chemicals, pharmaceuticals, electrical appliances and transport (Weaver 2000: 71–88; Halperin Donghi 1993: 253; Diaz Alejandro 2000).

In a short period, the region became one of the key recipients of US FDI, averaging between 40.0 per cent in 1950 and 31.4 per cent in 1957 of global US FDI, as illustrated in Table 2.1. Remarkably, the process unfolded on the basis of the existing social configuration which featured domestic-dependent ISI sectors and their corporatist welfare state generating tensions and divisions between the two industrial-oriented configurations. As a result, there was a marked process of

Table 2.1 US direct investment position in Latin America, 1950–79 (percentage composition, by regions in US$ billions)

	1950	*1957*	*1966*	*1979*
All areas	100	100	100	100
Developed countries	48.0	55.1	68.1	71.6
Developing countries	48.0	40.5	26.8	24.8
Latin America	(40.6)	(31.4)	(18.9)	(19.1)
Others	4.0	3.4	5.1	4.6

Source: Based on Griffith-Jones (1984: 28–35).

diversification of the structure of the regions' urban population as accompanied by the rise of new political tendencies and configurations of social forces.

Briefly, unlike the form that this had taken in Europe, the 'internationalisation of production' (Cox 1987: 244–253) in Latin America unfolded in a remarkably different manner and under rather different configurations of social forces, which maintained their impact for two decades. Remarkably, this time period is characterised by the political and ideological separation between national popular and liberal reformist groups, the latter in alliance with export primary sector elites, defining two projects in a scenario of pro- and anti-US–European financial projects (Halperin Donghi 1993: 253; Varas 1992; Diaz Alejandro 2000).

By the end of the 1940s and into the early 1950s, as US FDI expanded in the most industrialised countries of the region, the USA turned its eye towards the consolidation within the region of its new world hegemonic power. However, the task did not require the organisation of a new system, such as was demanded in Europe and East Asia, but was implemented through the existing 'Pan American Union', the hemispheric body dependent since the 1920s on the US Secretary of State and the State Department (Nef 1994; Halperin Donghi 1993: 248). The Pan American Union was the first expression of US domination over and alliance with the regional liberal and oligarchic elites, and the foundation upon which the Inter-American system was developed.

As new social processes began to displace traditional elites from power, this hemispheric body became the arena for regional new allies, framing and guiding hemispheric integration under US guidelines. However, despite reiterated Latin American claims for wide economic and political support for the creation of hemispheric institutions such as the World Bank, these did not find response from the USA. In fact, the USA had begun to concern itself with containing the expansion of the Soviet sphere of influence by laying the foundations for economic growth and military support for its allies in Europe and East Asia (Varas 1995). From then, and during the presidencies of Eisenhower, Kennedy, Johnson and Nixon, the USA's stance towards the region was dominated by the desire of the USA to maintain and demonstrate control over its own hemisphere, its 'backyard', and the region was seen largely as a homogenous zone by Washington (Payne 1996: 97).

The design and inception of the IDB

The first outcome of the Pan American Union came in 1947 with the creation of the first collective defence mechanism designed to protect US military interests. In 1948 the Pan American Union was renamed the Organization of American States (OAS) (Nef 1995). In the 1950s, the Eisenhower administrations (1953–61) persisted with emphasising security issues and US trade and financial expansion instead of regional development. By 1954, most of the military-led governments in the region received military assistance, but only when they showed commitment to US security concerns and accepted US FDI. The same year, the US administration authorised and supported the overthrow of the democratically elected government in Guatemala, branding its commitment to land reform as 'communist'. This regional climate, shaped by the stance of the USA to the region, made many Latin Americans resentful of US power, with Mexico and Argentina in particular developing important counter-hegemonic responses (Herring 1955; MacDonald 1985).

Briefly, the inception of the IDB within this context represented a hemispheric response against the backdrop of the rise and consolidation of the Pax Americana. Rather than a truly regional or Latin American institution, the IDB was created as a US-dependent hemispheric body, fulfilling in part the aspirations of regional elites, struggling together to find their way into a post-war world order from which they appeared to be almost completely marginalised. The IDB was conceived initially by its creators as a regional official bank with wide monetary powers over the region's governments, in accordance with the CEPAL guidelines and Quintadinha proposals addressed to create the first hemispheric financial institution (see below). Under different forms, the creation of a regional institution had long been the ambition of liberal elites including economists, politicians, representatives of big corporations, and key officials from north and south countries, all of whom aspired to an increasing involvement of the region with the USA (Tomassini 1999).

Actually, before and after World War II, some Latin American representatives had been appealing for a massive regional cooperation programme similar to the Marshall Plan, as was made clear by the Inter-American Economic Conference and Social Meeting at Quintadinha in 1954 inspired by Raul Prebisch and CEPAL. Nevertheless, the Truman and Eisenhower administrations consistently rejected such proposals, as they considered that Latin America played a peripheral role in the Cold War as, perhaps, it did not matter enough (Griffith-Jones 1984). In 1954, these initiatives found an echo in the US administration, supporting regional governments' call for the establishment of a group of experts from central banks and CEPAL to make a specific proposal to the OAS in Washington (Tussie 1995: 18).

However, the project soon began to take a different direction as the US administration, through the Secretary of the Treasury, George Humphrey, made clear that the USA would support but not finance the creation of such a regional organisation. In line with US foreign policy for the region, addressed to the avoidance of conflicts with the major countries and to gain regional access for US investments, the Eisenhower administration made it clear that financial resources should come from the private sector and the region's governments. If regional governments wished to form an association with the USA, they should concentrate on improving the climate for FDI. Hence, the historical aspiration of a regional official bank was realised through the inception of an agency for the promotion of FDI-attracting reforms (Griffith-Jones 1984).

On 30 December 1959, the Inter-American Development Bank was officially created by the OAS with the mandate 'to contribute to the acceleration of the process of economic and social development of the regional developing member countries' (under OAS 1959, Agreement Establishing the Inter-American Development Bank, Art. I/sec. 1 and Art. II/sec. 1). The IDB was an American institution within the context of US hegemony.

The shortfall of financial resources meant that it was only the embryo of the creature dreamt of by its sponsors, although it was firmly founded upon the tenet that development was a straightforward product of markets, demanding policies framed by long-term plans designed by official agencies to promote infrastructure for development and ISI policies nurtured by foreign capital, in particular US capital (Tomassini 1999; Tussie 1995). The mandatory function of the IDB was 'to utilize its own capital, funds raised by it in financial markets, and other available resources, for financing the development of member countries' and of 'nonregional countries which are members of the International Monetary Fund' (OAS 1959, section 2).

Originally, only members of the OAS were eligible for membership, the United States being the single non-borrowing member country, holding during the first decade 42.05 per cent of the voting power, allocated according to country capital subscription (OAS, Annual Report 1970). With headquarters in Washington and under the political umbrella and guidance of the main US financial and political institutions, the IDB came to be the third pillar of the Inter-American system along with the OAS and CEPAL, consolidating US hegemony in the region with its clearly defined functions. CEPAL was charged with providing technical support for national economic decision-making processes, the OAS was to deal with security issues, and the IDB was to address the problems of regional development and hemispheric integration.

As a result, the creation of the IDB was initially mainly symbolic. It represented a further historical step in the evolution and consolidation of hemispheric US hegemony through the regionalisation of production under FDI and the transformation of the Pan American Union. Nonetheless, at this stage at least, it did not play an important role in the financing of development in the region.

The Cold War and the internationalisation of the state

The early years of the IDB coincided with a period of unparalleled expansion in the world economy, in which 'development' meant the balance between defence of welfare and the liberal international order. However, two specific events shaped the scope of the IDB's role and policies during these decades. The first was the redirection of US FDI towards Europe and East Asia, demoting the internationalisation of production in the region while promoting the Cold War. The second was the consolidation of the dominant state form in South America: the military bureaucratic state. Actually, as the force of internationalisation of production moved into Europe, internationalisation of the state took on a growing relevance in a Latin America characterised by a great deal of regional political instability.

The process witnessed the internationalisation of the state under US hegemony through the consolidation of military-bureaucratic states in the region whose doctrines of national security assured US military and economic hegemony (Payne 1996: 97). The military-bureaucratic state was defined by the inclusion of the region in the Cold War through US foreign military assistance under the aegis of the Alliance for Progress (1961–69). Overall, this expressed the development of strong alliances between the USA and top elites in the region such as anti-communist military dictatorships, centre-right political forces, liberal intellectuals and exporters of primary commodities (Halperin Donghi 1993: 295–300; Nef 1994: 407–408). However, the significance of the inception of the IDB was diminished not only by the conditions the USA imposed upon its members, but even more so by the political and economic context of the Americas that assured it a negligible role as an RDB. As a result, the IDB would not become a significant economic actor until the creation of the Alliance for Progress in 1961 (Tussie 1995).

Until the end of the 1950s, the internationalisation of production in the region had received a mixed and short-lived impact from the Pax Americana's nurturing of the development of an externally dependent ISI sector. In the 1950s this dynamic changed, as the internationalisation of production took force in Europe through the Marshall Plan which absorbed the bulk of US FDI. Table 2.1 shows this tendency. There was a sharp decline in the US FDI flows to the region, dropping from 31.4 per cent in 1957 to 18.9 per cent in 1966. Europe presented an opposite case, where US FDI flows increased from 55.1 per cent in 1957 to 68.1 per cent in 1966, a result of currency convertibility and political agreements between the USA and Europe guaranteeing the repatriation of US capital and revenues (Griffith-Jones 1984).

Consequently, in the 1960s, the organisation of development financing was politically transformed, as the USA directed its official economic assistance to the region, with a flow of US official assistance reaching US$10 billion for the period 1960–69 (Griffith-Jones 1988: 34). Nonetheless, these disbursements were still small (US$4.8 billion) and directed mainly to military assistance in order to consolidate the new alliance between the USA and regional partners (ibid.). Overall, half of gross US economic assistance was addressed to repayments, amortisation of previous loans and accumulated interests; official assistance came to take the form of loans which expanded external debt (ibid.). Griffith-Jones concludes that, considering the total financial flows between the USA and Latin America, the net outflow of US revenues from the region exceeded the net inflow of US official funds to the region, showing the negative effect of US assistance (ibid.: 33–34).

In the 1960s, the USA's stance towards Latin America began to change, mainly motivated by political factors tied to the rise of economic and security concerns, with the Cuban Revolution as the turning point (Nef 1994; Abel and Lewis 1985; Varas 1995). As a result, in contrast to the economic form that the internationalisation of the state took in Europe, that is, their adjustment to the exigencies of the world economy, in Latin America the internationalisation of the state took on a military-bureaucratic state form, reinforced by US official financial aid and military assistance (Halperin Donghi 1993: 292–337). The bilateral stance of the USA towards the region favoured the diffusion of a National Security Doctrine which encouraged the armed forces to take an active role in ruling the region (Payne 1996). Nonetheless, the internationalisation of the state produced a counter-reaction, with a growing militant anti-Americanism of different social forces struggling around issues of redistribution of income and state control against the dominant liberal-oligarchic blocs aligned with the US hegemon (MacDonald 1985: 413).

Remarkably, despite the USA's influence in the region, the domestic coalitions tied to the domestic-based ISI processes in countries such as Argentina, Brazil, Chile and Uruguay managed to keep control over key resources contesting hegemony (Weaver 2000; Lewis 2003). As a result, by the 1950s and even the 1960s, the hemispheric integration of the South into the Pax Americana was a process which involved both growing levels of welfare and political instability. In fact, the outflow and shift of US FDI towards Europe even strengthened domestic-based industrial sectors and the role of corporatist states in the quest for more domestic consensus, while at the same time weakening the externally dependent industrial sector.

Nonetheless, the shift in US economic support towards Europe and East Asia soon encouraged those Latin American elites advocating a hemispheric partnership to reach for US support. Their requests found a place in the interests of the Kennedy administration, willing to support the 'developmentalist programme' through the IDB, although under its strong bilateral approach.

Developmentalism differed significantly from populist projects in terms of its social bases, state forms and relations to wider hegemonic forces. Developmentalism also focused on domestic industrial development but on the basis of direct alignments with US hegemony, in the hope of accessing FDI instead of domestic capital (with its particular relations with labour). Its configuration of social forces was narrower than populism and mainly based on new emergent social groups in alliance with top elites excluded from the past model. It adopted and employed the rhetoric and vocabulary of the Cold War and Keynesian economics as part of its strategies. In this regard, developmentalist projects led regional participation within the US-sponsored new Inter-American system and were deeply dependent on its official support – finance and military aid. The main political domestic target was to defeat populist coalitions in the struggle for hegemony, shaping a period featured by a hegemonic deadlock and limited democracies.

It had become clear to Washington that, without economic support, the region could end up penetrated and led by communism. The response to this was President Kennedy's Alliance for Progress, launched in 1961. The Alliance was founded on the belief that, in the face of growing anti-Americanism, contributing to the economic and social development of the uncommitted Latin American nations would lead to the growth of societies sympathetic to the US way of life (Griffith-Jones 1984). Accordingly, half of the money of the Alliance

> is for military assistance ... for the defence of countries directly threatened by aggression or subversion. More than 80 per cent of the money ... is in the form of loans ... and [to] be spent here in the United States on goods and services supplied by American businesses, and American workers.
>
> (President Kennedy, Press Conference, 5 July 1962)

The IDB as agency of development

Inspired by Rostow's (1960) modernisation theory of development, the Alliance fulfilled the expectations of liberal reformists, Christian democratic elites, and anti-communist forces in the region (Nef 1994). The first blueprint for the Alliance Plan emerged in the Quintadinha proposals, formulated with the partici-pation of Raul Prebisch and Felipe Herrera – first president of the IDB – who directly delivered it to President Kennedy (Griffith-Jones 1988: 32). Accordingly, they further warned the Kennedy administration not to appear to be promoting US foreign investment by means of the Alliance.

The spirit of the Alliance for Progress matched the 'developmentalist view'; nonetheless, the USA would cooperate economically, but only with those coun-tries willing to combat communism and make structural economic changes (Halperin Donghi 1993: 295). The character of the Alliance was purely bilateral and the OAS did not play any significant role during the following years. In addi-tion, the new US bilateralism represented a chance for some Latin American elites – and in particular the officer corps of armies – to align themselves with their northern neighbour, a chief element for the diffusion of the national security doc-trine as a justification for military activism in domestic affairs (Halperin Donghi 1993: 296). Briefly, after a decade of reforms under the Alliance, the outcome was that less than 2 per cent of economic growth benefited the poor, and there was a general deterioration in US–Latin American relations (Levinson and Onis 1970).

The Alliance for Progress defined the Bank's development mandate in its early years, financing social development in the hope of reducing social tensions and promoting political stability during the height of the Cold War (Tussie 1995: 20). In 1961, the Kennedy administration allocated US$394 million to the new Social Progress Trust Fund (SPTF) to be administered under a trust agreement by the IDB. The articles of agreement setting up the IDB require it 'to cooperate with the member countries to orient their development policies toward a better utiliza-tion of their resources' (quoted from Tussie 1995: 20). This was interpreted as a mandate to set up regional planning offices, organised through commissions com-posed of the OAS, the IDB and CEPAL, charged with exercising surveillance over access to the funds. Hence the Alliance for Progress not only defined the multilat-eral character of the institution but also its political character, not a few times pushing the IDB through its lending policies to support the US interests in the region.

The Alliance for Progress shaped the IDB's role and policies into the form of an agency of cooperation for development of the Americas, leading 'developmentalists' in the region to define the IDB both as the 'University of Development' and the 'water and sanitation bank' (Herrera 1970). Those labels were applied because of the character of its loans and assistance addressed to institutions of higher learning and its support to social infrastructure. With US$525 million of Alliance contributions, the operations of the Bank took off. The USA was the sole net donor country, holding 42.5 per cent of the voting power. It was the first multilateral institution to finance social projects, to make global loans and to support microlending in the region. It financed expansion of higher education and major tourism projects such as Cancun in Mexico (Tomassini 1999).

The first IDB loans were in housing, sanitation and education (Tomassini 1999). In the case of Chile alone, in the period between 1961 and 1973 the IDB approved 59 loans for US$305.7 million, which were addressed towards projects of agriculture, energy, transport, education, sanitation and urban development, giving evidence of the developmentalist character of the IDB. Education was a high priority, with several projects financed by the IDB for the Universidad Católica de Chile, Universidad de Chile, Universidad Austral and the Universidad de Concepcion. Even though the IDB had been designed to mediate between capital markets and borrowing member countries, its main contributions came mainly from official sources, turning the IDB into a financial cooperative for development rather than an RDB.

Regarding regionalisation, the IDB initially reflected CEPAL's pessimist view concerning the capacity of the region to compete with other regions, whereby the solution was regional trade integration (Bulmer-Thomas 2003: 289). The new RDB brought new winds of developmentalist integration, and a few months later the Latin America Free Trade Association (LAFTA) was launched by the Treaty of Montevideo and the Central American Common Market (CACM) by the Treaty of Managua in 1960. All these institutions supported regional integration, following a developmentalist path in the region; and so the IDB came to be known also as 'the bank for integration' (Tomassini 1999). Within the hemispheric trends, the IDB had to promote development through hemispheric trade integration, while blocking, at the same time, any expansionary movements of communist economies over the region. As a result, the IDB's development mandate was caught between the demands of Latin American countries for greater support and a US administration adopting an increasingly hard-line stance.

US hegemonic decline and rise of global governance

As US FDI shifted towards Europe and Asia in the 1960s, the world's major banks, supported by the role of the dollar as international currency, became multinationals in a massive expansion to meet the needs of the multinational corporations. During the 1960s, eight US banks had branches abroad; by 1975, this number reached 125 (Griffith-Jones 1988). However, two elements account for the development of international banking as the main source for financing development. The first is the rise of the main financial centres – New York, London, Frankfurt, Paris and Tokyo. The second is the encouragement given by the Federal Reserve to US banks to hold foreign deposits offshore (Germain 1997; Helleiner 1994). Both rendered a key role in the development of international finance after the massive international economic changes in the early 1970s.

The 1970s witnessed a massive growth in the presence of international commercial banks as sources of financing for development, particularly in Latin America. Governments no longer needed to go through the rituals meticulously created by the Alliance for Progress to justify their development objectives and specify the ways in which the money would be invested. Now ministers only had to offer government guarantees and the commercial lender would make funds available. The net contribution of private inflow from commercial banks to the financing of development in Latin America escalated from 9.3 per cent for the whole of the period 1966–70 to 43.8 per cent in the period 1971–75, reaching 88.0 per cent in 1977 and 92.7 per cent in 1978, as illustrated in Table 2.2. On the other hand, the net public inflow from multilateral sources collapsed from 15.7 per cent in 1966–70 to 3.1 per cent in 1978, with a significant fall in US bilateral support from 23.6 per cent in 1966–70 to 0.8 per cent in 1978.

International disorder and change during the early 1970s was the major factor triggering the coercive side of this hemispheric hegemony, acting through specific areas of states in an attempt to adjust economies and societies to the global order.

Table 2.2 Structure of net inflow of external resources to Latin America,[a] 1966–78 (US$ billions)

Percentage structure	Annual averages				
	1966–70	*1971–75*	*1976*	*1977*	*1978*
1. Net public inflow:	40.1	25.2	19.6	12.0	7.3
Multilateral	15.7	13.4	14.4	7.4	3.1
Bilateral	24.4	11.8	5.2	4.6	4.2
USA	23.6	6.8	2.6	1.7	0.8
Other countries[b]	0.8	5.0	2.6	2.9	3.4
2. Net private inflow:[c]	59.9	74.8	80.4	88.0	92.7
Banks[d]	9.3	43.8	61.0	48.3	56.6
FDI	33.3	26.2	12.4	20.1	16.0
3. Total:	100.0	100.0	100.0	100.0	100.0
Total, actual level (US$):	2,641.3	7,561.9	15,301.5	15,637.0	21,807.2

Source: Based on Griffith-Jones (1984: 28–35).

Notes
a Includes the member countries of the IDB.
b Includes socialist countries and developed except the USA.
c Includes credits for nationalisation.
d Includes financial institutions other than banks.

Briefly, the reaction took the form of the first wave of neoliberalisation processes in the region led by the dominant military-bureaucratic state form constructed during the previous decades (Frenkel 2003; Schvarzer 2003). International changes in the 1970s exacerbated US interventionist foreign policy in the region, encouraging a conservative programme directed towards the suppression of organised labour, privatisation, deindustrialisation, and denationalisation ruled by dictatorships, with the final integration of the region and subordination to US power (Halperin Donghi 1993: 341).

The Nixon administration assumed a low profile in regional affairs, although it played an active role in stopping any communist tendencies, as proved by its reiterated attempts to destabilise Chile's socialist government. The shift marked the end of the ISI developmentalist project and the rise of a model based on external debt. The time marked the rise of the first neoliberal programmes aimed at changing the political and economic conditions upon which the counter-hegemonic movements had based their power (Halperin Donghi 1993; Rapoport and Cervo 2002; Bulmer-Thomas 2003).

The shift took place in the context of a campaign of terror that flagrantly violated basic standards of human rights, eliminating almost a generation of political, economic and social leaders with a huge impact on the future development of the region. To maintain some degree of internal consensus, dictatorships blended policies of deindustrialisation and high social spending that increased fiscal deficit, and tackled this by borrowing from international banks. The redirection of countries – Argentina, Chile, Paraguay and Uruguay – towards an outward export-led model based on commodities duly followed the state-led policy of deindustrialisation. This was the means to bring an end to years of social struggle, and was defined by a continued shift from democratic to military rule (Halperin Donghi 1993; Weaver 2000: 199; Rapoport and Madrid 2002). Throughout this period, the integration of Latin American countries into the global economy set the basis for the internationalisation of finance in the region, a process interrupted by the debt crisis of the 1980s (Frenkel 2003: 40).

The access to large-scale commercial bank credits by Latin American countries enabled dictatorships – e.g. Chile in 1973, Uruguay in 1973, Argentina in 1976 – to retain power and implement reforms aimed at ameliorating social conflicts. The massive supply of liquidity by international commercial banks to Latin American countries also triggered the phenomenon of external debt in the region. Table 2.3 shows the escalation of the external debt for a sample of the region's countries from US$3.35 million in the 1970s, to $43.1 million in the 1980s and $73 million in the 1990s. As a result, Latin American countries entered into a massive process of external borrowing to cover fiscal deficits, triggering the inflationary spiral which dealt a blow to core developmentalist theory, undermining its relevance in the 1970s.

By the end of the 1970s, orthodox views started to prevail in the region and the IDB's power in overall regional development sharply declined. As multilateral financial regulation had become a function of monetary management by the US Federal Reserve and Treasury Department, the IDB remained in a sort of vacuum

Table 2.3 Growth of external debt in a selected group of Latin American countries, 1970–95 (total external debt, US$ billions)

	1970	1980	1990	1995
Argentina	5.2	27.2	62.2	89.7
Brazil	5.0	71.5	119.6	159.1
Chile	2.6	71.5	119.6	120.7
Mexico	6.0	57.4	104.4	165.7
Uruguay	0.3	1.6	4.4	5.3
Venezuela	1.0	29.3	33.2	35.3

Source: Based on World Bank (1998: 841–844).

until the mid-1970s. Nonetheless, the IDB was not the only regional institution to be unresponsive to the new changes; a similar situation was being experienced by the OAS and, especially, CEPAL. In the 1980s, CEPAL also responded to neoliberalism and its tenet of trickle-down economic effects by entering into a period of regional confusion, disorientation and redefinition of paradigms. The first attempt in this regard was led by its Secretary Executive, Enrique Iglesias in 1987, and the changes were reflected in the report 'Productive Transformation with Equity' in 1990 (Bielschowsky 1998).

In the 1970s, the role of the IDB in the financing of development was obscured by the emergence of massive private sources of capital, causing the Bank to play a marginal role in development financing but increasing its presence in social targets and development of infrastructure. Given the growth of international banking, the expected result was that the function of the IDB in development would diminish in relative if not in absolute terms, as private markets penetrated the terrain of public goods finance, previously the exclusive preserve of the Bank (Mistry 1995). Nonetheless, the financial bonanza allowed the RDBs to access funds under better conditions, concentrating their loans on long-run projects and making significant profits (Sagasti 2002). At the same time, and because of the pressure on the United States during the Cold War, the shortfall of resources was aggravated by conflicts within the US administration regarding the IDB's lending programme.

As a result, the Bank, under the presidency of Ortiz Mena, focused on new strategic targets of development. The first of these were the poorest regional economies, since global capital markets were unprepared to provide finance until minimal conditions propitious to capitalist development were achieved. Another new target was social investment in human capital, the type that capital markets did not finance. The other central target became institutional infrastructure, essential for market economies to function properly – judicial systems, property rights, accounting systems, public administration and political governance (Mistry 1995).

In the 1970s the IDB faced a globalised world and changing times, yet did not shift its developmentalist approach. Pushed by the political and ideological inertia accumulated during its first decades, and by the complex mechanisms used by the Alliance for Progress to control aid for development, the IDB confronted the shortfall in financial resources by enlarging the Bank's membership towards European and Asian countries. The change was political rather than technical and financial, strengthening the international position of the Bank by seeking additional official contributions (Tomassini 1999). The step up was taken to enlarge the presence of non-borrowing member countries.

In 1972, an amendment to the charter allowing the admission of Canada was opposed by Chile and Peru, due to the alteration of the voting power, but soon it was decreed that the voting power of the member countries could not fall below 53.5 per cent. Subsequent to this, other incorporations were accepted with further amendments in the mid-1970s, including the admission of Switzerland, Austria, Belgium, Denmark, Finland, France, Germany, Israel, Italy, Japan, the Netherlands, Spain, Sweden and the United Kingdom.

In the 1970s, the IDB remained loyal to the region and, despite increasing US pressure, managed to deliver further support to the region. In 1972, with the dispute over the nationalisation of US firms in Chile and Peru, the region's countries led by Argentina responded to US pressure by suggesting that the IDB's headquarters be moved from Washington to Latin America (Tussie 1995: 27). Another dispute took place in January 1971, concerning two agreed loans to Chile: US$7 million for the Catholic University and $4.6 million for the Universidad Austral, the last of the IDB's loans to be made to Chile during the Allende administration.

However, the roots of the major IDB changes can be found in the period of the Reagan administration. Reagan's strategy, a 'Second Cold War', was aimed at the defeat of Third World nationalism, interpreted as the advance of communism and the Soviet system, through a economic showdown and arms race. The strategy, a mixture of consent and coercion, was directed against the core of the historical coalitions in the region, aimed at weakening trade unions, dismantling public welfare and promoting privatisation of state-owned assets. Economically, the approach sought to reduce inflation to foster free capital flows, forcing submission to monetarist macroeconomic management through central banks, and export-led growth imposed by IFIs and allied countries. Hegemony had given way to domination and the name of the new path of development for Latin America was now 'structural adjustment', showing that the power of the United States still remained unquestionable (Gamble and Payne 1996: 14).

The neoconservative revolution only worsened an already deteriorating situation in Latin America, continuing the decline initiated by the dictatorships. The second oil shock in 1979, the drop in commodity prices and the rise of US interest rates increased debt service costs exponentially, triggering a regional debt crisis and the 'lost decade'. The result was a debacle for the region, now extremely subordinated to external financing of development and suffering serious internal fiscal weaknesses. With Mexico's declaration of moratoria on its external obligations, an escalation of fiscal crises spread throughout the region. The external money supposedly fuelling development left, throwing Latin America into further poverty and recession. According to CEPAL (1983), total net capital inflows to Latin America fell by 55.0 per cent between 1981 and 1982, a fall accounted for by the withdrawal of private credit. The region's US$400 billion debt offers mute testimony to the massive over-reliance of Latin America's economy upon external financing of development.

With the collapse of military regimes and their external debt-based models of development a new stage began to appear. The Latin American debt crises of the 1980s paved the way for the consolidation of the agency of the neoliberal global hegemony in the region, with finance as the principal regulator of development and determinant of the production of welfare (Cox 1987: 267). The debt crisis brought to centre stage the actions of IFIs, central banks and governments of industrial countries, in contrast to the 1970s when industrial countries and IFIs had almost abandoned the field to the actions of private banks (Griffith-Jones 1988; Krugman 1995). Overall, in the 1980s and led by the USA, the global management of debt crises became functional regarding the needs of international banking system but dysfunctional regarding the development of the region (Griffith-Jones 1988: 12). By mid-1985, it was evident that the international financial order exerted agency, and that the possibilities for new democracies in the region to finance development depended on global financial integration.

In the mid-1980s, the new democracies had to respond to the changing global political and economic conditions under the heavy burden of public debt and the IFIs' conditions, fettered by a decade of deindustrialisation, social deterioration, and above all the absence, owing to their elimination by the state, of a generation of political and economic leaders. Constrained internally and externally in its alternatives for development, the region experienced a historical change in its strategies, defining a new stance in the main hemispheric institutions – the IDB, OAS and CEPAL. Since then, the climate of relations between the region's countries and the rest of the world, particularly the USA, has changed beyond recognition (Phillips 1999: 73).

The shift took the form of large-scale integration into the global economy through domestic reforms addressed at redefining the financing of development and reformulating the production of domestic welfare. The shift brought about key changes in foreign relations, mostly within the Americas, giving way to an extensive process of regional integration in the form of open regionalism. This new regionalism was the result of a broad shift from import-substitution to export-oriented strategies of development taking place in the region (Payne 1996), coming in the form of a series of free-trade agreements aimed at eventually creating a hemispheric free-trade association from Anchorage to Tierra del Fuego (Grugel 1999).

In 1987, the situation seemed to improve for the region when US Treasury Secretary Nicholas Brady formulated a new strategy for dealing with debtors: the issuance of treasury bonds to countries committed to executing economic reforms and adjustment programmes supervised by the IMF and WB. The debt crisis and stagnation in the region marked a downturn for the IDB. Debt crises nearly broke the Bank in the late 1980s, with the result that the IDB had not only become part of the debt problem but was accused together with the CEPAL strategy of being part of the cause of the crisis (Tussie 1994). To survive, the IDB needed a radical change. In addition, as the focus changed from economic development to financial survival, the Bank lost its niche, which was aggravated by two factors. The first was the decision of treasury departments of the donor nations to elevate economic adjustment policies to top priority and place a firewall around new lending and capital flows to the region. The second was that bilateral aid began to diminish rapidly as the developed nations sought to stem their own haemorrhaging budget deficits.

The IDB was unprepared to cope with the most severe financial crises in the region. Problems emerged such as the Bank's indebtedness, absence of maintenance funds, budget cuts, and so forth. Worst of all, the institution remained at the centre in the struggle between the Reagan administration and deeply indebted large countries such as Mexico, Argentina and Venezuela. In addition, the situation for the Bank worsened after Honduras, Peru, Panama and Nicaragua went into arrears. To deal with the situation, the Seventh Replenishment – the mechanism of the Bank to get fresh funds – was needed for the IDB to again be a supplier of capital to the region. Before it would sanction substantially higher loan disbursements, however, Washington required and demanded a radical change in the IDB's policies (Scheman 1997).

The deterioration of the relations between the IDB's borrower member countries and the US administration had become official since the early 1970s, in particular reflected in disputes over loans for Chile, Peru and Venezuela. In 1988, the conflict reached its highest point when the USA stated that it did not trust any bank dominated by borrowers to execute the conditions attached to loans. In consequence, the USA demanded more voting power inside the IDB and its subordination to guidelines of the World Bank, a conflict seen as the main reason behind the resignation of Ortiz Mena in 1988 (Lewis 1988). It is clear that the IDB as a hemispheric institution could not overcome US influence and interests in the region. By the end of the 1980s and reflecting new changes, the IDB's response towards the neoliberal policies came to converge with US demands on the region and with the new stance of Latin American countries, all of which found its expression of radical institutional changes towards the market governance under the administration of Enrique Iglesias.

Financial globalisation, new regionalism and consensus formation

After two decades marked by dictatorial repression, deindustrialisation, debt crises and the emergence of restricted democracies, the 1990s opened a new period in the region defined by the internationalisation of finance, the rise of the hemispheric consensus around neoliberal strategies of development, democracy, and new regionalism as states responded by reinserting the region within the global economy, in turn reshaping the region. It is within these political economic processes that the regional agency of development, the IDB, became the leading hemispheric development bank. During this historical stage, the Bank experienced three key shifts in its directions and policies in South America, an analysis of which can provide relevant insights into the political economic character of the institutions. The first period, 1989–94, saw its inclusion into the political economic framework of the IMF and World Bank for the region and Washington Consensus guidelines as a result of US demands and countries' new regional stance. During the second period, 1994–96, the IDB reformulated and shifted its approach for the region as a result of widespread financial crises and poor results of its strategies. The final period, 1997–2000, is signalled mainly by the role of the Bank in the growing deteriorating economic and social situation of Argentina, with the final crises in 2001.

By the early 1990s, the structures of a new world order had already emerged 'with no clearly definable institutional structure in place to govern the global economy' (Cox 1997: 60). It featured a transnational economy driven by a vulnerable financial system decoupled from production, macro-regions as frameworks of national capital accumulation, reshaping of the limits of sovereignty, the emergence of new social forces and the ascent of world state-cities (Cox 2000; Germain 1997). This deep historical transformation redefined the framework of development strategies and put states into a deep process of reorganisation, facing the prospect of uneven globalisation and stringent financial constraints, blurring the boundary between the domestic and international (Payne 2004; Grugel 2001).

By the early 1990s, export-led models, under the neoliberal tenets of the conservative Anglo-Saxon model, had become the dominant strategy for the Americas defined by the Washington Consensus. The Consensus was the expression of a hemispheric compromise defined by a 'loose elite network of influential and agencies, sharing a common set of ideas', performing a new governance function in the region (Naim 1999). The conviction and promise of the Consensus was that the costs of global deregulation of capital flows, labour and commodity markets – dislocating and making imperative a reorganisation in the domestic production of welfare – were 'transitional' and would be compensated by benefits in economic growth, rising standards of living and a narrowing of the gap between rich and poor (Stiglitz 2002).

Export-led growth strategies based on free-market governance became the paradigm for the policies of IFIs and most of the region's governments for a decade under the surveillance of the IMF and the WB. It was supposed that the neoliberal Consensus would move savings from developed to developing countries, lower the cost of financing development through the use of capital markets and increase economic growth. Instead, from the 1970s, under the liberalisation processes savings flowed from developing to developed countries, interest rates rose, economic growth slowed down, let alone the very modest results compared with the social outcomes of ISI strategies (Eatwell 1996; Astorga *et al.* 2002). Briefly, the neoliberal tenets of the Consensus were addressed to reinforcing economic globalisation, separating the economic realm from the political in order to make competitiveness and self-regulated markets the determining factor of development (Cox 1996a).

In the 1990s the organisation of the financing of development thus changed radically. The pool of international private capital had began to develop far beyond the capacity of the developed world to absorb it, offering Latin America, a net producer of financial revenues, unlimited possibilities for financing. Figure 2.1 illustrates these global financial flows to the region, and these became more diversified

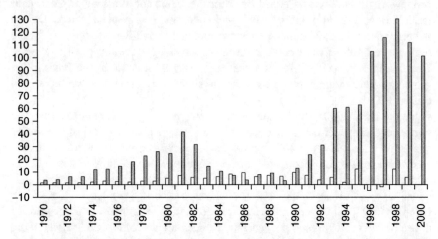

Figure 2.1 Net flow of official (*unshaded*) and private (*shaded*) resources towards Latin America and the Caribbean, 1970–2000 (US$ billions). (Based on Sagasti 2002: 16.)

into FDI, portfolio flows – bonds and equities – and other investments, with 50 per cent in the form of short-term liquid funds characterised by high volatility (Sagasti 2002: 16). Between 1991 and 1993, portfolio flows rose significantly and stopped after 1994 because of the Mexican debt crisis, only to again recover in 1996. Of particular note is that the Brady Plan made it possible for the biggest Latin American economies to access and use international bond markets to finance development, which in turn left them exposed to international financial shocks such as the Tequila, Russian, Thai and Brazilian crises.

In the 1990s, Latin America turned to increasing its cooperation with the USA, voting with it at the United Nations, participating in the Gulf War, Somalia, Cyprus, and in other military exercises showing its new commitment. This shift in the hitherto inward-looking strategies of Latin American countries following the end of the Cold War came in hand with the process of re-democratisation, which redefined the role of armed forces in the region and the region insertion into the post-Cold War agenda. In addition, the turn towards democratic governance and human rights was soon reflected in changes in the main hemispheric institutions, the OAS, CEPAL and the IDB. Countries became eager to comply with the right policy framework, and with the multilateral rules for economic and political stability, in exchange for international support for their access to private financial resources for development (Kuwayama 1993; CEPAL 1994; Bulmer-Thomas 1996).

The shift brought about a new hemispheric scenario, characterised by a complex web of bilateral reforms and regional trade agreements. This shift was triggered by the end of the US global hegemony which was superseded and slowly replaced, at least in part, by a form of open regionalism which re-engaged the USA with its own hemisphere, so making its presence in the region once again a critical factor (Payne 1996: 93). At the centre of this shift was the Bush's Enterprise for the Americas Initiative (EAI) in 1990, which consolidated the tendency initiated by the debt crises towards the redefinition of a new map of relations within the Americas, and consolidated a new map of its subregions.

Three components of the EAI were key to the restructuring of debt, the promotion of investment in the region via the IDB, and free-trade agreements with selected countries in the region with the aim of creating a hemispheric free-trade system (Payne 1996: 104). The relevance of the EAI was summed up in the words of Peter Hakim, from the IDB: 'Of every dollar Latin America spends on imports, 50 cents came to the United States' (cited by Payne 1996: 107). Thus, as a direct outcome of this initiative, in August 1992, the USA, Canada and Mexico signed the NAFTA treaty, triggering a wave of similar agreements within the region. However, for its influence in the long run, the most remarkable outcome was the detachment of Mexico from the region and the growing strengthening of the bonds between Southern Cone states around the Argentine–Brazilian axis, redefining the Latin American map.

In this context, the launching of the Southern Common Market (Mercosur) and the relaunching of the Caribbean Community (CARICOM), Central American Common Market (CACM) and the Andean Community (AC) were in the first instance state-led responses to the development challenges imposed by globalisation in the region. The new option was to work with Washington in liberalisation, in order to be allowed to gain access to capital markets as a resource for development, in compensation for unpopular reform programmes. Mercosur represents the most powerful set of countries outside of North America, with Brazil largely defining the progress and structures of the FTAA in South America (Phillips 1999).

In the 1990s, the new regionalism in Latin America was conceived of as an 'open regionalism' defining the complementarity of trade arrangements between neighbours, and the multilateral trade strategies linking them to the rest of the world (Phillips 1999: 77). The Latin American style of regionalism reflects world tendencies in terms of globalisation, emphasising economic liberalisation addressed to economic objectives and difficulties in political coordination between its biggest partners, that is, Brazil and Argentina.

The IDB as the regional bank of the Americas

The transformation of the IDB into a regional bank was a process politically and ideologically driven by states, which does not reduce the importance of the Enrique Iglesias leadership, but integrates it into the wider analytical context. At the centre of the agential process appears a mix among external conditions, needs of survival, and old ambitions to bring into reality the long-time aspirations of the Bank founders.

The first step towards this change was taken by the US Republican administrations, producing the traumatic process of internal reforms and adaptation of IDB structure and instruments that lasted three years from 1988 to 1991. Conflicts between the Bank and the US government came with the Reagan administration, which had been seeking greater influence at the Bank. However, Ortiz Mena's swan-song gesture of defiance infuriated administration officials, by refusing to nominate James Conrow, deputy assistant treasury secretary, when the United States delayed the increase in the IDB's resources. Washington traditionally has had the right to name the vice-president of the Bank, and now the president of the IDB was an obstacle to that (Scheman 1997).

Indeed, the Bank was desperately short on funds, and money would come only from debt-trapped members such as Argentina, Brazil and Mexico. Many feared that in order to survive, the IDB would have to accept the US demands for change, ending 30 years of relative developmentalist control. Assuming diplomatic defeat, the search was oriented then to a candidate to preside over the Bank who was able to bridge the gap with the US administration and negotiate a regulated transformation that was vital (Lewis 1988: 3). Iglesias achieved this, and his administration would stand as the landmark of the rise of the RDB.

If the Bank changed, it would participate in the massive process of debt rescheduling for Latin America led by the Bush administration and would reach a major regional status. The US contribution would represent 70 per cent of the Bank's convertible currency resources, enabling and benefiting the IDB with a doubling in its rate of lending to the region. The US proposal for IDB's restructuring was rather clear: veto power on lending of at least the USA and Canada, institutional downsizing, involvement in the strategy of debt rescheduling for Latin America, free-market lending policies, subordination of the lending policies to the endorsement of the IMF, working together with the WB, and the IDB's executive vice president position for James Conrow institutionalising the US Treasury surveillance of the IDB.

As a result, the debt rescheduling under the Brady Plan became a twofold opportunity for the Bank. First, it was a chance to survive, in the midst of a dramatic hemispheric change, and second, it would permit the IDB to assume a major role in the liberalisation process taking place in the region, especially in its major member borrowing countries. Consequently, the IDB shifted in its structures and policies, and achieved renewed financial resources, under the surveillance of the US Treasury Department. However, the size of its lending arms would still be small for the size and political influence of a country such as Argentina enjoying the support of the US conservative administration and in the midst of well-advanced pro-market reforms.

The change was a political decision, ideologically accompanied with what later would come to be called the Washington Consensus and its hemispheric network of Washington and Latin American officials, corporate representatives and intellectuals. This network was beyond the limits of Washington, and would became the main source of recruitment of the Bretton Woods institutions including the IDB, further consolidating Washington's influence over the region's government. This hemispheric network evolved initially in the shadow of Washington's new strategy for the region, soon finding a place among elites with a dominant position over the design and instrumentation of the new prescriptions for Latin America.

The process was quickly permeated by the ideas produced by business schools and US academic departments and think-tanks. Ideas, prescriptions and policy recommendations addressed to eradicate the roots of Latin American instability, became the 'doctrine of development' thanks to the ideological dynamics of the hemispheric network (Naim 1999).

For the first time, there was a clear and optimistic consensus in the hemisphere about what the international community should do with developing countries, something grasped and summarised in ten ideas by John Williamson in 1989. The 'consensus' was rooted in common ground about what was wrong with Latin American development according to US mainstream economics and politics; something whereby Latin America's misfortunes were the result of historical lack of trade and financial openness, bureaucratic–authoritarian states, populism, institutional weakness and fragile property rights, all built upon corruption, political instability and crony capitalism (O'Donnell 1973; Haber 2002; Levitsky and Murillo 2005).

The consensus was an enthusiastic self-fulfilling credo. Even as popular a magazine as *Business Week* in 1992 praised the hemispheric network as 'the shock troops of change', 'a new generation of leaders, many of them educated in the US. That is a continental network of Harvard, Chicago, and Stanford grads', 'back home atop business and government ministries spreading a new market mind-set' (Baker and Weiner 1992). And highlighting the social dynamics of the network consensus it followed that '[t]hey're using old school ties to reach across Latin America's border, signing … free-trade agreements with fellow alumni'. The magazine considered 'America as one big market to compete with the European and Asian blocs'. As a result, Latin American governments needed a new race of economists to deal with the transformation, and who better for the job than the English-speaking economists, many with classmates now in the banks and the IMF (Baker and Weiner 1992: 51–54). The new formula for development was simple: privatise everything in sight, from toll roads to sewers, crush inflation, slash tariffs to world levels, open the doors to foreign investment, and sign free-trade pacts with neighbours, particularly with the USA (Baker and Weiner 1992).

The whole new credo of development for Latin American countries was laid on the extension of the neoclassical postulate that the 'unfettered market is the best guarantor of human well-being' due to the rational behaviour of economic actors. Accordingly, public bond and tax financing always finds its limit as the 'omniscient market will force government to keep its finance from blowing up' (Taylor 2004: 199–217). The translation of this premise into reality found excellent conditions in the mid-1980s as high international liquidity and low US interest rates favoured replacing existent capital and interest debt with commercial banks for long-term public bonds under the Brady Plan. Thanks to the visible hand of politics, now investors might use public bonds to purchase, almost without risk, state assets under privatisation programmes.

Policy options such as debt rescheduling, privatisation and financial reforms came to be part of the same, inseparable political economic process, something induced from creditors and multilateral institutions to favour external interests and, at the same time, converging with domestic options seeking to reposition powerful domestic actors. The process resumed within the IFI–state complex sustained by specific social configurations at the very base of coalition pro-reforms, which in turn, marked the roles of multilateral institutions and instruments within this governed interdependence (Murillo 2001; Weiss 2003b; Etchemendy 2005).

It was within this set of historical processes that Enrique Iglesias' administration became the symbol of the historical shift of the IDB towards pro-market governance policies. Iglesias had led the negotiations among member countries that resulted in the IDB's Seventh and Eighth Capital Increases in 1989 and 1994, from US$26.5 billion and $40 billion respectively. Enrique Iglesias was already an experienced official in Latin American affairs, conscious of the confusion, disorientation, and imperative need for a redefinition of the region's strategies for development. As a result, the Bank broadened and deepened its research efforts, establishing specialised offices (including one in Europe) for the first time devoted to economic investigation and the analysis of sustainable development issues in collaboration and under the guidelines of development of the IMF and WB dominating in Washington.

The changes revitalised the Bank under the new view of 'policy-based' loans addressed by country performance instead of projects, that is, access to multilateral funds in exchange for domestic reforms. The 'Seven Replenishments' reflected the newly empowered IDB increasing its lending and political capacity in the region. The changes and innovations brought about made some of the region's governments enthusiastic about the new Bank's machinery, policies and renewed professional staff, mostly economists bound to important US universities such as Maryland and others now occupying CEPAL's think-tank role. The IDB assumed a major role in promoting reforms that facilitated access to external financing, which governments demanded in order to materialise structural reforms designed to attract private capital by improving the macroeconomic environment. In sum, the 1990s were a time of the rise and consolidation of the IDB as an official RDB actively involved in debt swap for privatisations. The IDB's lending policies had been designed along developmentalist guidelines of CEPAL; now it was the US academic centres that exerted their ideological leadership.

The transformation of the IDB in the 1990s into an RDB with a set of instruments, areas and dependent institutions – predominantly under the control of economists – expressed the belief that policy-free markets and sound money were the key to economic growth domestically and internationally. In all cases, the changes reflected the enlargement of finance-related sectors in the belief that reorganising the financing of development would facilitate domestic private capital formation. Overall, the new institutional instruments came to develop a transformative system of rewards and punishments around the region, supporting and rewarding those Latin American states involved with the Washington Consensus along the lines set by the IMF and WB.

Inevitably, the IDB entered into areas of lending which would have been ideologically and politically inconceivable a decade ago, such as projects to strengthen democratic institutions, reform judiciary systems, deregulate labour markets and privatise public services. Among the most important innovations of the period was the radical shift from the state towards the private sector in the IDB's financing of infrastructure. Under the Eight General Capital Increase, the IDB was allowed to provide long-term direct financing and guarantees for private sector participation in large infrastructure and public services projects without government guarantee. These projects include a power generation plant in Honduras, a merchant power plant in Peru, gas transportation in Peru, water and sanitation in Argentina, and the first use of IDB guarantees to cover currency convertibility for a project in Colombia (Tomassini 1999).

In fact, since the foundation of the IDB, infrastructure support through the public sector has been the largest component of its lending operations – transport, power, water and sanitation and telecommunications – defining in turn its role as a supporter of countries' development strategies. But, since the establishment of the Inter-American Investment Corporation (IIC) in 1989 and the Multilateral Investment Fund (MIF), the Bank began to encourage private sector activities in infrastructure, with a significant increase in privatisation facility occurring between 1995 and 1997, going from US$128 million in 1995 to $280 million in 1997 (Sustainable Development Department (SDS/ENV), IDB 1998b). As shown in Figure 2.2, between the periods 1970–80 and 1991–2000, the IDB's loans to the

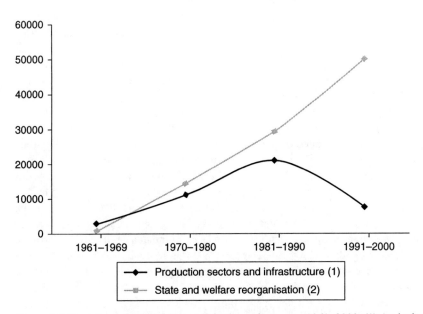

Figure 2.2 Evolution of IDB lending policies by main targets, 1960–2000. (1) Agriculture, fisheries, industry, mining, tourism, science and technology, and energy, transport and communications. (2) State reform and modernisation, export finance, pre-investment and others. Welfare includes sanitation, urban development, education, social investment, health, environment, microenterprises (also microtourism). (Based on IDB annual reports.)

region tripled in value, reaching a total of $5.96 billion, revealing the quantitative significance of the IDB's lending policies in the financing of development in Latin America.

To summarise, the new role, financial structure and lending policies of the IDB became a powerful device for supporting governments committed to withdrawing states from historical areas of development such as public infrastructure and labour markets. Completing the plan of neoliberal globalisation, such devices represented a political and economic incentive to reduce barriers to industrial foreign goods for domestic consumption and encourage economic openness. Accordingly, member nations were called upon to extend legal protection to foreign investors and create more efficient financial markets by improving supervision of banks and security markets, removing restrictions on entry into capital markets, and liberalising credit and interest rates.

The step forward in the IDB's market governance approach became central in its strategies, now centred on consolidating access by the international private sector to areas historically under state control, such as telecommunications, electricity and transportation. Complementing these PSD strategies were IIC and MIF support for the development of projects such as IMPSAT's hydro-electrical project in Argentina and similar operations in Colombia, Ecuador, Mexico, Peru and Venezuela. All were complemented by technical assistance from the public sector arm of the Bank, granted by the MIF, encouraging private sector participation in infrastructure and the privatisation processes, as in the case of Guyana Electricity Company (GEC) (IDB 2003e: 14). In addition, the Bank's changes along the lines of pro-market governance gave further expression to the current impact of globalisation upon the region manifested in its support for the new open regionalism.

In 1994, a hemispheric summit took place, the first since 1967. The creation of NAFTA and the possibility of its spread to the rest of the region ensured that the IDB would develop additional instruments in support of adjustment to free trade in borrowing countries. The Bank's embrace of the US 'Enterprise for the Americas Initiative' (EAI), launched by President George Bush Senior, may be understood in this context. Of the three main components of EAI, the investment area was placed in the hands of the IDB, providing the institution with a financial and political instrument to foster regionalism under the Anglo-Saxon model of capitalism, regardless of any regional capitalist configuration. In short, the EAI reflected a reassertion of the hemispheric character of the IDB under US hegemony, demonstrating the capacity of the USA to set the terms of the debate about development in the region together with the IMF and the WB (Payne 2005: 76).

The first four years of the 1990s were characterised by regional optimism based on the neoliberal credo, which turned out to be a disaster waiting to happen. As different scholars show, this was chiefly due to three factors, each indicating the power of global finance in development: debt, external financing of development and aid (Bulmer-Thomas 2003; Payne 2005: 138). The debt-based model of development of dictatorship had a huge cost. Years of reliance on debt financing and growing dependence on external financing of development had provided the new global financial governance with the necessary leverage to demand countries' domestic adjustment in exchange for financial aid. In 1994, Mexico's decision to float the peso was unexpected. The 'tequila effect' soon spread through the region, triggering a massive outflow of foreign capital, particularly hitting those economies now opened up by neoliberal reforms. However, the region's countries and Mexico more or less faced up to the situation, helped by the regional response and support of its main trade partner, the USA.

The financial turbulence in foreign and equity markets affected Asian economies, whose security markets plummeted in January 1995. It would not be until 1997, with the devaluation of the Thai currency, that a new financial crisis would spill over, via Russia, to Brazil and later to Argentina, shaking these countries and revealing the fragility and instability of development strategies based on external financing of development and the liberal production of welfare. By the end of the 1990s, as a result of the spill-over of financial crises, the main concern of development came to be centred on the international financial architecture and in particular on the role of the IMF and the WB. By this time, it had become clear that the main body with responsibility for the financial architecture and its stability was the G7, which issued directives to the IMF and the other IFIs, and which also sought to include developing countries in order to strengthen the global structure and absorb discontent (Payne 2005: 139; Germain 2002: 21).

By the end of the 1990s, it was clear that globalisation in its neoliberal form, as promoted by the Washington Consensus, had gone too far (Rodrik 1997). Because of spreading financial crises and social deterioration, by the end of the 1990s the IFIs' role in development finance came under the spotlight, through crisis-prevention and bail-outs to governments in trouble. The first critique came from the Clinton administration (1999), emphasising that the IMF should focus on preventing crises and provide official lending only to those countries that could not access capital markets (Payne 2005: 143). However, it was in 2000 that these critiques came to a head, through the report of the Meltzer Commission to the US Congress, chaired by the prestigious monetarist Allan Meltzer.

The Meltzer Report called for a redefinition of the roles and a reduction of the financial resources of the IMF, WB, and Regional Development Banks, in particular the IDB. As regards the IMF, the Meltzer Report advised that it reduce its function to that of a lender of last resort to countries that met specific financial preconditions, while the WB should provide grants to the poorest countries, instead of official aid (International Financial Institutions Commission 2000). These suggested changes affecting the IFIs soon found an echo and a counter-action, in particular a defence of the functions of Regional Development Banks such as the IDB made by the Commission on the Role of the MDBs in Emerging Markets, chaired by Paul Volcker, former Chairman of the Trilateral Commission and Princeton University Professor, before the US Congress. Despite nuances in the debate around the new role for the IFIs, the Meltzer proposals did not find an echo in the Clinton administration, something which was to change in 2001.

In 2001, the Bush administration came into office with most of its senior officers enrolled in the Republican tradition of hostility to the Bretton Woods institutions and UN system, exemplified by its Treasury Secretary, Paul O'Neill, who led the appointment of the Republican economist Anne Krueger as First Managing Director of the IMF. The Bush administration took a conservative approach towards the IFIs, defining the official framework and, in 2001, applying it to what was one of the most important financial crises – Argentina – a crisis in which the IDB played a significant role. In short, the 1990s international financial architecture showed a mix between the new and the old, although as Payne points out, '[t]he architects themselves have remained essentially the same' (2005: 145).

Conclusion

This chapter has given an account of the political and economic stages and processes in the Americas that have historically shaped the role of the IDB and its involvement in domestic and regional developments. The chapter analysed the political and economic nature of the IDB by using the theoretical framework of new IPE, as defined in Chapter 1. The purpose of the study was to prove, and to determine to what extent, a Coxian version of IPE could report critically on the political economic nature of the IDB.

The task contained a twofold challenge. The first was that any analytical finding had to match the complex network of economic, social and political events defining the different stages of development in the Americas and in Southern America. The second challenge was that the approach had to account for and be able to identify the main processes shaping and defining the role, direction and impact of the IDB in development finance and welfare outcomes. In this regard, the analysis has shown that the nature of the world's leading RDB follows a pattern historically bound to the political and economic developments unfolding in the Americas. As a result, the re-readings of the analysis lead us to four conclusions relevant to the aims of this investigation and to subsequent chapters.

The first major re-reading is that despite the participation by Latin American countries in the IDB's decision-making processes, the political economic nature of the IDB has been hemispheric rather than Latin American. In accordance with this analysis, the IDB's policies have obeyed two historical mandates which, though unwritten, are clear. The first mandate, from its inception to the debt crises in the 1980s, defined the IDB's role of economic and ideological promotion of hemispheric integration into the US hegemony by providing intellectual leadership and financial support to regional strategies of development under the so-called developmentalism. The second, between the end of the 1980s up to the end of the 1990s, appears related to the consolidation of the global economy driven by capital markets as a source of financing of development and reorganisation of welfare along neoliberal and liberal lines.

The second major re-reading reveals four major historical stages which defined changes in the IDB's role and lending policies within Latin America's political economy. The first stage is identified here as the evolution and consolidation of US hegemony in the region, through the transformation of the Pan American Union into the Inter-American system. The second stage features what is named here as the hemispherisation of the state. The evidence suggests that this is the time of the IDB's take-off, but as a regional, cooperative agency of development under the tight control of its single and major donor. This was probably one of the most difficult periods for the IDB, since it was caught in the middle of growing hemispheric tensions. The third historical phase in the region is defined by the decline of the USA, the end of Bretton Woods and the hemispheric hegemonic reaction in the form of dictatorships and the internationalisation of production and financing of development. The fourth period marks the historical change of the IDB, that is, its transformation from an agency of development into a RDB as the United States acted to reassert its economic hegemony in the region through the Washington Consensus and 'new open regionalism'. The analysis has shown that the main ideological and institutional transformation of the IDB is apparent in the new mandate of the institution: promoting the global economic integration of the region's economies. This can be seen in the radical changes wrought to the financing of development, to economic openness, privatisation and state reforms.

3 The IDB's role in the South American political economy in the 1990s

Introduction

This chapter aims to analyse the development role of the IDB in the processes of neoliberal reforms promoted by the IFI–state complex managing the global economy in the 1990s, and pursued by South American countries. In so doing, it focuses on the political economic leverage of the Bank *vis-à-vis* the global and regional political economic agency and structure, and analyses the IDB's role and participation in the stages of the evolving regional political economy which were identified in Chapter 2.

It is argued here that, as a result of the complex set of changes in the 1970s and 1980s, in the 1990s the IDB became integrated within the regional structure of global governance. Consequently, its development function was redefined and reoriented towards global market integration, capital expansion, and generating and reinforcing consensus among domestic and international actors around the management of the global economy. Consequently, the IDB's development function was reshaped for new capabilities, not present in previous stages, such as its capacity to adapt or frame policies, and to justify and legitimise specific projects of development along the global guidelines of development. A key assumption for understanding this is that the IDB's development view, and lending and assistance policies, reflect power relations and social changes at the time under scrutiny at global and regional level. As a result, the Bank's approach to development necessarily reflected the dominant neoliberal tendencies at international and domestic level, and was consistent with the rise, consolidation and decline of a regime subject to international finances such as the Argentine convertibility regime in the 1990s.

The chapter is divided into two main sections. The first section examines the position and relevance of the IDB within the structure of global and regional governance, highlighting the complex interaction of regional institutions and recipient countries shaping partnerships in the states of different IDB regions. This section outlines how these relationships and the Bank's role have varied according to the political economy of specific countries and how this is reflected in the use of different IDB policies and instruments. Finally, the section identifies the connections between development approaches followed by the Bank, its lending targets and the chief areas of national development most impacted by them, erecting an analytical framework within which IDB lending and policies throughout the period can be appraised.

The second section is devoted to the examination and qualitative assessment of the Bank's policies throughout the three main stages of hegemonic change in South America in the 1990s. The first period to be analysed is identified here as hegemonic convergence (1990-93). The next period to be addressed (1994-97) is characterised by growing financial instability and tensions, characterised by the emergence of the Bank's so-called countercyclical development function. Finally, the chapter moves on to consider the last stage of development (1997–2000), signalled by a steady retreat from the reforms made during hegemonic change shaping a new structured scenario for governments and IFIs. Finally, the chapter ends with a short conclusion summarising the main findings.

The role and relevance of the IDB in development in the 1990s

IDB, global governance and the role of multilateral lending in Latin America

As shown in Chapter 2, the role of the IDB has been significantly influenced by the evolution of US hegemony in the hemispheric and world economy, extending from the hemispheric institutions bound to US regional hegemony to what Cox calls the *nébuleuses* or governance without government (2000: 77). It also became clear that, by the end of the 1980s, the IDB had emerged as an important regional driver of the Washington Consensus, with the general role of promoting regional consensus on global financial integration around guidelines set by the global hegemon.

It is common to approach MDBs and RDBs by focusing upon their agency, measured by the rationality and financial efficiency with which these institutions implement their development mandates (Rodrik 1995). The result is that MDBs and RDBs are seen primarily as technical institutions driven by a mandate to promote development in the regions where they make loans. The IDB, for example, is mandated 'to contribute to the acceleration of the process of economic and social development of the regional developing member countries, individually and collectively' (IDB 1995a). As a member of the staff claimed:

> The development mandate of the Bank has been always the same, and everyone in the institution interprets and works under it. This is like the constitution of the United States . . . it never changes . . . What may change in each epoch is the interpretation of this mandate and how it is translated into reality.
>
> Anonymous interview 05/2004)

However, rather than as a matter of interpretation, the IDB's development mandate is subject to the dynamics of development, as stated by another official of the IDB:

> [The IDB] is a dynamic institution whose development function changes according to the challenges in the regional scenario . . . . Up to the 1970s, our

function was to promote physical infrastructure for development, but at the time of Reagan and Thatcher, the role changed to the promotion of structural reforms and the preparation of countries for globalisation . . . . If one looks at the evolution of the lending operations, one can see the ideological changes and influences over the IDB . . . . But the biggest changes came in the 1990s . . . in particular after the Tequila crisis, accompanied by an increase in the financial role of the Bank in support of the globalisation of [countries] . . . . First, crudely, by supporting privatisations; afterwards, by deepening structural adjustment . . . and finally, helping in the [financial] rescue . . . battered by international financial crisis.

(Anonymous interview 05/2004)

However, there are two dimensions defining the changing dynamics of the Bank's development function and the uneven influence of the IDB in the region's different countries. The first is that, since lender and borrower countries provide the main capital and the Bank operates as a finance cooperative, its structure of governance comprises a complex interaction between states and the regional financial institutions. This structural legitimacy, beyond its technical expertise and capacity to act in international capital markets, rests on the participation of countries in its governance (Griffith-Jones 2002b). The second is that even though all the region's members are included in its corporate governance, the influence of the IDB necessarily varies from one country to another.

For instance, the guidelines and conditionalities set by its governance for lending and policing access to official financing can be less for smaller countries – Ecuador, Bolivia and Paraguay – than bigger borrowers with large stakes in the Bank – Mexico, Brazil and Argentina. Briefly, therefore, the importance of the IDB's role in a country's development has an uneven character, and is defined by the size and participation of the country in the Bank's structure of governance, and by the economic strategy pursued by the country in the particular stage of its development.

In the 1990s, the Bretton Woods institutions came to be charged with promoting the new structural reforms in two ways. The first was by conditioning access to any sources of external development financing and endorsing government policies aligned with the Washington's approach. The second was by propagating and generating consensus around the new neoliberal guidelines of development through its networks. Within this framework, there was a particular division of labour between the major IFIs. Hence the IMF became responsible for the surveillance and approval of the macroeconomic viability of government policies, whilst the World Bank and the IDB assumed the task of promoting and financing those structural reforms regarded as necessary to end Latin America's economic stagnation. In short, the mission of the whole system was to prepare and adjust domestic economies to the tendencies of the global economy and to transfer resources into private hands. The process was set in motion by obliging countries to adopt market-oriented reforms, translated at the national level into neoliberal economic measures of fiscal, economic and social policy, as officially recognised by the IDB (RE-260, IDB 2002d; RE-288, IDB 2003b; RE-299, IDB 2004a).

The system worked rather simply, following a clear sequence of stages. In order to provide access to external sources of financing, whether official lending or endorsement for their participation in capital markets, the IDB required member countries to implement macroeconomic policies and structural reforms. These were materialised in the so-called Structural Adjustment Programmes (SAPs) signed with each country (RE-299, IDB 2004a) and endorsed and certified by the IMF. This process of conditionalities worked, but only when the country's government was committed to these reforms. For the Bank, the first impact of this was a significant increase in its role through lending committed to the reform of strategic areas of development – mainly state reforms, equalling the World Bank's lending to the region. The second impact consisted of a sharp decline in concessional funding for poor countries (Griffith-Jones 1994: v).

This was a radical quantitative and qualitative change in the IDB lending policies. Nonetheless, it should not be understood as merely the result of an imposition from above, but as a hegemonic result involving the participation of recipient governments. The process was generated by a historical convergence produced by the globalisation of the economy and domestic responses to it and related to structural changes taking place since the 1970s in the region, as described in Chapter 2. Paradoxically, and as result of the IDB's subordination to and inclusion within the management of the global economy, the Bank became in the 1990s, despite the modest outcome of the structural transformations, the largest regional multilateral source of financing of development for Latin America, and the world's leading RDB. Table 3.1 illustrates this, providing an idea of the size of the IDB's financial resources destined for Latin American in relation to other MDBs' lending to the region. The Bank accounts for nearly 50 per cent of the entire financial resources destined by MDBs for the region. It is clear that IDB and multilateral lending brought about an increase in the burden of the region's debt, which by itself offers only a partial explanation of the IDB's importance in development.

A short assessment of multilateral lending policies in the region shows that, despite the increasing allocation of financial resources and technical assistance by the Bank and other MDBs, recipient countries have, since the 1980s, unfortunately experienced a significant deterioration in the unequal distribution of income.

Table 3.1 Multilateral lending to Latin America by MDBs, 1991–2000 (US$ millions)

Institution	Amount
World Bank	59,969.40
Inter-American Development Bank	59,612.00
Central American Bank of Economic Integration	3,047.90
Andean Development Corporation (CAF)	2,996.40
Development Bank of the Caribbean (CABEI)	119.60
Cuenca del Plata Development Fund	26.90
Bank of Development of North Americas	297.10
TOTAL:	126,069.30

Source: Based on Sagasti (2002: 14).

In fact, there was a rise in the number of poor people from 135.9 million, 40.5 per cent, to 211.4 million, 43.8 per cent of the population in 1999 (CEPAL 2000). Unemployment increased steadily from 5.7 per cent in 1991 to 10.7 per cent in 2003, and there has been a significant decline in welfare measured in terms of financing of social policy. As a point of fact, after a decade of economic modernisation through pro-market reforms, the IDB has officially acknowledged its role in weakening the state's capacity to perform strategic functions, leading to the unfolding, since 2002, of an important process of reformulating its policies for the region (RE-260, IDB 2002d; RE-287, IDB 2003a; RE-288, IDB 2003b; RE-299, IDB 2004a).

In the 1990s, the position of the IDB and other MDBs in the international financial system resulted in them playing a vital role in the promotion of global integration through market-leading development. They mobilised and channelled financial sources in a manner different from other agencies. Actually, RDBs interact with the whole set of international institutions, governments, private investors, pension funds, credit rating agencies, commercial and investment banks, and domestic groups such as civil society organisations, offering a varied range of services (Culpeper 1993; Tussie 1995; Sagasti 2002; Sagasti *et al.* 2001). Beyond that, what is important for this investigation is that these interventions were mainly addressed to key areas of development such as productive sectors, infrastructure, welfare production and delivery, and state reform.

To appreciate in full the significance of these interventions, the approach must go beyond an emphasis on the financial side of the IDB policies but bearing *caveats* in mind. The first is that even though the size of IDB lending is small in relation to the total flow of resources from international multilateral institutions, its contribution to the region in the 1990s still matters, since the Bank acted in coordination with the rest of MDBs and in particular with the World Bank. The second is that the region's countries – in particular the larger countries – are key members of the IDB's structure of governance; hence the Bank's role in development must be interpreted within the framework of the interplay between states and regional institutions (Griffith-Jones 2002b; Birdsall 2003).

IDB lending policies and technical assistance are, therefore, more clearly understandable in the context of the role they play in political economy, in terms of the consensus-generating role played in their borrower country as a result of its more active or passive interplay with governments and the major IFIs. This role can be more integrally appreciated and assessed in two ways. The first is by identifying the type of IDB–government relationship existent at each stage, areas targeted and main instruments used. The second is by tracing the political, social, economic and ideological forms which the IDB's propagation and legitimation of pro-market reforms assumed at a domestic level (see Chapter 1).

Politically, we must explore the extent to which the IDB contributed or participated in the absorption of political forces into the new framework of development. Socially, we must analyse the Bank's participation and contribution to the process of co-option and absorption of sectors of organised labour and local organisations. Economically, it is necessary to trace and assess the extent to which the IDB backed structural reforms. Ideologically, it is necessary to examine the participation and contribution of the Bank to the dissemination and promotion of the new approach to development and reform.

It is important to notice that the Bank's role and the development strategies pursued by governments of larger member countries constituted an inseparable part of the political economic IFI–state complex given their regional and multilateral nature. This concept is central and must be included in the analysis if we are to comprehend the IDB's role, interventions by areas and its interconnections with the region's government strategies as well as the uneven conditions of development existent at the domestic level. As a result, the IDB's role in regional development is assumed in this investigation to be defined by the dynamics of the global financial hegemony and the character it has taken in the region as a whole, and how it has adopted and adapted domestically in relation to the countries' development strategies.

In this regard, the consensus-generation role of the IDB emerges defined by the Bank's ability to adapt a hegemonic tendency to regional policy guidelines, the framing of policy alternatives, and the ability to legitimise through support and justification specific domestic political projects. These three elements are present in the Bank's interventions in the region and are traceable in its strategies, development targets, instruments and programmes. As a result, it is noticeable that at a regional level the IDB played an important financial and ideological role, fuelling integration between domestic and international actors behind a common project and assimilating opposing positions. The exercise of this role was tied to a complex set of financial, research and academic networks, playing a central role in knowledge production and transmission (with particular attention to academia and the media), and the legitimation of a particular ideological form of economic globalisation.

In political economic terms, the IDB is more than a Bank, given its capacity to access global capital markets and at the same time, domestic actors. In fact, the regional leadership of the Bank has been defined and recognised by its 'capacity to access the domestic' and engenders 'a feeling of ownership' in the region owing to three key elements (Iglesias 2004: 84). The first is the presence and support of industrialised countries, which allow the Bank to access sophisticated capital markets to obtain financial resources under the umbrella of industrialised countries. The other side of this coin is the chief capacity of the IDB to access recipient countries, as well as domestic actors – NGOs and the private sector – achieving a widespread acceptance of its involvement in regional initiatives. The third factor is that IDB officials are usually recruited from its network of associated institutions, former officials of Latin American administrations and US universities. They represent a powerful ideological hemispheric elite network with significant participation in the shape of the Bank's interventions. They constitute a new sort of hemispheric social strata, which exerts influence and frames policies through technical means, given their strategic institutional position within the regional and global governance. These former government officers, intellectuals and technicians have climbed the corporate ladder in Washington and are no longer dependent on their original states to achieve prestige. However, this network consensus is neither uniform in its interests nor homogenous in its approaches to development. In fact, the network is the scenario in which market-led and polity-led perspectives struggle for the directions of development reflecting and justifying specific social interests.

The IDB coexists in a dialectical way with this hemispheric social network, shaping it and shaped by it, as far as both keep themselves aligned with the dominant hemispheric tendencies. Within this framework, the Bank expresses a leading consensual and ideological role as institutional referent of a group of different think-tanks and financial academic institutions which taken together play a chief role in the generation of a consensus around the dominant economic view of development in the region. This consensus-formation network constitutes a central element of the political economy of the IDB's development function, allowing the Bank to retain its individuality while seeking to be 'one step ahead of the policymakers' (Tussie 1995: 114–117).

Table 3.2 briefly lists some of the main financial institutions and think-tanks associated with the World Bank and the IDB, featuring a network of academic institutions mainly oriented to macroeconomic and financial studies. For instance, the Latin American Research Network associated with the IDB includes internationally and regionally acknowledged academic institutions, including the Fundacion de Investigaciones Economicas Latin Americanas (FIEL), Universidad Torcuato Di Tella, Universidad del CEMA in Argentina, CIESS-Econometric SRL in Bolivia, Facultade de Economia e Administracao in Brazil, Instituto de

Table 3.2 Main MDBs and their associated groups in Latin America

World Bank Group	Inter-American Development Bank Group
The International Bank for Reconstruction and Development(IBRD)	The Multilateral Investment Fund (MIF)
The International Development Association(IDA)	The Inter-American Investment Corporation
The International Finance Corporation (IFC)	The Social Development Institute
The Multilateral Investment Guarantee Agency (MIGA)	The Institute for the Integration of Latin America and the Caribbean (INTAL)
The International Centre for Settlement of Investment Disputes (ICSID)	Latin American Network of Central Banks and Finance Ministries
	The Latin American Research Network
	The Capital Markets Network on Latin American Financial Issues
	The Latin American Financial Network (LFN)

Source: Based on IDB official information.

Economía – Pontifica Universidad Católica de Chile, Universidad de Chile, Centro de Analisis y Difusion Economica del Paraguay, and Facultad de Ciencias Empresariales y Economia, Universidad de Montevideo, Uruguay, to mention but a few.

IDB changes in the 1990s

The 1990s brought about a substantial modification in the IDB's development role, lending policies and target areas, in order to promote the new pro-market development agenda. The shift was reflected in the enlargement of the Bank's financial departments, as well as the creation of a new set of sister institutions (MIF and IIC). They were created to reinforce the IDB's role directed to the promotion of regional private capital accumulation, primarily through the introduction of 'policy-based lending' to induce Latin American governments to adopt neoliberal reforms. With that, the IDB's new role, policies and targets of development, along with the rest of the IFIs, evolved to become a complex transformative system of incentives and punishments to promote global financial integration along the guidelines of the Washington Consensus.

The IDB's development mandate in this period was dominated by two complementary approaches, which officially guided the IDB's actions: the Structural Adjustment Programmes (SAPs) developed initially by the World Bank in the period 1990–94, and the Second Generation of Reforms (SGRs) between 1996 and 2001, created by the IMF. SAPs and SGRs were the dialectical outcome of structural changes taking place in the global and regional economy. They were met with widespread enthusiasm in some countries and reticence in others, since the positive condition of the global economy made it realisable to overcome what was considered to be the critical obstacle to development: overblown states and underdeveloped markets.

Removing this obstacle entailed reducing government intervention in economies, especially through privatisation; and increasing labour market mobility, especially through reducing welfare protectionism (RE-287, IDB 2003a: 1–2). Henceforth, the development framework focused on macroeconomic policies, implemented through the well-known SAPs. These were officially justified by their positive results in reducing inflation and increasing exports, but were also the target of vast criticism, since they ensured debt repayment through economic openness, reducing welfare spending, and worsening social conditions in recipient countries. According to the evidence, throughout half a decade SAPs had a negative impact on unemployment and poverty while increasing imports. Social safety nets were unable to compensate for flaws introduced by SAPs (Deacon *et al.* 1997; Welch and Oringer 1998). SAPs followed a single recipe, designed without serious reference to the social conditions in recipient countries, resulting in severe consequences in development financing and welfare production (Dasgupta and Ratha 2000; Taylor and Ros 2000; Taylor 2001; Stiglitz 2002; RE-288, IDB 2003b).

SAPs developed the basic principles of market-orientation of the IFIs' interventions addressed to stimulating the supply side of the economy. Accordingly, development was blocked by fiscal imbalances, distorting economic regulations and capital formation generated by industrial subsidies and labour market protection. The centrepiece of the approach was the fiscal problem, whereby governments were conceived as part of the problem, given their inefficiency and corruption; and the solution was to privatise the public sector, reduce the scale of government spending and abandon any policy that 'altered any prices that would otherwise be set by the impersonal forces of the market' (Leys 1996b: 18).

The second approach to development pursued by the IDB in the 1990s was the SGRs. These reforms did not modify the macroeconomic principles of the SAPs, but rather augmented them by placing major emphasis on microeconomic factors, institutions and the organisation of welfare, all based on a major, yet restricted, limitation of state participation. SGRs emerged as the result of the financial crisis in the 1990s, in particular the Tequila crisis – caused by the devaluation of the Mexican peso in December 1994 – followed a few years later by the East Asian and Russian financial crises (RE-287, IDB 2003a: 3).

By 1994, IFIs (including the IDB), came to assume that what was missing in the SAP model was the scant importance it attached to the role of the banking sector and capital markets and the imperative of fiscal prudence and sound monetary policies. This strategy, by and large, directly secured a desirable environment for international investors through raising market confidence and reforming and reducing spending on health, education and the military, as principally defined by the IMF for the MDBs and adopted by the IDB (Wood 1997; RE-287, IDB 2003a). After a decade of multilateral lending directed to structural reforms, the IDB officially recognised that it 'has created a large outstanding stock of debt whose service ... constitutes a major fiscal obligation for most borrowers' (RE-300, IDB 2004b: 4). In fact, the flow of multilateral lending to Latin America during the 1990s was almost equal to the repayment obligations of recipient countries (ibid.). Table 3.3 illustrates the IDB's two central development approaches in the 1990s, the resultant lending targets and objectives, the central outcomes and the requisite macroeconomic policies. The table presents a typology of SAPs and SGRs, identifying their central features and elements: the mechanism by which these resources are allocated, their development objectives, the chief actor or development driver, the lending targets pursued by the IDB, and the macroeconomic policies demanded of recipient countries before being given access to lending. Noticeably, both models display a strong emphasis on the deconstruction of state intervention in development financing and welfare production, regarding this as the key to activating the market's role in development.

The dominant approach to development defined the new IDB's mission in the period, and in so doing, the Bank was adapted to address the new changes introduced in the region through new areas and institutions: the Private Sector Department (PSD), established in 1994; the Inter-American Investment Corporation (IIC), created in 1988; and the Multilateral Investment Fund (MIF), established in 1992. Together with the institutional innovations, armies of economists came to take

Table 3.3 Economic development models and the IDB's lending targets, 1990–2001

	1990–95	1995–2001
	Structural Adjustment Program (SAP) 'New Economic Model'	*Second Generation Reforms (SGR)* 'New Governance Model'
Resource allocation mechanism	Free market	Free market; selective government intervention permitted provided it has no impact on fiscal deficit
Strategic objective	Macroeconomic stability	Financial stability Increasing competitiveness
Development driver	Private sector	Majority private, but in combination with efforts by public sector
Lending targets in growth	Reform of the state Privatisation of state assets Privatisation of official banks Promotion of the private sector in development (big players)	Promotion of private sector in development Reform of the state Institutional transparency Government accountability Privatisation of state assets Privatisation of official banks Labour market reforms Federal Civil Service Reform of provincial states Emergency
Macroeconomic policies demanded of recipient countries	Fiscal discipline Free trade Price and interest rate liberalisation Privatisation Liberalisation of investment Elimination of subsidies to domestic industries Protection of private economic right and investment	Emphasis on competitiveness-oriented policies Same macroeconomic measures as SAP model Strengthening market self-regulation Investment in human resources/retraining Labour market reform Pension system reform
Lending targets in social welfare	Liberalisation of labour markets National decentralisation in health, education and basic assistance policies for family and childhood Programmes for displaced workers	National decentralisation in health, education Pension system reforms Poverty reduction Labour market flexibilisation Programmes for youth, women and indigenous people

Source: Based on various IDB/OVE reports and interviews.

over and subordinate areas traditionally considered to be key pieces of social development. Since then the PSD has provided long-term financing for private infrastructure, mainly without government guarantees, signalling the capacity of the IDB to relate directly to domestic actors.

The IIC was created to provide loans to small and medium-sized enterprises and to finance equity investments without government guarantees, complemented by the MIF which was charged with promoting reforms of investment policies and the expansion of the private sector. The latter was also supported by the Technical Cooperation Facility (TCF), directed to aiding the transition to market economies through the reform of investment laws, laws in intellectual property, commercial laws, tax systems and labour laws. Complementing these, the Human Resource Facility (HRF) was established to provide grants to government or education institutions to help develop the human resource bases needed for an expanded private sector, such as training schemes to facilitate privatisations or the downsizing of the public sector. Finally, the Small Enterprise Facility (SEF) provides loans and equity investment to micro-enterprises.

The IDB operated by providing long-term debt finance through loans for individual projects, aimed at creating productive assets through net transfers of resources. The IDB's operations were classified, according to their different characteristics, into four strategic instruments or financial channels: (1) investment loans for promoting private sector participation in development; (2) policy-based loans for several uses in exchange for structural reforms; (3) concessional loans with preferential rates, available only to low-income countries; (4) emergency loans, whose approval requires the endorsement of the World Bank and the IMF, for countries facing liquidity problems in times of reforms or international turbulence. Policy-based loans (PBL) were originally denominated as sector lending designed to disburse quickly in response to proof of compliance with policy changes.

PBLs were addressed to the twin objectives of policy reform and the financing of countries' balance of payment needs (RE-300, IDB 2004b). Emergency loans are a variant of PBLs created in 1998 for extreme situations and come with a higher interest rate (over 400 basis points over LIBOR rates). In all cases, projects are designed in conjunction with country authorities and executed by the borrower. In 1989 the IDB created a new lending instrument – sector loans – which specified the policy reforms it was to finance while preventing the loans from being used to purchase imports (RE-300, IDB 2004b). PBLs and emergency loans were both constructed on the basis of detailed policy 'conditions', defining in detail the changes to laws, regulations or institutions that the recipient country was obliged to undertake. In addition, every PBL and emergency loan had to demonstrate 'fulfilment of a satisfactory macroeconomic framework' (OA-330, IDB 1998a) and show that it did not lead to a rise in imports (AB-1704, IDB 1994).

However, as the IDB's nature is to intervene in development, the central political-economic element within the division between PBLs and investment instruments was the location of its corporate governance. Table 3.4 provides a

Table 3.4 IDB global–regional dynamic of instruments, governance and approach to development

Elements	Globally defined	Regionally defined
Development approach	Defined elsewhere and intended to support, promote and legitimise global economic inclusion–expansion	Defined in-house and intended to support, promote and legitimise global insertion, regional cohesion and political stability
Financial source	Capital markets and G-7	Capital markets and Member countries
Governance axis	Anchored in the IMF-WB inter-coordination and defined by G-7	Defined internally in a bargaining process subject to the size of the country and relations with lender and borrower countries
Core policy instrument	Sector and emergency loans (highly policy based)	Investment policies and loans (defined in common agreement with the sovereign)
Source of legitimacy	External state–state relations with G-7 and IMF and WB support	Regional state–state relations and domestic support

Source: Based on various IDB reports and interviews.

summary of these power locations, approaches, instruments and sources. As can be seen from the table, there is a structural division between those instruments defined by the global financial governance, by the IDB–IFIs complex, and those defined regionally, by the IDB–state members complex, with both centres coexisting and defining the complex nature of the Bank's corporate governance.

IDB lending targets and strategic areas of national development

Given the increasing importance of capital flows in the financing of development of Latin American economies in the 1990s, IFIs, governments committed to the pro-market reforms and mainstream economists have for a long time been concerned with the interconnections between capital flows and multilateral lending. There the major issue of contention has been whether or not official lending has had a positive or a negative effect on the management of capital movements, financing of development and welfare restructuring (Rodrik 1995; Garret and Mitchell 1999).

The economic multilateral approach defines these relations positively in terms of countercyclical financing, that is, multilateral lending counterbalances volatile private capital flows, whereupon the political economy of exchange rates becomes the key macroeconomic issue in the relation between the domestic and international economy (Frieden and Stein 2001; Titelman 2002; Sagasti *et al.* 2001). On the other hand, a more pessimistic view – led by development scholars – finds that there is no direct correlation between private capital flows and multilateral lending. They argue that multilateral lending has in point of fact followed global capital flows, rushing in when times are good, and queuing up to withdraw in times of severe crisis, with a negative overall impact on development financing and welfare production (Rodrik 1995; Stiglitz 2002; Weisbrot and Baker 2002; Frenkel 2003).

Dealing with such complex economic issues goes beyond the scope of this research. However, it is assumed here that, since the IDB has privileged access to global capital markets, multilateral lending can exert a major negative or positive effect on capital flows, the latter being configured by market conditions and tendencies set in motion by economic actors at the domestic and international levels. This point is vital for this investigation in two ways. First, it shows the ideological dimension of the IDB's multilateral lending. This is so because, given that the mandate of the IDB and MDBs is to foster rapid development in recipient countries, the changing notion of development informing the IDB's development targets and policies must be understood if we are to comprehend the *effectiveness* of IDB policies in the key strategic areas of national development. Second, it expresses the structural dimension of multilateral lending as it shows the intergoverned international–domestic character at the very basis of the IDB's role as well as its capacities to depoliticise and economise development issues.

Having identified the evolution of the concept of development which guides IDB policies in Latin America, it is time to identify the chief areas addressed by the IDB's lending and assistance policies and their relation with those strategic areas which define the organisation of the financing of development and production of welfare. Scholars with an optimistic view of the role of the IDB and other MDBs and RDBs in development argue that these institutions play an effective, positive role in three distinct ways. The first is by promoting better access to international capital markets for recipient countries. Another is by playing a countercyclical role in times when international private capital becomes scarce. Finally, others consider that they facilitate the access to external financial sources that yield high social returns and welfare reorganisation (Culpeper 1999; Sagasti *et al.* 2001; Titelman 2002). Accordingly, three major strategic areas of development are identified for the IDB:

- investments in the production sector; infrastructure, including agriculture, fisheries, industry, mining, tourism, science and technology; and infrastructure encompassing energy, transport and communications;
- welfare production, which comprises sanitation, urban development, education, health, social investment, environment, and micro-enterprises;
- state reform, meaning mainly the retreat of the state from product and labour markets, state decentralization, changes in laws and institutions, and particularly the dismantling of state regulation of markets.

As a result, the importance of the IDB's role in development is appraised here through the extent to which it contributes, both positively and negatively, in the short and long term, to key areas related to development financing and welfare production. Rather than an emphasis upon the size of lending, it focuses on the orientation pursued in key areas of development, whereby the figures below are mainly indicative of the policy targets followed by the IDB and recipient governments.

Figure 3.1 shows the evolution of IDB lending for the region and its distribution by country during this period. What is interesting in this figure is the significant correlation between the IDB's lending cycles and the three main stages identified in the changing political economy of South America and Argentina during the 1990s, as analysed in Chapters 2 and 3. The first period, of hegemonic convergence, lasted between 1990 and 1994, was signalled by an international and regional hegemonic convergence of the dominant interests forging strategic state–IFI partnerships following two decades of economic change. The second period, 1994–96, was characterised by the escalation of regional and international tensions as a result of increasing structural differentiation between the domestic and international.

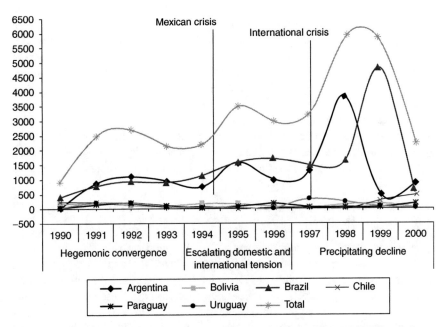

Figure 3.1 IDB annual loan approvals in South America, 1990–2000 (US$ millions). Loan approvals reflect the amounts approved, which are not necessarily equal to disbursements for any given year since an approved operation may not be disbursed until the following year. (Based on IDB annual reports.)

Finally, the third phase between 1997 and 2000 featured an accelerated decline in neoliberal policies, capital flows, multilateral lending and the rise of increasing social tensions. In addition, the dominant influence of Brazil and Argentina in the cycle of the IDB lending is clear, as is the fact that the smaller countries such as Bolivia, Chile, Paraguay and Uruguay became financially almost insignificant.

It is important to note that the series of stages mentioned, rather than marking isolated inflection points, signify the presence of international–domestic changes in the political economy of South America and in its chief regional financial institution, defined by Brazil and Argentina in terms of access to multilateral lending, and by their influence upon IDB lending and policies. Similar recognition of these phases can also be found in several IDB reports regarding the evolution of the notion of development pursued by the Bank and the changing dynamics of its lending to countries such as Argentina (RE-260, IDB 2002d; RE-288, IDB 2003b; RE-299, IDB 2004a). Outstanding throughout these reports is the recognition of the Bank's failure to articulate a clear concept of what constitutes 'development' and the absence, during this time, of country background reports (RE-260, IDB 2002d: 4; RE-288, IDB 2003b).

As shown in Figure 2.2 in Chapter 2, the historical evolution of IDB lending targets in the strategic areas of development mentioned revealed a sharp transformation in the 1990s over previous decades, with a significant concentration on welfare production and state reorganisation. Figure 3.2 shows more empirical evidence of this, illustrating the evolution of IDB lending in relation to the two broader strategic areas of production sector promotion and state reform, the latter including welfare reform. As the figure reveals, the allocation of lending for state and welfare reorganisation grew considerably in the 1990s, despite being marked by two major drops prior to 1994 and in 1997, coinciding with the Mexican and Asian crises, and an abrupt fall after 1999 in the aftermath of the crisis in Argentina. The allocation of lending to production sectors and infrastructure diminished in the period 1994–96, only to recover its average after 1997. The most salient result that emerges from the data is that IDB lending targets seem to be directed mainly towards state reorganisation along the lines set by the SAP and SGR models of development rather than to the promotion of productive sectors.

The IDB's role in the political economic stages of South America in the 1990s

Provided with new funds and renewed political support after the difficult process of the Seventh Replenishment (1989), in the early 1990s the IDB executed a substantial modification of its developmental approach, institutional areas, and lending policies and targets of development, increasing its influence in regional development as shown above. Throughout this stage, the role of the Bank in development came to be reinforced by the three elements already described. The first element was the incorporation of its lending policies and sources within IMF and WB strategies, which amplified the power of the IDB in recipient countries. The second factor behind this was the Bank's leadership over small regional financial

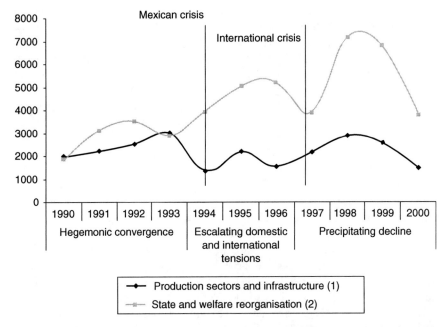

Figure 3.2 IDB lending according to targets of production and state reorganisation in South
America, 1990–2000 (US$ millions). (1) Agriculture, fisheries, industry, min-
ing, tourism, science and technology, and energy, transport and communications. (2) State reform and modernisation, export finance, pre-investment and
others. Welfare includes sanitation, urban development, education, social
investment, health, environment, microenterprises (also microtourism) (occa-
sionally debt-service and rescheduling as chapter shows analyses in more
detail). (Based on IDB annual reports.)

institutions, think-tanks, research centres, and academic centres, and its prestige,
based on technical expertise among politicians, increased its capacity to produce
consensus around the demands of the global economy. The final factor was the
new capacity of the IDB to condition countries' access to its sources to their participation in the Brady Plan and debt rescheduling. By so doing, the IDB added something that no other regional financial institution ever had before, that is, political
power to guarantee the execution by its borrowers of the new set of global policies
(see Tables 3.3 and 3.4).

This new capacity translated into a set of instruments able to provide wider political powers to the MDBs in order to make SAPs and SGRs effective in recipient
countries through the unfolding of a two-way process in which countries benefited
from access to international capital flows in exchange of domestic adjustments
(Griffith-Jones 1994; Birdsall 2002). The dynamic of this political power was based
on complex relations between the Bank, main donors and recipient countries, within
which the largest nations, such as Brazil and Argentina, stand out as countries able

to bargain with the institution in relation to the imposition of the policy orientation. Thus, conditions and reforms involving the participation of the Bank were the result of agreements between governments adopting reform programmes and Bretton Woods institutions committed to financial and technical support.

The process started with the inclusion by governments of structural reforms in their development strategies and their translation into domestic policies. The process involved, first, negotiations and agreements, defined previously, between top officials, finance ministers and the IDB staff; second, the design of its instrumentation by IDB officials, to be subsequently agreed and ratified between government officials and technical staff in the recipient country. Both sides were informed by a general multilateral diagnosis of the roots of stagnation and the regional obstacles standing in the way of development (RE-260, IDB 2002d; RE-288, IDB 2003b). Accordingly, it was assumed officially that the critical obstacles to development were 'overblown states and underdeveloped markets', and IDB interventions were directed towards 'reduc[ing] the scope of state activity and economic intervention, and provid[ing] a regulatory environment that incentivises and promotes private economic participation' (RE-260, IDB 2002d: 9). However, a close look at the evolution of IDB lending does not show an unvarying pattern in the directions of reform set by the SAP and SGR models. Instead, this presents a differentiated figure marked by rises and declines in the allocation of IDB lending to the welfare, state, infrastructure and production sectors, closely associated to major events in the global and regional economy in the 1990s.

Indeed, the variable pattern and changing targets of IDB lending emerges related to the changing dynamics, nature and aims of global finances and governance. Figure 3.3 illustrates the distribution of IDB loans by target sectors in the 1990s – production sectors and physical infrastructure, welfare production, and state reform. The importance of the figure is the correlation between the political economic stages identified for the region and the shifting emphasis on the various developmental targets by the IDB. It can be seen from Figure 3.3 that, in relative terms, the focus on state reform and welfare production occupies the centre of IDB policies in the period. Additionally, the course of the IDB's targeted 'state reforms' follows the same pattern as the fluctuating conditions of the global economy, defined by the impact of financial crises in Mexico in 1994 and in Asia in 1997. Moreover, IDB policies addressed to 'welfare production' show continuous growth throughout the decade, with two peaks, each one just after the main international financial crises, and an abrupt decline in 1999 and 2000. Finally, it is important to note that even though 'production sector and infrastructure' were central objectives for the Bank and governments, the reality is that, state reforms and production of welfare represented the major developmental targets constitute the bulk of financing in the 1990s.

Convergence within the new global hegemony (1990–93)

During the period 1990–93, the role of the IDB's lending and government policies in South America shows, in terms of agency, an unambiguous alignment to the

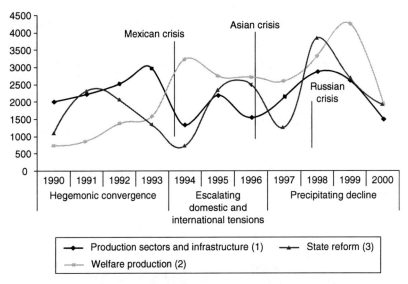

Figure 3.3 Distribution of IDB loans by sector to South America in the 1990s (US$ millions). (1) Agriculture, fisheries, industry, mining, tourism, science and technology. (2) Sanitation, urban development, education, social investment, health, environment, micro-enterprises. (3) State reform and modernisation, finance, trade (occasionally debt service and debt rescheduling). (Based on IDB annual reports.)

Washington Consensus and to development policies expressed in the form of the SAPs. The period was characterised by a historical convergence of interests and solid alliances based on a diagnosis of the roots of stagnation that was shared by domestic and international actors.

The stage is signalled by widespread optimism among international financial intermediaries, investors, domestic industrial sectors and officials in Washington and South American governments that market-driven reforms would permit restructuring and the integration of economic actors into the new global trends, fostering faster growth and improved welfare (RE-260, IDB 2002d; Krugman 1995). State reform – mostly in the form of reduced public spending and privatisation – came to be key to the fight against inflation and the achievement of the macroeconomic stability necessary to attract capital flows. Briefly, this economic rule picked up from developed economies came to be the rational and absolute rule of development under which countries attempted to reorganise their political economy (Lora *et al.* 2004).

This positive ideological atmosphere was fuelled by two elements: first, the positive results of neoliberal reforms in OECD countries and in particular in Pinochet's Chile, supported by the Reagan administration and by massive financial flows from MDBs (Griffith-Jones 1994); second, the upsurge in capital flows

Table 3.5 Summary of IDB's main policies, targets and devices in financing development and welfare, 1990–2000

	1990–94	*1994–96*	*1997–2000*
IDB's role and lending policies	Defined in coordination with the World Bank and the IMF, and addressed to promote market-driven reforms SAP policies	Countercyclical lending Country access to capital markets SGR policies State reform Private sector promotion	Countercyclical lending SGR policies Emergency loans State reform Private sector promotion Welfare production reform
Role of the state	Reduction of state in development Development led by markets and private sector	Reduction of state in development, now driven by financial markets and private sector	Selective state action to contain social conflict during transition
State institutions/ areas to transform	Federal civil service reform Privatisation of state assets and official banks Property rights Labour law	Provincial banks Judicial reform Provincial and Federal fiscal sector	Retirement and pension national system Federal civil service
Sources of financing of development	Privatisation Capital flows (short-term) Multilateral lending	Capital flow (short-term) Trade and corporate acquisition and merger Multilateral lending PBL loans	Multilateral lending Emergency loans Capital flow (short-term)
Spending approach	Centred on reduction of fiscal spending and economic subsidies State fiscal decentralisation	State reforms Social and infrastructure sectors	Social development and emergency
Changes in the social welfare structure	Labour market deregulation Fiscal decentralisation Assistentialism Conversion of human resources Microenterprises	Deepening labour market deregulation Provincial pension system Decentralisation of health, education and basic assistance policies related to family	National pension system Unemployment Decentralised welfare in municipalities

Source: Based on annual IDB and OVE reports.

to Latin America following 1989, determined by high-yielding profit opportunities
– concentrated mainly in Brazil and Argentina – that came to an abrupt end with
the Mexican financial crisis. These capital flows were largely composed of short-
term funds and portfolio investments with FDI making up a minor portion
(Kaminsky *et al.* 2001). However, despite this, the danger of crisis was dismissed
and little consideration was given to the contagion of crises across international
capital markets caused by international herd movements (Frenkel 2003: 41).

Given the empowerment of the IDB by the Washington Consensus and its historical capacity to access domestic actors in the region, in the 1990s the IDB was
able to enter into areas of lending which would have been inconceivable under the
ISI-CEPAL developmentalist models. The IDB now was targeting labour markets,
social security, pension funds, state decentralisation, design of financial institutions, trade judiciary reform, state accountability and corruption (Espinoza
Carranza 2002). Throughout this period, IDB lending and policies aimed at forging a new role for the state in development, one shaped by the reduction of its role
in growth and welfare and based on pro-market reforms. Accordingly, key targets
for the IDB were privatisations, fiscal decentralisation to local governments,
federal civil service reform, privatisation of state assets and official banks, elimination of subsidies, market deregulation, property rights and labour market
deregulation.

In order to reorganise the financing of development, reforms were centred on
trade and finance, specifying the dismantling of industrial subsidies and privatisations, as the means to reduce fiscal deficits, attract capital flows and encourage private sector participation in development (RE-258, IDB 2002c). As a result,
privatisation of state assets and capital flows came to be the centre around which
IDB policies promoted the reorganisation of development financing. Driven by
economic assumptions, the IDB's policies subordinated welfare production to the
fiscal and conjunctural constraints of the market-driven transformation. In this
regard, its policies translated into policies directed towards labour market deregulation, decentralisation, the reduction of fiscal spending on health and education
and compensatory social policies such as training programmes for displaced workers and microenterprises.

Consequently, despite the size of IDB lending to the region, its lending and policies came to play a significant role in South American development. It is worth
noting that when capital flows to the region restarted in the early 1990s, short-
term, interest-sensitive portfolio investment represented 66 per cent of gross
inflows compared with only 26 per cent to Asia, while FDI to Latin America was
only 30 per cent of gross inflows compared with 45 per cent to Asia (MIF/GN-
78-3, IDB 2003g). Hence, during the period of convergence the reorganisation of
financing of development was driven by an explosive mix of short-term capital
flows and the one-off proceeds of privatisation. Furthermore, the over-reliance on
external sources in financing promoted by the IDB not only presented quantitative
limitations upon recipient countries, e.g. by market-regulating institutions, but an
increase in countries' over-exposure to external changes as capital flows were

highly unpredictable and subject to the conditions and trends of the global political economy (RE-260, IDB 2002d).

Economic openness and liberalisation of countries' capital accounts followed, with the financing of development tied to privatisation and to the behaviour of global finances, with serious implications for regional development (Eatwell and Taylor 1999; Ocampo 2002; Kaminsky *et al.* 2001). In terms of financing of development, the early stages of this period show the positive impact of IDB policies, as these contributed to countries' creditworthiness in international capital markets (Griffith-Jones 1994). The effect was amplified by the privatisation processes, as the region's countries obtained significant domestic revenues to finance reforms, support social costs and service debt. These results inspired optimism among IDB and government officials about the potential of private sector participation in development, expressed in the continuity of its support to production sectors and infrastructure targets as Figure 3.4 presents (RE-287, IDB 2003a; RE-303, IDB 2004c).

The high financial liquidity of the economy and the new reforms created a positive context for an economic, political and social convergence of domestic and international interests. International banks and investors, and major domestic industrial interests, benefited from openness by taking advantage of privatisations

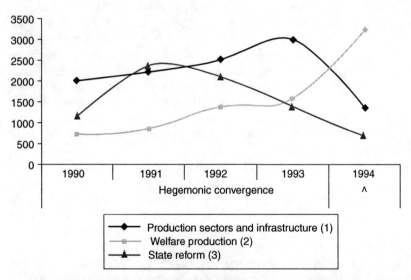

Figure 3.4 Evolution of IDB lending to South America by chief development targets, 1990–93 (US$ millions). (1) Agriculture, fisheries, industry, mining, tourism, science and technology. (2) Sanitation, urban development, education, social investment, health, environment, micro-enterprises. (3) State reform and modernisation, finance, trade (occasionally service debt and debt rescheduling).(Based on IDB annual reports.)

and the guarantees created by the financial engineering of the Brady Plan. Finance and trade openness stimulated upper- and middle-class consumption, and politicians benefited from renewed legitimacy and social support fostered by economic stability.

However, it was mostly domestic and international big players that were being favoured, and trade and financial deregulation had began to harm small and medium industrial enterprises through an indiscriminate openness to imports, although the social impact had not yet become widespread. Policy-induced high interest rates and overvalued exchange rates guaranteed huge returns, thus attracting massive short-term capital flows into the region. A decline in the dollar price of imported consumer goods, induced by tariff reduction, overvalued currencies and dollar-denominated wages, triggered luxury consumption by the middle and upper classes in countries such as Brazil and Argentina but hid deterioration in the conditions of labour (Palma 1998: 14; Taylor and Ros 2000).

As South American countries shifted from protected to open economies, the IDB accepted the diagnosis that labour contracts and quality of employment guaranteed by state regulation also had to change to labour market regulation. The economistic notion of human resources as economic means of growth replaced the social concept of labour as agent and generator of collective welfare, with two policies driving the shift: deregulation of labour markets and privatisation. Deregulation of labour markets was considered to be vital to the needs of the pro-market development, whereby existing labour legislation, institutions and access to political power created economic rigidities (MIF/GN-78-8, IDB 2003i). The credo of labour flexibility became a chief element of the IDB's conditions, which came to promote revision and elimination of historical labour legislation and the adoption of the idea of flexibility in labour regulation. In cases such as Argentina, this approach was enthusiastically followed by governments and justified by the need to execute privatisation of state assets (Griffith-Jones 1994; Bronstein 1995).

Now, newly privatised companies had the right to hire only those skilled workers functional to their competitive strategies, reshaping the conditions of their workforces. On the one hand, this weakened the labour unions' power to influence companies' actions affecting workers, including salaries, social benefits and labour conditions. On the other hand, there was the growing emergence of a new stratum of people outside of labour markets and changes in the composition of the labour force, in which growing unemployment and the increasing preponderance of low-skilled workers was associated with a deindustrialisation process affecting high-skilled workers (Frenkel 2004; Ros 2004).

A new marginalised social segment emerged, comprising those who had failed to enrol either into the new conditions of labour demanded by markets or in the micro-enterprises and retraining programmes promoted by central and local governments, the IDB and the WB. The mounting political presence of this new sector was ameliorated temporarily by the economic effect of labour indemnifications delivered by states with the financial support of MDBs, as well as the consumption boom, but would emerge later as one of the major social issues associated with the reforms.

Despite these social elements undermining the basis of IDB and government policies, four important events maintained enthusiasm for the neoliberal structural reforms in the early 1990s. These were:

- the successful implementation of the Real Plan in Brazil;
- the Convertibility Plan in Argentina, which soon lowered inflation in Latin America's largest economies to levels in developed countries;
- the integration of Mexico into the North American Free Trade Agreement (NAFTA) in partnership with Canada and the United States;
- growing regional trade in South America as tariff barriers dropped.

The optimism was shattered in 1994 with the Tequila crisis in Mexico, which, despite its severe impact on Argentina, did not undermine the confidence of Washington institutions and top economists in pro-market reforms (Lora *et al.* 2004). The end of the period was signalled by a sharp decline in the production sector and infrastructure-oriented IDB policies, and increasing the Bank's attention to welfare and state reforms as chief areas of development.

Influenced by the work of Calvo *et al.* (1993), the dominant idea in the IDB was that if some countries undergoing deep structural reforms were able to overcome the shock, and even grow – as in the cases of Chile and the OECD – then external factors must play a fundamental role in determining the misfortunes of some countries. Macroeconomic volatility was the problem, although domestic reforms could still isolate countries and absorb external shocks. Countries should pursue deeper structural reforms, including denominating debt in foreign currency, and tying debt more closely to fiscal spending (Lora *et al.* 2004). National officials in countries such as Brazil and Argentina concurred with the diagnosis; more reforms were needed; in particular, the capital account should be liberalised in order to attract capital flow and maintain the macroeconomic stability required for development to be financed. The formula was a complete deepening of pro-market change based on more reductions in tariff barriers, independent central banks targeting inflation, a sound banking system, labour market deregulation, and more privatisations.

Increasing financial instability and social tensions (1994–96)

During the period 1994–96, the IDB's role in development in the region became defined by a steady exhaustion of the model of development financing based on capital flows and privatisations, with an increasing differentiation in the economic and political community of interests at the base of development models. The process also featured a continuous deterioration in social conditions as a result of the impact of market-led reforms and the dismantling of welfare, with political systems trapped between the success of economic stability and growing social deterioration. As a result, the IDB's development function shifted again, triggered by the so-called Tequila crisis, but within the same pro-market pattern, deepening its financial role, this time by assuming a so-called countercyclical role through financial rescues.

Rescue packages coordinated by IFIs and governments were addressed mainly to neutralising regional and global financial disruption arising from the globalisation of national economies, and drew the World Bank and the IDB into deeper involvement in the region. In all cases, the multilateral interventions appeared directed to averting default on dollar debt obligations so as to avoid damaging investments, thereby overcoming short-term dollar liquidity crises and preventing their contagious spread to other emerging markets. In this way the new countercyclical role of the IDB emerged, defined by and subordinated to the economic and political imperatives of averting the risks accompanying the globalisation of development financing arising from the imperfections of global capital markets. This change was demanded by the major industrialised states and implemented by the IFIs. A former director of the IDB offered a similar interpretation:

> To understand the IDB's new role after the Tequila crisis, you have to understand how the gamut of multilateral institutions in Washington actually functioned and the priorities of the North Americans and Europeans within the Bank... Behind the macroeconomic justifications for the new counter-cyclical role lay many real interests... In fact, usually the technical justifications took form only after measures like this were implemented.
>
> (Anonymous interview 05/2004)

The Tequila crisis represented a sharp reversal in reform-financing capital flows, a phenomenon also expressed at a regional level, affecting the US government's NAFTA project and its economic and political interests in the region (Rodrik and Velazco 1999). In short, sudden access to large amounts of external financing had inflated Mexico's bubble, leading to a liquidity crisis as it exhausted its dollar reserves in an attempt to honour its debts, seriously threatening the US NAFTA strategy (Palma 1998; Krugman 1995). The rescue packages to Mexico, Argentina and other countries prompted a debate concerning the countercyclical role of the IFIs, with the US right wing leading the chorus of criticism.

Nonetheless, following the dominant ideas in Washington, the IDB interpreted Mexico's 1994 debt crisis as a balance-of-payment problem highlighting the vulnerability of capital-importing countries to abrupt reversals. Volatility had reduced economic growth (Lora *et al.* 2004). The IMF certified the path of recovery by endorsing more pro-market reforms, expressed during the period as a significant increase in lending targeted to state reform and continuous support for welfare reorganisation, as Figure 3.5 illustrates.

As a result of the impact of massive bailouts to Mexico, scholars positively judged the efficacy of official bailout packages as sources of sizable support and as means to avoid default, settling the issue about the importance of crisis resolution for both national and international policymakers (Calvo and Mendoza 1996; Cline 2002; Lora *et al.* 2004). Thus, the possibility that the policies and approaches pursued by the MDBs and IFIs contained inherent failures was dismissed, and a divorce between the domestic and global economy was assumed. By the same token, it was an error in the IDB's diagnosis that capital flow volatility and

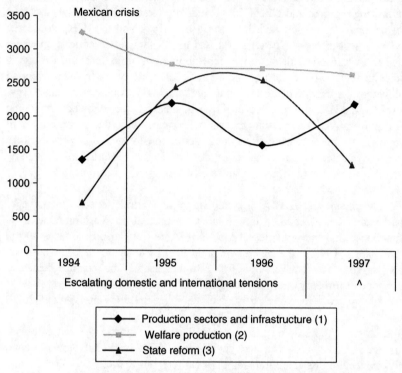

Figure 3.5 Evolution of IDB lending to South America by chief development targets, 1994–97 (US$ millions). (1) Agriculture, fisheries, industry, mining, tourism, science and technology. (2) Sanitation, urban development, education, social investment, health, environment, microenterprises. (3) State reform and modernisation, finance, trade (occasionally debt service and debt rescheduling). (Based on IDB annual reports.)

international interest rates were the major causes menacing regional growth and that institutional domestic changes should henceforth play a major role (RE-258, IDB 2002c).

The introduction of the SGRs further defined the path of recovery by including microeconomic factors, labour, judicial institutions, and new finance regulators in the targeting model; and in particular by specifying reform in the organisation of welfare, changes in the provincial or federal pension systems and decentralisation of health and education. In addition, major attention was placed upon the efficiency of the banking sector and on the essential impact of fiscal prudence and monetary policy on the financing of development. Implicitly, SGRs concerned finance, and so they sought, directly or indirectly, to secure and guarantee the sound fiscal environment required by international and domestic investors. Significantly, the IDB, in an attempt to ameliorate the dominant social liberal orthodoxy, now considered that social reform should be central to economic reform (Wood 1997; RE-287, IDB 2003a). Accordingly, in July 1994, the IDB created the Inter-American Institute for Social Development (INDES), in order to train public sector and non-governmental organisation employees to reinforce the administration of the social sector and to promote the participation of NGOs in social policy.

However, as development shifted towards deeper pro-market reforms, the negative social consequences of the reorganisation of welfare, the increasingly regressive distribution of income, and social tensions became gradually more amplified by the decentralisation or de-concentration of key public areas, particularly in the delivery of health and education. Drawing on the theories and experiences of fiscal federalism in the mid-1980s, in the early 1990s the IDB advocated decentralisation as another antidote to fiscal deficits, with the added benefit of promoting citizen participation (RE-250, IDB 2001b).

Fiscal stress, it was felt, showed the vulnerability of large central governments and created incentives for politicians and trade union actors to support the domestic economic reform. Decentralisation does not appear to have followed a common pattern in the region and to have instead been shaped by the main political forces and structural conditions of each country, as the cases of Chile and Argentina show. In the case of Chile the process was addressed to reduce regional constituencies and concentrate power around the capital. In Argentina, however, it was directed to reducing the central fiscal deficit and towards involving provinces and municipalities in the neoliberal coalition by devolving social responsibilities to them – all processes in which the IDB played a chief role (Willis *et al.* 1999).

Gradually a contradiction started to emerge in the Bank between economic outcomes and social costs. The macroeconomic and institutional results of reforms were read as successes of the Bank's policies, since these implied 'a change in law or regulation, [intended] to have the outcome of improved performance of the economy as a whole', changes which were tied to the IDB's conditions (RE-258, IDB 2002c: 22). In 1994 the Bank began to perceive the growing social deterioration, understanding this to be a transient cost of reforms and the result of labour market rigidities.

It responded by reinforcing social mandates addressed to 'enhancing social equity' and prioritisation of investment targeted at reducing poverty (RE-288, IDB 2003b). However, during this period, the IDB appeared more concerned with the promotion of pro-market policies and institutional change rather than with their outcomes. The presence of IDB financial and technical support within federal or provincial administrations became synonymous with government. And 'government' came to mean politicians and professionals in tune with the new wind of change: modernism, efficiency, commitment to reforms, and, above all, possession of the resources necessary to drive change.

IDB policies should help to remove distortions in market prices, and therefore improve the efficient use of productive resources, including human resources, and hence state and welfare production should necessarily be the main targets of its lending and policies. Figure 3.5 presents the evolution of IDB lending to South America by developmental targets in the period 1994–97. As the figure shows, the major contributions of IDB lending were addressed to welfare production, while state reform rose in 1995–96. It is worth noting that despite the Bank being authorised to lend directly to the private sector, this area does not show significant growth compared to lending targeted towards welfare production and state reforms (RE-303, IDB 2004c).

In terms of the political options taken by the major countries – Brazil and Argentina – the period 1994–97 was a time of growing influence of, and differentiation between, regional economic interests. Differing from Argentina, where policies addressed to deindustrialisation became more acute, Brazil gave priority to stimulating regional trade, particularly with Argentina, through major fiscal and financial incentives to industrial sectors. Argentina, for its part, pursued a strategy of openness in trade and finance favouring a massive process of mergers and acquisitions between domestic and international corporations and the development of the service sector (Kulfas 2001; Nochteff 2001; Basualdo 2001, 2003).

In 1997, the unexpected happened, and the East and Southeast Asian countries that had pursued rapid domestic financial liberalisation and capital account liberalisation anchoring the financing of development to the dynamics of capital flows and the global economy, suddenly collapsed. Macroeconomic policies and monetary stability could not prevent vulnerability without imposing other costs on welfare (Stiglitz 2002). The new financial crisis rapidly terminated the Asian miracle, spreading trouble to countries whose strategies of development financing entailed a high exposure to capital flows, such as Russia, Brazil and, finally, Argentina.

The decline of transformismo (1997–2000)

During the period 1997–2000, the role of the IDB in the region's development was defined by three elements. The first element is the policy inertia resulting from its assumptions and diagnosis about the origin of the crisis and the social deterioration, within which two improvements in its policies stand out: emergency lending and poverty reduction strategies. The second element is the subordination to the leading actions of IFIs and endorsement of their policies. The final element is the development of the IDB's regional commitments, as it began to perceive the increasing social deterioration produced by market-led reforms and above all by the impact of the dismantling of the state.

The period has been appraised in two opposing ways: as a time of loose direction by the Bank (RE-299, IDB 2004a), and as a time of major commitments with South America. A glance at Figure 3.6 shows the continuity and the increase in the IDB's lending and in its welfare production policies, which experienced an abrupt drop in 2000 following the tendency of capital flows to converge on the largest countries in the region. The state reform target seems also to have received a renewed impulse from the Bank following the Asian crisis, something in tune with the official diagnosis about the positive role of reforms. Something similar occurs

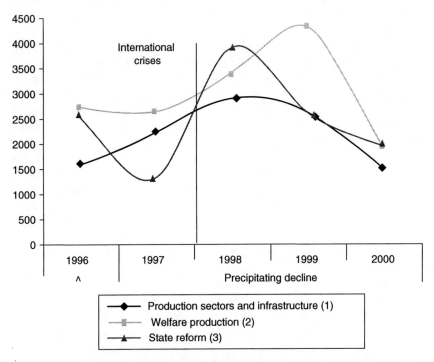

Figure 3.6 Evolution of IDB lending to South America, by chief development targets, 1997–2000 (US$ millions). (1) Agriculture, fisheries, industry, mining, tourism, science and technology. (2) Sanitation, urban development, education, social investment, health, environment, micro-enterprises. (3) State reform and modernisation, finance, trade (occasionally debt service and debt rescheduling). (Based on IDB annual reports.)

with production sectors and with infrastructure, both appearing to recover their dynamics of the early 1990s, only to suddenly decline in 2000, together with the rest of the IDB's lending targets.

For neoliberal macroeconomics, still the IDB's dominant view of development, diagnosis of the causes of the Asian crisis focused on the sudden halt in capital flows, damaging economic activity in countries implementing reforms. It became evident that the structure of debt had something to do with these countries' inability to freely float their exchange rates, diagnosed as a 'fear of floating' (Lora *et al.* 2004: 10; Calvo and Reinhart 1999). This idea led to two kinds of policy responses, both tacitly favouring diverse international and regional interests. The first suggested that market credibility could only be restored by dollarising the economy; something officially criticised as it increased incentives to borrow and lend in foreign currency (Hausmann 1999; Sachs and Larrain 1999; Calvo 2000a). This option clearly benefited foreign investors in particular, by erasing currency risk. The second option aimed at improving the defences of emerging market countries by creating a basket of bonds to control speculative attacks (Eichengreen and Hausman 2004). This option was perhaps more favourable to trade, to the region's states and to large industrial actors.

Whatever the policy option, the IDB as a multilateral institution was caught in the financial trap generated by market-driven reforms which it itself had promoted and the interplay of international and domestic sectional interests. The financing of development based on external finance, private or official, tended to generate fiscal collapse as high country risk premiums made external financing more expensive (Frenkel 2003: 41). Reorganising welfare production along social liberal guidelines exacerbated other economic contradictions, in particular those experienced by unprotected social sectors and especially workers, children, women and the elderly of large urban districts (Deacon *et al.* 1997: 62; Yeates 2005: 5). It is worth noting that despite the international capital markets' growing negative perceptions and heightened risk assessment, and despite the gradual distancing of the IMF and WB, the IDB assumed in this period a more aggressive stance in terms of support to the region, and in particular to countries in trouble. This stance exemplified the major political role being played by the IDB in the region's development; something which did not fit well the approach of its technical staff.

By 1998, the crisis in international finance had become chronic, particularly affecting emerging countries attempting to finance development through capital markets. Within this context, the industrialised countries and IFIs designed a set of measures, to be coordinated by the IMF and MDBs, to rescue countries in free fall. In essence, the measures were addressed in the first place to providing liquidity to troubled countries in order to avoid bank runs and the exodus of capital, thus reducing the pressure on domestic currencies and growth. The second objective was to ensure financing of basic social programmes vital to reduce social conflicts and, at the same time, attempt to generate consensus between the major actors around the deepening of adjustment programmes (RE-251, IDB 2001c: 3–17). The IDB's Board of Governors authorised the rollout of a new variant of fast-disbursing policy-based lending for countries which had fallen victim to contagion, a facility also made conditional on structural reforms (RE-300, IDB 2004b). Table 3.6 illustrates the approvals of emergency loans to Latin America. More significant than the size of lending is the presence of the region's larger countries, Argentina and Brazil, denoting their important presence in the configuration of the IDB policies.

In 1997, the IDB introduced, as the centrepiece of its policy, the 'Strategy for Poverty Reduction' (GN-1894-5, IDB 1997a), which according to the IDB's official evaluation seriously lacked 'a diagnostic section' and 'an analytical discussion of the poverty issues facing the region', and overemphasised the management of resources rather than the effectiveness of social targets. This 'call[ed] into question whether the interventions proposed' were the most appropriate for the region or only reflected a general framework applied to the region (RE-288, IDB 2003b: 5). The IDB argued that 'a strategy of poverty elimination is to help the poor earn their way out of poverty' (RE-288, IDB 2003b: 5); in order to achieve this, the economy must create the conditions for jobs to be made available to the poor.

Table 3.6 IDB emergency loans to Latin America, 1990s (US$ billions)

Country	Amount	Year
Argentina	2.50	1998
Brazil	1.20	1999
Brazil	2.20	1999
Colombia	0.35	1998
Colombia	0.30	1999
Jamaica	0.01	1999
Peru	0.31	1999
Colombia	0.50	1999

Source: IDB/OVE, RE-300 (IDB 2004b: 42).

Briefly, in terms of welfare production, the IDB's efforts were addressed to employment generation, understood to be the by-product of private sector activity. Therefore, any effort to increase welfare should be directed to the promotion of private sector involvement in development, deregulation of labour markets and privatisation of social security, with the state playing a compensatory or minimal role (RE-288, IDB 2003b). Highlighting the safety-net character given to the social policy, the IDB officially recognised that 'a main feature of the 1997 strategy is its clear reflection of the pro-market consensus that emerged in the eighties, in which government interventions are necessary only as a compensatory mechanism and to ensure minimum standards of living' (RE-288, IDB 2003b: 6).

However, the masterstroke of these welfare reforms was the promotion of the structural reform of the pension sector (Barrientos 2004; Haagh and Helgo 2002; Gough and Wood 2004; Mesa-Lago 1996, 2004; Mesa-Lago and Muller 2004). The 'new pension orthodoxy' demanded massive domestic involvement and large financial support and coordination with the World Bank and the IMF in the region (Mesa-Lago 1996). The new structural policy was oriented to pressurising governments to develop an adequate legal, regulatory and institutional framework that would encourage private sector participation, which in the region generally ended in their takeover by large international financial operators (Huber and Stephens 2000). The policies aimed to replace fully funded public pension plans with systems of individually funded pension accounts.

The change, based on the 'successful' Chilean experience of the 1980s was, rooted in an economic rationale, through which public social security systems could be transformed into national domestic schemes to further foster economic growth. Privatisations of pension systems, as carried out in the 1990s, were promoted by the MDBs, RDBs and governments. As a matter of fact, great controversy continues to surround the privatisation of pension systems, including in relation to the impact of such reforms on the financial crisis of the 1990s, as these are judged to have weakened the fiscal sector and amplified the deterioration of social welfare. According to the evidence, such socio-structural reforms led to a decline of labour force coverage, a failure to pay contributions, imperfect competition among large pension funds, a dubious impact on national savings, high and prolonged costs of the transition and concentration of investment portfolios (Hernandez 2003; Mesa-Lago 2004; Mesa-Lago and Muller 2004).

Conclusion

The aim of this chapter was to explore the relevance and analyse the role of the IDB in the processes of neoliberal reforms, promoted by the IFI–state complex managing the global economy, and pursued by South American countries during the 1990s. It appraised the influence of the IDB first within the regional political economy and then in relation to its distinct stages, as identified in Chapter 2, in order to inspect its role in regional development. The chapter has attempted to appraise the political economic nature of the Bank's policies by examining it within the context of the historical political economic processes which have shaped regional development in the period. This approach was chosen in preference to the alternative: abstracting the IDB from this context and examining its internal mechanisms and discourse.

Accordingly, the chapter has attempted to grasp the IDB's multilateral nature by giving an account of its quantitative and qualitative influence in development in the light of the more integral IPE approach. Appealing to the notion of hegemony and the indissolubility of domestic–international and economic–political relations, the chapter has highlighted the transformative hegemonic political economic nature of the IDB. It has been argued that this nature is rooted in the generation of consensus, across the region and in recipient countries, around the demands of the global economy, through an ideological process and emphasis on strategic areas of development.

In this regard, the dynamic relations between the IDB and recipient states have been outlined, identifying the main development approaches pursued throughout the period and their translation into lending targets and policies, as a method of appraising their leverage in chief areas of development – state reform, promotion of productive sectors and welfare production. As a result, the interdependent nature of its policies received special attention, particularly regarding development financing and welfare production.

The final part of the chapter was devoted to the IDB's role in development throughout each regional political economic stage identified in preceding chapters. This section showed the changing nature of the IDB policies and how they responded to changing international–domestic and economic–political dynamics of South American development, consisting of the rise, consolidation and sharp decline of pro-market reforms in the region in the light of agency and structural changes.

Consequently, a changing historical and social pattern in the orientations of development of the IDB has been shown, from the enthusiastic adoption of neoliberal reforms as a result of an alignment of the region's countries with the Washington Consensus, to the rise of international financial troubles increasing the failures of reforms, and finally towards a steady slowing in the reforms and a distancing of governments from global market-driven integration strategies. Significantly, this fact triggered the political side of the institution based on its commitment to the region, although not abandoning existing paradigms of development. The whole process was marked by the weakening of regional *transformismo* and the danger, mostly due to the significant social deterioration, that some countries could become detached from global economic governance as financial crises spread.

4   Argentina in the political economy of the Americas

Introduction

The precise relationship between political and economic factors in propelling Argentina into the social, political and financial crisis of 2001 is still a matter of contention. Notwithstanding the vast array and diversity of academic works, the most popular and dominant views are centred on the analysis of two factors. First is the macroeconomic mismanagement of the economy, focusing on the rigidity of the convertibility/currency board (*The Economist* 2002). The second factor is the inherent weakness of the political system to sustain a fiscal discipline and the obstacles it imposed on the consolidation of a stable and open economic environment (Mussa 2002; Loser 2006). Common to both sets of academic literature is the divorce between the dynamics of the economic and political spheres and the international and domestic factors playing a role in the debacle, and something similar can be observed regarding the influence of hemispheric and regional factors. This chapter discusses, in a critical historical perspective, the relations between hegemony, economic regimes and political systems and their impact on the organisation of the financing of development, as central elements at the very base of the financial crisis in 2001.

Following the theoretical framework developed in Chapter 2, this chapter explores the political economy of Argentina in order to develop a critical understanding of the research questions of this thesis. The first is the extent to which a new IPE of Southern America can tell us something different about the stages of development which this country has shared with its regional neighbours, i.e. about the dynamics between economics and politics, in the domestic, regional and international realms, as elements shaping the country's political economy. The second question is the extent to which the options and organisation of the financing of development in each stage were subordinated to one or other pole of these complex and inseparable dynamics and their specific configurations of social forces and state forms. Finally, and in particular, to what extent can the neoliberal reforms of the 1990s be explained in relation to regional tendencies that have begun to unfold since the 1970s? That is relevant as in the long run these process ended in the midst of growing tensions and contradictions, with a sharp decline of neoliberal reforms by the end of the century with a significant participation of the IFIs.

The chapter's main sections identify three main historical stages in the political economy of Argentina which have shaped the organisation of the financing of development from the 1940s until 2000. The first is the historical transition between British hegemony and the rise and consolidation of US hegemony in the region, which, in Argentina, coincided with the rise of Peronism. The second stage is the process that lasted between the downfall of Peronism and the installation of dictatorship in the 1970s, signalling the arrival of the so-called *developmentalist* period, the rise of the dictatorship and the democratic transition in the 1980s. Then the third section portrays the consolidation, apogee and decline of Argentine *transformismo* and of the neoliberal–conservative hegemony which it expressed, a period that included both the Menem and De La Rua administrations and which ended in the crisis of 2001. The section highlights the main structural and agency tendencies which defined the organisation of the financing of development during the Argentine *transformismo*. It examines the rising tensions and contradictions which led to its decline, the collapse of the convertibility regime and the fall of the Alliance administration. Finally, in the conclusion, the chapter offers a brief summary of the main elements concerning the analysis of Argentine political economy and the financing of development in the light of what is called here the New Political Economy of South America.

Argentina under US hemispheric hegemony

The Peronist coalition, or criollo *development in a conservative nation*

From 1910 to the 1940s was a key period in defining the political economy of Argentina and the emergence of new social, economic and political configurations that would shape, within the context of the changing regional hegemony in the Americas, the structure and direction of Argentina up to the 1980s (see Appendix C). The liberal oligarchic hegemony ruling the nation ended in the 1930s. It ended after four sessions of limited formal democracy and liberal reforms, with hegemony turning into dominance through the 'oligarch restoration' led by the armed forces and conservative elites, initiating the period known as the 'Infamous Decade' (*La Década Infame*). The process appears as a structural reaction, an attempt to return to the liberal order characterised by economic insertion based on primary export structures (Diaz Alejandro 1970, 2000; Rock 1987: 163–212; Rapoport 1988; Lewis 2003; Halperin Donghi 1993: 215–223; Bulmer-Thomas 2003: 232–235).

Paradoxically, this period featured unprecedented repression, political corruption, and social deterioration in the country; and an unexpected economic recovery following the Great Depression of 1929. The change was stimulated by the substitution of traditional imports by emergent industrial processes, a movement starting in the 1910s, and signalling the ascendancy of industrial workers as a new social and political force during the following decades (Diaz Alejandro 1970; Villanueva 1972; Rapoport 2002: 225).

Because of its flirtations with Fascist and Nazi politics, the old conservative–liberal coalition regime of the 1930s increased the tensions and contradictions within the model, and helped to provoke the historic convergence of varied social forces and the forging of a national movement based on labour, popular sectors, business and military organisations (Diaz Alejandro 1970: 107–108; Murmis and Portantiero 1971; Rock 1987: 175). By 1943, and after a series of *coups d'état*, a new coalition of political forces overwhelmed the conservatives as the armed forces and other ruling elites found a place within a new emergent national coalition. The change sparked a new role for the state in the economy and in welfare, signalled by the greatest income distribution in the history of the country, rapid growth through industrialisation, organisation of labour and social reforms – a process accompanied by prolonged unsettled relations between Argentina and the USA.

In parallel, with the ascendancy of the USA, the whole of the Americas was pushed into a process of realignment in accordance with new tendencies and new institutions established by US power. As a result, South American countries became increasingly subordinated to the strengthened and widened functions of the Pan-American organisation which the USA sponsored as a means of assuring US hemispheric hegemony over security, finance and trade (Varas 1992; Halperin Donghi 1993: 215; Rapoport 2002). Nonetheless, the process was not uncontested, with major resistance coming from those countries competing with the USA in primary export trade, massive processes of immigration and significant development of the domestic- oriented manufacturing sector and of the labour force, with strong past links with Europe. Within this framework, Argentina did not represent a different case, except for harsher treatment from the USA than other neutrals, 'despite its large material contributions to the Allied cause' (MacDonald 1980: 365).

The Peronist period was the time of a counter-hegemonic movement based on a poly-class coalition in which workers and employers were bound together by corporatist arrangements which sought to regulate both the domestic economy and its relation to the international economy (Murmis and Portantiero 1971). The Peronist government was distributional and industrial rather than one addressed to import substitution, and was interested not so much in industrialisation via international insertion as in reorganising national labour and industry on a corporative basis in order to sustain incomes, protect distribution and strengthen domestic industry (see Appendix C). Within this framework, the state played a central role in the distribution of resources and delivering the major public services such as transport, education, primary health and social security and wide access to electricity, gas and other public services (Franco 2002: 131; Rapoport 1988).

Despite the economic mistakes of the Peronist administration, some facts are undisputable: between 1946 and 1952, wage increases reached 56 per cent per annum; 70 per cent of the labour force enjoyed social protection. In a nutshell, the country had the highest standard of living in the region; and the participation of workers in income distribution reached 51 per cent (Lanata 2003: 77). Externally, in the ten years after 1946 the relations between Argentina and the USA were signalled increasingly by a sequence of conflict, distance, and again conflict. In this regard, the United States moved from aggression to a cautious stance towards the Peronist administration, and once again towards intervention in Argentina's domestic affairs to prevent the Peronists from returning to government after 1955. Argentina was outside of the arc of influence of the US Monroe doctrine and, as well as other South American countries, competed in trade with the US primary sector (MacDonald 1985: 413; Rapoport 2002: 227; Escude and Cisneros 2000).

In short, this was a *criollo development* – domestically fed and bred by the blend of different cultures with all of their tensions, contradictions and limitations. A multiclass alliance of workers, immigrants and small and new entrepreneurs nurtured nationalistic and popular policies such as increasing consumption, employment, social protection and economic security for the masses (Diaz Alejandro 1970: 126; Murmis and Portantiero 1971). The development strategy followed by Argentina represented an alternative option to countries with a similar level of development, such as Australia and Canada, although it took a different approach to these countries in its international integration and its domestic development. Peronism was strongly directed towards family welfare and consumption, and gave particular emphasis to its non-alignment with the USA; this is highly relevant, in addition to domestic factors, to a full understanding of the collapse of Peronist development strategy (Di Tella and Dornbusch 1989; Rapoport 2002; Halperin Donghi 1993).

The Peronist plan was based on an erroneous diagnosis of the post-World War II international scenario, with a direct impact upon the bottleneck which confronted the Peronist economic strategy: its necessity of external financing for development (Di Tella and Dornbusch 1989: 19). That was because domestic-based ISI and rural sectors were unable to fuel the levels of industrialisation and income distribution demanded by the strategy (Rock 1987: 262–319; Diaz Alejandro 1989: 86–88). By pursuing its path, the Peronist administration amplified the pre-existing hostility of the USA towards the Latin American region and its reluctance to support Argentina. Isolated from postwar trade, limited in its conception of economic sovereignty in a hemisphere increasingly falling under US control, and domestically weakened and divided, in the mid-1950s the Peronist administration was left at the mercy of the liberal–conservative opposition. The new alliance was based on a new configuration of social forces represented by the alliance of some sectors of the armed forces, traditional export groups, bankers, liberal intellectuals and the powerful Catholic Church (Franco 2002).

The Peronist administration sought to found a New Political Economy, avoiding both the pure Anglo-Saxon capitalist and Soviet communist models (Portantiero 1989: 16–26; Di Tella and Dornbusch 1989). It pursued a re-foundation of the country on the basis of social justice, political independence and economic sovereignty, which defined the so-called 'Third Position'. The political project represented the legitimisation and institutionalisation of the past decades of domestic struggles toward international autonomy and welfare expansion. It was based on a coordinated and regulated economy by the state, an inclusive political system based on corporatist relations, and a welfare regime reflecting the grassroots organisation of its social structure, mediated and controlled by labour unions (Repetto and Alonso 2004).

During World War II, Argentina was the major obstacle to the United States' attempts to organise the region behind its war aims, with Buenos Aires repeatedly blocking US proposals (Halperin Donghi 1993: 216). The United States' response was to seek alternative means to overthrow Peron's administration, engaging in a long struggle which combined diplomatic and economic pressure (MacDonald 1985: 405). However, opinions in the USA about Peronism were divided. For those against it, such as Spruille Braden, State Department Secretary (1945–47), Peron was an anti-capitalist nationalist, an Axis sympathiser who was either paving the way for communism or providing the basis for Argentine–Soviet cooperation against the USA (ibid.: 406). For others, such as Messersmith, Bruce and Griffis, successive US ambassadors to Buenos Aires after 1946, 'there was no acceptable alternative to Peron' (ibid.: 407). In their view, the opposition gathered together the most 'irresponsible elements' in the country, and any alternative government would be a 'reactionary military regime' attacking Peron's social programme and so paving the way to communism (ibid.: 407). The Peronist programme, in addition, offered a unique opportunity, since only the USA could provide the capital goods and investments required by Argentina's Five Year Plan (ibid.: 407). By mid-1947, the new position had triumphed, and the Peronist administration was invited to join the new hemispheric security pact at the Rio Conference in 1947 (see Appendix C).

Nonetheless, Washington remained hostile to key aspects of the Peronist administration, in particular its 'Third Position', challenging US authority over the hemisphere. The Third Position was an international pragmatic response to the United States' economic and political hostility by then, and a way to make clear to the new Soviet Bloc the independent regional orientation of the country. Worsening the situation, Peronism had developed its Third Position in the economic realm, through bilateralism, high tariffs, industrial protection, income redistribution and labour protection and, above all, with state trading through the Argentine Institute for Exchange (IAPI). On top of this it firmly refused to join the WB, the IMF or the GATT, avoiding borrowing from the multilateral system given its massive reserves (MacDonald 1985: 407). In Washington it was considered that a great part of the blame for this lay at the door of the Peronists' 'extremist wing' represented by Eva Peron and Miranda, head of IAPI, and their position should be discredited and weakened.

Washington's chance came in 1947: the Argentine government had staked its political future on the Five Year Plan, and US financial assistance could be used to undermine the extremists (MacDonald 1985: 408). In return for financial support, Washington demanded restrictions on the IAPI, better conditions for foreign investment and ratification of the Rio treaty (Rock 1987: 274–276). As the country did not agree, in early 1948 the USA excluded it from the trade benefits of the Marshall Plan, with the result that Europe would be provided exclusively with the USA, Canada and other British Commonwealth grains, while Argentina could only supply secondary markets such as Spain and Brazil (Rock 1987: 292).

In 1950, US–Argentine relations improved with US State Department support for the Peronist administration's application for an Eximbank loan of US$125 million (Rock 1987: 301). Responding to the new stance, the Argentine administration began to align with the USA, but it reaffirmed its Third Position again at the outbreak of the Korean War, ending the brief 1947 to 1950 honeymoon. Following this, the USA began a policy of 'masterly inaction' towards those supporting Third Positions or proposing a middle way between capitalism and communist strategies of development (MacDonald 1985: 412). Despite the shift in the Peronist administration in its last years, there was no guarantee that it would again take up the Third Position, and it was made clear to its successors that no middle position would be allowed in the hemisphere. As history shows, the Revolución Libertadora (Liberty Revolution) and Frondizi administrations responded to this hemispheric policy by enthusiastically joining the Bretton Woods institutions, closely cooperating with the OAS and CEPAL, embracing Wall Street and driving the country into debt (Rapoport 1988).

Hegemonic deadlock turns into dominance and coercion

Democracy for minorities and dictatorships in the Cold War

On 20 September 1955 the Peronist administration was overthrown by a military–civil coalition aimed at restoring the conservative–liberal system of the 1930s, through the transformation of some elements of the Peronist coalition and through subordinating others by force, and by these means assuring the integration of Argentina into the US-designed inter-American system (Halperin Donghi 1993; Escude and Cisneros 2000: 11; Ramos 1983: 176–177). The period from 1955 to 1983 marked a crucial period in the history of the political economy of Argentina, one characterised by the country's international economic integration within the framework of the Cold War (see Appendix C). Domestically, the process featured a hegemonic deadlock existing from the Revolución Libertadora or Oligarchic Restoration up to the dictatorship of 1976 (Franco 2002: 145).

This hegemonic deadlock, or the 'impossible regime', resulted from an undefined struggle by the liberal–conservative civil–military coalition against the Peronist populist coalition and its main organisational pillars, the General Economic Confederation (CGE) and the General Central of Workers (CGT), and left-wing forces. In this regard, welfare regime was a centre piece for both, populist and developmentalist, as it nurtured, in part, both social structure and coalitions, which defined the political limits of financing development in Argentina in subsequent decades (Portantiero 1973; O'Donnell 1973, 1997).

The restoration of the conservative–liberal project took place through a vast political and social purge characterised by the persecution of any Peronist element in the armed forces, the dissolution and proscription of the Peronist party and military intervention in the CGT. It also banned every social organisation related to social security and the prohibition of all Peronist insignia and slogans – even the very mention of Peron's name. A wage freeze was decreed, hundreds of union leaders were arrested and put in prison, and 60,000 more were expelled and banned (Rock 1987: 334-335; Ramos 1983: 177–179). After Peron, and with the new military–economic alignment of Argentina into the inter-American system, there ensued a long period of growing social and political divisions, with military–civil coalitions struggling to regain prosperity and growth and to maintain the proscription and persecution of the Peronist movement (Basualdo 2001: 30; Portantiero 1973).

The process slowly led into a sort of differentiation between politics and economics, whereby economic progress became incompatible with representative government and social rights, and military rule intervened frequently to sustain the conservative hegemony. The final result was political instability, violence and repression which, by the 1970s, convulsed the country. The stage marks the beginning of the externalisation of the Argentine financing of development, the internationalisation of its economy and the subordination of the state to the guidelines of the major IFIs. Argentina was now within the framework of US global hegemony and pursued the new developmentalist strategy. The developmentalist period lasted between 1955 and 1972 (Rapoport 1988; Azpiazu *et al*. 1989; Franco 2002).

Until 1943, Raul Prebisch was director of Argentina's Central Bank. In 1955, when secretary-general of CEPAL, he was commissioned by Revolución Libertadora to suggest economic reforms. Strikingly, Prebisch's plan presented not a developmentalist but a strongly liberal approach, emphasising the deregulation of the economy and market-driven international integration. Its proposals notably included the country's integration into Bretton Woods institutions, the promotion of international trade through freer use of devaluation and the complete dismantling of IAPI. In addition, it extended to privatisation of state assets and public banks, reduction of government spending, cessation of price controls, subsidies and export taxes, and the promotion of FDI and multilateral loans (Scalabrini Ortiz 1998; Rock 1987; Rapoport 1988; Escude and Cisneros 2000).

By 1956 much of the programme had been accomplished and Argentina had achieved admission to the Bretton Woods system (Rock 1987: 335; Ramos 1983: 180–183). With this, the country reversed its strategy of development in order to return to the traditional agroexport development strategy, repositioning traditional liberal elites and their 'intelligentsia' in power with the firm purpose of dismantling the corporative Peronist state (Escude and Cisneros 2000; Szusterman 1989; Ramos 1983: 183). With that, the military had thrown a democratic government from power, but not the structures and social relations that sustained it.

Despite Aramburu's success in achieving a balance-of-payments surplus – thanks mainly to devaluation, a freeze on wages and the inflow of short-term capital from abroad to fuel the export of primary products –the deepening of the new external-oriented strategy of development did not take off until the Frondizi administration. Promising to legalise Peronism, Frondizi achieved power in 1958, and his strategy was synonymous with developmentalism, with industrialisation based on foreign capital to accelerate growth in strategic sectors such as metalwork, energy, heavy chemicals, transport and communications. The developmentalist strategy launched by the Frondizi administration led to an expansion of public spending, triggering significant inflation as a result of a struggle around income distribution (see Appendix C). The deficit was controlled, with monetary emission and external borrowing transferring resources from primary activities to subsidise the industrial sector and, at the same time, allowing the repatriation of profits for transnational companies, consolidating the external-oriented industrial sector, mainly driven by US and European investments (Rapoport 1988: 556–559; Azpiazu *et al.* 1989).

The Frondizi administration therefore adopted the developmentalist programme based on guidelines established by CEPAL and the Bretton Woods institutions (Halperin Donghi 1993). It was clear to the Frondizi administration that President Kennedy wanted access to US FDI and Bretton Woods support to go to regional allies in countries who were loyal to the USA and committed to moderate reforms. In 1963 it became clearer still that the Alliance for Progress was the key and the new CEPAL's developmentalist idea aiming at hemispheric security and economic integration was the model to follow (Rock 1987: 340). For the Frondizi administration, CEPAL's ISI guaranteed US support and access to FDI and to military assistance, all key instruments to assist in the transformation and absorption of industrial and labour sectors traditionally part of the Peronist coalition.

However, Europe and East Asia had become the focus for FDI, and the developmentalist administration responded to the absence of capital to fuel fast industrial development by accessing, with the support of the USA in the IMF, WB and IDB, official assistance in the form of loans reaching US$329 million in support of the new strategy of development (Escude and Cisneros 2000: 31). Given the size of the IDB, it is not surprising that its participation in such an operation was not the same as that of the big official banks, and so the IDB's lending was concentrated mainly in the modernisation of the agricultural sector and support for public infrastructure, providing 70 per cent of these loans.

Unsurprisingly, by 1961, Argentina needed to roll back accumulated debts (Diaz Alejandro 1970: 196). In the shadow of Argentine hemispheric alignment, the Frondizi administration had developed the major process of internationalisation of production in the country, signalled by the arrival of prominent multinational companies (see Appendix C). This is the time of the arrival of large firms such as Ford, Renault, FIAT, Peugeot, Citroen, and later Duperial, Firestone and Coca-Cola, whose interests were defined by the access and control of chief industrial segments of the domestic market (Rock 1987: 328; Kosacoff 1999: 56; Escude and Cisneros 2000).

A glance at Table 4.1 shows the origin of these foreign investments, within which the most prominent are those of US, Swiss, British, German and Italian origin. Soon the new pro-FDI industrial policy became a source of contention between the Frondizi administration and Peronism. But this was not the only reason behind the rupture of the alliance. Another source was the issue of the conditions related to foreign borrowing associated with CEPAL's ISI development, and in particular its debts to Bretton Woods institutions. In fact, official loans came about with significant demands in government spending cuts, high interest rates, higher public service prices, cessation of subsidies, and wide measures oriented to liberalising the economy and correcting distortions in relative prices which distorted the distribution of income in favour of labour.

Table 4.1 Origin of foreign direct investment, 1958–65 (percentage of the whole)

Country	Percentage
United States	55.1
Switzerland	9.8
United Kingdom	8.1
West Germany	6.7
Italy	5.6
Holland	5.3
France	3.7
Canada	2.2
Others	3.5
TOTAL:	*100.0*

Source: Martorelli (1969: 107) cited by Escude and Cisneros (2000: 39).

In short, the policies accompanying the strategy of external financing soon led to recession, unemployment and falling wages and salaries – stabilising, perhaps, the balance of payments but renewing political instability and increasing the country's indebtedness, in addition to the political problems that Frondizi himself generated. In 1962, as Frondizi's party lost the congressional elections to a resurgent Peronist movement, the armed forces reacted immediately and declared illegal the national electoral process, dissolved the congress and overthrew Frondizi (Halperin Donghi 1993: 314).

The period 1963–76 was characterised by the unstable and violent character of the struggle within the dominant military–civil coalition and also the response to each side by the national and popular coalitions. A prominent feature of this turmoil was the confrontation between conservatives and liberals, supported by different factions in the armed forces seeking to occupy and control the power left by the proscribed Peronist movement. Now they were confronting the new generations of Peronist militants and organisations which were also inspired by the Cuban revolution and the events of May 1968 in France. This process culminated in the hegemonic reaction of 1976, marking the beginning of the darkest period of Argentine history: the dictatorship.

By 1964, it was clear that the incorporation of Argentina and other Latin American nations into the hemispheric order would demand something more than increases in official aid through a reprise of the Marshall Plan. As reformist governments such as the Frondizi and Illia administrations had proved unable to deal with social unrest, the new Johnson administration in Washington began to favour right-wing dictators over liberal reformers, and it was easy to find Argentine collaborators (see Appendix C).

The new 'Nixon Doctrine', based on the Rockefeller Report (1965), openly legitimised the use of military coercion, abuses of human rights and the dismantling of the welfare state and industrial policies to solve the hegemonic deadlock (Nef 1994: 408). But far from producing stability, military rule and free-market policies made Argentina ungovernable. In 1965, economic incentives and external support were not enough, amplifying an already deteriorating political situation. Fears mounted, among the military forces and the powerful externally oriented industrial sector grouped in the Argentine Industrial Union (UIA), that government concessions to labour unions and the growing presence of the Peronist business union, the CGE, would open the door to the return of Peronism (Escude and Cisneros 2000).

From then until 1973, Argentine political life came to be characterised by three periods of military attempts to achieve a balance among growth, political stability and international alignment, all in a permanent domestic struggle to prevent the reemergence of the Peronist movement. The first period was 1966–70 with administration of Juan Carlos Ongania. The second period was 1970–71 during the Roberto Levingston administration. The third was 1971–73 under Alejandro Lanusse's government. Interestingly, the three military governments demonstrated an intransigent commitment to keeping close relations with the USA and combating communism (Escude and Cisneros 2000). By the early 1970s, the country was falling out of institutional control, and armed struggle arrived with four main groups engaged in armed insurgency and disputing the scenario: the Montoneros, the Fuerzas Armadas Peronistas (FAP), the Fuerzas Armadas Revolucionarias (FAR), and Ejercito Revolucionario del Pueblo (ERP).

Dictatorship as a final solution and new beginning

In 1972 the military government called for elections, and even though Peron was not allowed to participate he was authorised to return from exile. Workers, labour and business unions, centre and left-wing forces, and all popular classes envisioned some sort of restoration of the late 1940s. Finally, in 1973, with 60 per cent of the votes, the 78-year-old Peron began, in the middle of the major political struggles of the country, his third elected term as President. After the failed attempt to restore the kernel of the past Peronist policies based on income distribution, full employment and social reform, supporting the CGT and CGE and marginalising the left-wing sectors of his movement, Peron died in 1974, shattering the political system (see Appendix C).

By the end of 1975, the government was universally reviled, due to both the economic crisis and the continued armed struggle. Facing a democratic government isolated and without support, on 24 March 1976 the military forces embarked again on a new government. This time, however, they had the firm objective of dismantling the sources of power of the Peronist state, breaking up in addition the developmentalist ISI strategy, and imposing a new economic model based on finance and the supremacy of capital over labour (Rock 1987: 366; Basualdo 2001). The plan was neither Peronism nor developmentalism. In terms of political economy, the period witnessed the transition from hegemony to dominance and coercion whereby the conservative and liberal sectors confronting decades-long hegemonic deadlock head-on, aimed to pull up the national and popular and developmentalist coalition by its roots. This structural change was later to play a key role in the democratic transition in the 1980s, and in the re-emergence of the neoliberal–conservative coalition and its convergence with the rise of global financial governance (Basualdo 2001; O'Donnell 2001).

The US administration saw Martinez de Hoz, economic minister, as a guarantee for US foreign economic policy in the region, and General Videla as a stabilising factor (Escude and Cisneros 2000). The new strategy of the dictatorship was composed of two complementary and inseparable projects, the economic programme and the military war against 'subversion and terrorism', which led to the disappearance and murder of 30,000 people (Franco 2002). The dictatorship harvested unexpected support in the country, such as that from the Communist Party and other political forces (Rock 1987; Lewis 2000).

The economic plan, following the monetarist theories of Chicago and increasingly adopted by the IFIs, was the first orthodox and monetarist attempt to dismantle the state as a source of employment and union power, as well as end its role as a chief agent in the distribution of resources. The plan was based on freezing and lowering wages, eliminating taxes on agricultural goods, reducing tariffs on imports of industrial products and eliminating subsidies. In addition, the government eliminated social compensation and spending on housing and health, increasing public tariffs, and, especially, the liberalisation of capital markets, the financing of public spending through external borrowing and the privatisation of state assets (Escude and Cisneros 2000). The neoliberal plan came to rest heavily on foreign loans and investments. An outstanding role was played by commercial banks and also by official and private financial institutions willing to support the experiment. Among these featured the IMF, the WB, the IDB, Export-Import Bank (Eximbank), Austrian banks, Interunión-Banque, Atlantic International Bank Ltd., Canadian-American Bank S.A., Centrale Rabonbank, European-Arab Bank S.A., Marine Midland Bank, Tokai Bank, Bank of Boston, Deutsche Bank, Citibank, Bank of America and Chase Manhattan (Escude and Cisneros 2000).

By 1983, 68.5 per cent of Argentina's external debt was in the hands of commercial banks, while debt under the control of Bretton Woods institutions ascended to 15.9 per cent, as Table 4.2 illustrates. It meant that, altogether, by 1983 commercial banks and Bretton Woods institutions controlled 84.4 per cent of the total debt of the country. It is noteworthy that the development of Argentina's

Table 4.2 Composition of external debt by creditor, 1983 (US$ millions)

Type	Amount	Percentage
Bilateral	1,654	3.7
Multilateral	1,760	3.9
IMF	1,173	2.7
Bonds	4,208	9.3
Commercial banks	30,899	68.5
Others	5,393	12.0
TOTAL:	*45,087*	*100.0*

Source: Bouzas (ed.) (1988: 73), cited by Escude and Cisneros (2000: 50).

debt burden took place under a mixture of models based on external financing and export-led growth, reflecting the coalition of forces sustaining the dictatorship (Rock 1987: 370; Azpiazu *et al.* 1989; Bulmer-Thomas 2003). Argentina's external debt jumped from 18.6 per cent of GDP – inherited from the times of developmentalism – to 60 per cent in 1982 during the dictatorship, with an important role played by the re-equipment of military forces prior to the Falklands/Malvinas conflict, as Table 4.3 illustrates.

Within a few years, the restructuring initiated by the dictatorship had deeply altered economic and social conditions in the country. The dictatorship had achieved a diversified, although unconsolidated, agroexport-led model fuelled by financial liberalisation, but one which produced recession, widespread unemployment and an explosive growth in external debt. Salaried workers received 43 per cent of national income in 1974; by 1977 this had shrunk to 31 per cent (Lozano 2001; Altimir *et al.* 2002).

By the end of the 1980s the recessive effects of the neoliberal experiment were obvious, and leaving aside the military repression, the weakening of the economy by trade and financial openness, as well as costly military rearmament, worsened the economic situation and brought the financial system near to collapse (Rock 1987: 372–374). Firms struggled to survive by renegotiating loans, a wave a bankruptcies began, devaluation triggered capital flight of nearly US$2 billion, and interest charges on debt escalated to 30 per cent of exports. In March 1982, the CGT organised a strike under the slogan '*Paz, Pan y Trabajo*' – 'Peace, Bread and Jobs' – but suffered atrocious repression with 1,800 workers detained.

The dictatorship had imposed its power through the primitive tactic of fighting a domestic or external enemy, and now it sought to transform a legitimate diplomatic claim to sovereignty versus colonial rights into a war between a dictatorship and a democracy. The dictatorship had been searching for a national objective to

Table 4.3 Relation of external debt and GDP, 1975–85 (US$ millions)

Year	Total debt (public plus private, US$ millions)	Debt/PBI (percentage)
1975	7,875	18.6
1976	8,279	18.6
1977	9,679	19.2
1978	12,496	23.9
1979	19,034	30.2
1980	27,162	37.3
1981	35,671	48.1
1982	43,634	60.3
1983	44,781	59.5
1984	47,821	60.5
1985	48,312	64.5

Source: Dornbusch and de Pablo (1988: 191), cited by Escude and Cisneros (2000: 51).

contain popular opposition, beginning with a campaign against domestic subversion, after Chile; and finally it hoped that the recuperation of the Falklands/ Malvinas Islands would provide it with the political time it needed to reorganise its hegemony. But the reality defined a different and paradoxical history, wherein the military's defeat in the Falklands/Malvinas Islands marked the demise of its dictatorship, and soon, in the face of increasing social unrest, the military government was compelled to call for new elections. However, the defeat of a military government did not mean a change in the configuration of the social forces at its very basis, which would extend its influence and project into the next decade (Rock 1987: 374–379; Franco 2002).

Neoliberal–conservative emergence underlying the democratic transition

From a political economic point of view, it is clear that, despite the fall of the Argentine dictatorship, the dominant sectors and coalitions that emerged during a decade of conservative and repressive policies were capable of articulating new alliances which converged with global tendencies shaping the conditions of the democratic transition (see Appendix C). They therefore helped to produce the Argentine *transformismo*, a hegemony based on international–domestic alliances capable of co-opting subaltern sectors and carrying forward the adjustment of Argentine society to the new conditions of accumulation emerging at international and regional levels, within a democratic system (Cox 1996b: 130; Basualdo 2001; O'Donnell 2001; Taylor 2005). The democratic openness in Argentina is thus signalled by the transformation of the dominant coalitions, leftovers of the dictatorship, allying themselves now with foreign sectors. This new configuration of forces converged around a similar diagnosis concerning the way the new democracy should implement the adjustments necessary for Argentine society to conform to the new global conditions, and the transformation of the political system required to achieve this (Rapoport 1988; Basualdo 2001).

This is a period characterised by debt crises and capital flows, and by the consolidation of a dependent financial structure driven by conflict between dominant economic groups, foreign capital and banks. Within this framework, the economy oscillated between stagnation and economic crises, led by a political system trapped into a pessimist realist view of the probable as the only alternative of national development. That is, a political system whose strategies meant meekly following the orders given by the consortium of foreign financial interests and IFIs. This gave rise to a particular hegemonic transformist structure, a complex particularly able to align the domestic to the international guidelines of capital expansion via political democratic process. In short, what is clear, throughout the *transformismo* stage emerging in the democratic transition, is the permanent dominant influence of economic sectors over the political system, in particular the so-called *capitanes de la industria* – captains of industry – the social and economic base that had emerged under the umbrella of the dictatorship (Kosacoff 1999; Basualdo 2001: 43–50; Rapoport 2002).

The post-dictatorship transformation was characterised by its capacity to increasingly subordinate the policies of the main democratic institutions to a new pattern of accumulation and global integration, deepening Argentina's participation in an increasingly globalised economy while co-opting the demands of subaltern sectors. In addition, since political parties were key institutional engines in democracy, they reflected the main tendencies of this historical social change. It is no surprise, then, that Argentina's political parties played a central role in the process of national adjustment to the global economy. They were the first political institutions to experience the effects of globalisation and carry through central alterations of the core base of Peronism and developmentalism, in order to redefine and legitimise the reorganisation of the financing of development.

The bonds between the economic leaders and the main political parties, including the Peronist electoral machine, were constant themes during a period of ideological change, in which dominant political sectors and economic businesses increasingly integrated intellectual sectors. As a result of decades of persecution and annihilation, no political body possessed power enough to play a key role in leading the political system. So it was the dominant economic sectors, those bound to the domestic concentrations of capital and finance, which assumed first place in the task of conditioning the political parties that administered the government, playing a much more important role than external creditors or the IFIs (Verbitsky 1993a, b; Basualdo 2001: 50–51).

It is here that neoliberal global ideas finally fitted with the conservative national project, with the latter coming around to the view that only state restructuring through privatisations and financial and trade openness could fuel the necessary growth. Conditioned by the new global financial settings, the government could no longer fuel domestic development managing fiscal deficit as it did through the developmentalist period. In 1989, expectation of devaluation provoked a run on the dollar, and triggered the hyperinflationary crisis which destroyed both the economic plans and the constitutional government. It is noteworthy that the hyperinflationary crisis did not represent a typical cyclical crisis related to either import substitution or redistributive strategies, but a crisis arising from two elements. The first element was from the removal of structural elements – mainly the state from the economy. The second was linked with the global integration of the country along the guidelines of the IFIs nurturing the increasing power within the political system of financial sectors which emerged during the dictatorship (Bouzas and Keifman 1990; Basualdo 2001: 54; Repetto and Alonso 2004).

By the end of the 1980s the Alfonsin administration had already shifted its political economy to what it called 'positive adjustment', that is, to a strategy based on the expansion of exports and the liberalisation of domestic markets aimed at attracting FDI, as the only means to pay back external debt and achieve economic growth (Basualdo 2001: 41–42). From this perspective, the financial and political crisis seems related to the impossibility of removing structural restrictions on the new economic model, given the struggle for the control and directions of development between dominant and differentiated sectors. Thus the crisis and fall of democratic government in 1989 rested on the attempts by hegemonic groups to strengthen the structural conditions necessary to consolidate their position, yet this appears to be a political crisis triggered by an economic plot led by the dominant actors. As a result, the hyperinflationary crisis represented another step towards realigning the domestic with the international. In fact, it led in the following years to an unprecedented and historical convergence between dominant industrial and financial sectors and to the detachment of the political system from society overseen by the bipartisan system consisting of two major political parties, the Radicals and the Peronists.

Argentine *transformismo* and the neoliberal–conservative order

It is a commonplace to analyse the Menem administration as an abrupt change in the political economy of Argentina, resulting from external pressures and the domestic adoption of the policies of the Washington Consensus through necessity rather than conviction (Murillo 2001). Nonetheless, from a critical approach, it becomes clear that the Menem administration constituted a further step in the country's liberal internationalisation. The administration represented the consolidation of the neoliberal and conservative hegemonic processes, which have been taking place in Argentina and other South American countries – for instance, Chile, Uruguay, Paraguay and Bolivia – since the mid-1970s. And by the same token, it is clear why the De La Rua administration later was not so much an alternative to the previous administration but represented continuity with it; and why, trapped by circumstances, its attempt to build a different social alliance failed.

A critical analysis of the structural changes of 1989–2001 reveals the presence of four key stages, leading to the development of the neoliberal–conservative hegemony and to a development strategy for Argentina. The process is characterised by the continuing global financial integration led increasingly by the government–IFIs partnership carried out from the end of the dictatorship to the collapse of convertibility. The change deserves particular attention in order to understand the social character of the unfolding, consolidation and the collapse of this new regime in its relation to the rise of global governance and the role of IFIs, including the IDB.

The first period identifiable is from 1989 to 1991 and represents the rise of Argentine *transformismo*, a process under way since the decline of the dictatorship. The second stage (1991–94) constitutes the time of the consolidation of this order and regime. The third period (1994–98) saw the dissolution of the political economic coalition and the rising tensions and contradictions of the convertibility regime, whilst the final stage (1998–2001) represents the period of decline and collapse of the neoliberal–conservative model of development.

Figure 4.1 presents the evolution of the financing of development throughout the political economic stages mentioned. As can be seen, each stage is markedly defined by the dominance of the central source of the financing of development. For instance, privatisation emerges as the central source of the consolidation stage of the convertibility regime. Mergers and acquisitions dominate the second stage of rising tension within the regime, and both decline as main sources of

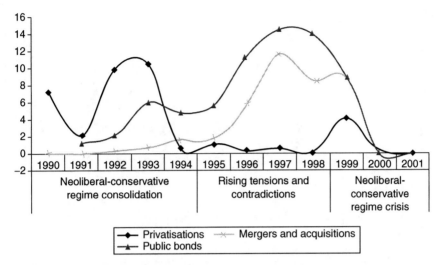

Figure 4.1 Argentina, evolution of the financing of development by main source, 1990–2001 (US$ billions). (Based on Basualdo 2001, Dal Din 2000, and Ministry of Economy, Government of Argentina.)

financing during the last stage of decline and crisis. The figure is also relevant as it shows the growing presence of public bonds or public borrowing in the financing of development throughout the period, a key element considered to be at the root of the financial crisis and which, since the second stage, exceeds the other sources.

One of the defining factors conditioning the organisation of the financing of development, noticeable throughout all the stages, was the growing importance of the transference abroad of financial resources, increasing almost in proportion to the gross external debt and to interest payments on it, as Figure 4.2 illustrates.

Towards neoliberal–conservative hegemony

The first stage, between 1989 and 1991, witnessed the final transition towards the new neoliberal–conservative *transformismo* initiated in the mid-1970s. The period was characterised mainly by the convergence of interests between dominant domestic and international groups *vis-à-vis* the state and IFIs with differential elements defining the participation of the IDB, as we shall see in Chapters 5 and 6. The stage was marked by a shift in the Argentine political system in conformity with its commitments to the new dominant neoliberal–conservative *transformismo*, which began to detach the state from its historical social domestic configurations and reshaped it. The stage is also characterised by a deep crisis of restructuring expressed by hyperinflation shocks jolting the political system.

The nature of the Argentine *transformismo* was characterised by its capacity to absorb, adapt, frame and legitimise the convertibility project. It created and based

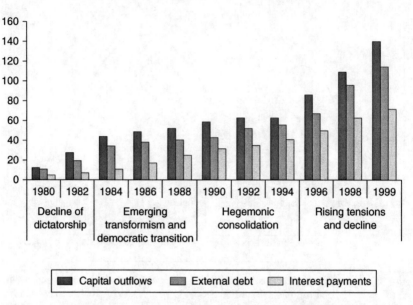

Figure 4.2 Argentina, cumulative capital outflows, external debt and interest payments, 1980–91 (US$ billions). (Based on Basualdo 2001: 37, and Economic Information, Ministry of Economy, Government of Argentina.)

itself on a complex pro-globalisation coalition of intellectuals, political forces, economic actors, labour unions and local governments. This was a historical confluence of three key elements shaping the neoliberal hegemony and the state–IFIs partnership in the country. The first element was the rise of global political economic governance following the decline of US hegemony. The second factor was the subordination of the political system to directions established by economic and especially domestic and international financial actors. The final element was a shift in the reorganisation of the financing of development, a crucial element in domestic economic adjustment to the exigencies of a globalised economy (Cox and Schechter 2002: 81; Basualdo 2001: 63).

It is noteworthy that initially the Menem administration sought support from domestic economic sectors at a time of major struggles between powerful foreign and domestic economic actors, with the government firmly supporting the domestic actors. An example of this was the designation of a prominent member of the economic domestic group Bunge and Born, Miguel Angel Roig, as economic minister, institutionalising the struggle (Azpiazu 2002; Azpiazu and Basualdo 2002). Nonetheless, overwhelmed by external pressures from IFIs, creditors and domestic actors, soon the Menem administration commenced a set of reforms addressed to reorganising the public sector and the transfer of state resources to the private sector (Basualdo 2001: 59). The first measure in this regard was the Law of Economic Emergence (25.561), whose first step materialised in the opening of the capital account, and accompanied by the eradication of subsidies, the opening of imports, and the elimination of any other form of state industrial incentive. The second was the Law of State Reform, intervening in every public-owned company in order to draw up a schedule for the transfer of state assets to the private sector.

But as the measures could not stop capital outflows and hyperinflation, the conservative regime's transition towards favouring domestic economic actors was halted in March 1991. Surprisingly, the process led to the conformation of a wider coalition between domestic and international economic actors, opening the door to the convergence of two institutional elements. The first was the Domingo Cavallo's Convertibility Plan (Law 23.098), whose convergence with external supporters of the Brady Plan allowed state assets to be transferred to the domestic and foreign private sector, eliminating the conflict of interests between domestic industrial sectors and foreign financial sectors. The second was the reform and extension to the membership of the Argentine Supreme Court of Justice, a vital reform that allowed the Executive to legitimise its concentration of political power and its rule through official decrees (Levitsky 2003; Levitsky and Murillo 2005).

What is noteworthy here is that this period represents a transition towards anchoring domestic–external relations upon state–IFI relations. This, together with a convergence between domestic measures set in motion by the Menem administration with those established by global financial governance acting through the Brady Plan, shaped the conditions for the next stage, 1991–94. This convergence was based on the international and domestic shared diagnosis and efforts oriented to repositioning and reinserting the country within the international financial system driven by the alliance with the Clinton Administration and its support in the Bretton Woods institutions. The impact was immediate, and in a short time Argentina had gained access to external official and private borrowing with the support of the international financial community. Convinced by the idea that this had defined the beginning of a new path of market-led development, the government only had to permit foreign and domestic investors to use public debt in the form of bonds to acquire state assets. The whole process marked an unprecedented period of financial bonanza signalled by massive transferences of state assets to the international and domestic private sectors. This stage is characterised by the internationalisation and regionalisation of public utilities, a process centrally subordinated to privatisation of state assets with a significant participation of the IFIs and in particular the World Bank and the IDB. By this time, the cooperative dynamics between the government and the IFIs reflected a deep alliance or partnership based on financial globalisation and founded on common ideas concerning changes in the central guidelines of development. The process, in a nutshell, was fostered and accompanied by powerful domestic and regional social forces arrayed behind the market-led tenets of development.

Also notable for this investigation were the institutional changes following this process. Actually, since political parties played a chief role in the democracy, the political system experienced a deep shift as it was subject to the process of domestic adjustment to the new global economic conditions, adopting a transformative character in line and coordinated with the global financial governance. The transformation of the political system became a central piece in the process as it permitted the government to materialise a globalisation strategy within the democratic framework. The change tacitly aimed to expand the power of capital but would limit social inclusion in order to define a new social structure, a new Argentina (Palermo 1994). Political parties became electoral machines, reorganised under business guidelines, and driven by elites of political operators, recruited on the basis of influence and access to strategic areas and sectors such as business sectors, military, labour unions, provinces, the church and intellectuality. The main political parties thus came to be institutions defined by vertical contractual rules which replaced social and ideological bonds. Within this, the state and IFIs acted as the source of power producing huge political transformation. It made politicians or militants into members of a new profession, the political operators, and politics a matter of political marketing and discourse analysis. As a result, the political system came to be aligned and subordinated to the intergoverned process of financial globalisation of the country (Basualdo 2001; Levitsky 2003).

The course was accompanied by the rise of a particular ideological atmosphere characterised by a set of beliefs subordinated to specific economic assumptions, which were popularised by government, media and dominant social forces. One of these powerful beliefs was that without external official and financial support there would be no way to sustain the financing of development. As a corollary of the above, it became a dominant idea that it was no longer feasible to protect labour markets, whereby the state could no longer finance universal rights such as access to education and health. Another fostered idea was that, given the historical failures of politicians to manage the country, new externally experienced and foreign-educated technicians should be invited to restructure and manage state affairs in the spirit of a new national beginning and the need to forget the past. Given the depth of the hyperinflationary crises and the responsibility of state mismanagement, development should be redefined, but this time along the guidelines of the new development strategy. Inspired by the Washington Consensus, the new approach of development recognised that an increasingly globalised economy had left the country with only one option: openness and integration in association with developed countries (Rock 2002: 65).

Apogee of the neoliberal–conservative hegemony

The process of hegemonic consolidation of the neoliberal–conservative *transformismo* took place during the period 1991–94 of the Menem administration characterised by the strategies, policies and perspectives of the international and domestic coalition pro reform. This was the time of major structural changes in Argentina, defined by an externally based reorganisation of the financing of development and the restructuring of the labour force, accompanied by a state-based changing process of class and status differentiation.

At the base of the change was the alignment of, and interdependence between, the convertibility regime and the Brady Plan, which was also reflected in the interdependence and coordinated strategies between the Argentine government and the

IFIs. The changes were of such structural magnitude that by anchoring national finance to international markets while globalising and regionalising public utilities, the financing of development became dependent upon the ability of the Argentine *transformismo* to attain external support in the process of reforms and control and to co-opt any domestic opposition. This was a governed, interdependent political process, through which the country's financing of development came to be tied to the dynamics of international capital markets, and the globalisation of the economy to the generation of domestic–international partnerships with IFIs in which MDBs and the IDB played significant roles (Vitelli 2001; Kulfas and Schorr 2003).

The first guarantee implemented by the Menem administration to foster domestic–international partnerships was to restrict domestic control of money, an option with two important implications. The first was to subordinate the level of economic activity to a growing fiscal surplus. The second was that such surplus could be nurtured only through trade surplus, capital inflows or external borrowing from international capital markets and/or IFIs in which the key element was the cost of external borrowing. For the government, it was vital to keep low country rate risks rather than debt reduction in the negotiations of the Brady Plan with international commercial banks and IFIs, including the IDB (Vitelli 2001; Rapoport 2002).

The direct cost of the renegotiation under the Brady Plan for Argentina was US$3.4 billion, of which $2.9 billion were lent by IFIs, including the IDB, in exchange mostly for privatisations. The Brady Plan did not mean a significant impact in the reduction of debt but its transformation, providing the government with major control upon its management. In fact, the main impact was the conversion of the liabilities of bank creditors in long-term public obligations in the form of 30-year bonds secured by the US Treasury bonds that investors now could acquire for nominal values to buy public assets at real prices. The government used privatisation to manage the country's internal and external debt and fiscal deficit via debt–equity swaps (Damill 2002; Damill *et al.* 2005). In debt–equity swaps, bank debts were replaced with an equity investment. For instance, privatised state assets were used in exchange for external public debt owed to a foreign creditor.

As a result, the period was signalled by a massive transfer of state assets to domestic and international groups, through privatisations. This process was carried out with substantial financial and political presence of the WB and the IDB and capital markets to transfer ownership and to cushion the social impact of the changes. The process was characterised by high levels of coordination between domestic and international officials synchronising their actions. It was only then that the structural changes initiated during the dictatorship historically succeeded, in the presence of a disarticulated domestic response, and finally removing the structural and institutional obstacles in the way of the country's neoliberal global integration (Azpiazu 2002; Stiglitz 2002; Rapoport 2002; Rodrik 2003).

Between 1991 and 1994, the neoliberal–conservative alliance attained the level of institutional and structural hegemony necessary for the re-foundation of the country on the new neoliberal–conservative bases. In this sense, it represents a historical attempt made to change state–economy–society relations in which the financing of development would be mediated by market-driven forces. This was ahistorical convergence with the consensus, at domestic and international level, about the need for a structural change consisting of the transference of state assets to the private sector through a deep state reform and economic openness, with global economic integration as the central goal. In agency terms, there was a confluence between the main pillars of the Convertibility Plan, the Brady Plan, and the new Washington Consensus policies, with multilateral lending policies and assistance subordinated to the IMF's guidelines (Escude and Cisneros 2000). The Brady Plan was basically the bridge to return to and access external financing of development through debt swaps for privatisation, the Consensus the legitimising ideology, and the Convertibility Plan – the strategy of international–domestic alliances – three inseparable elements of the same globalising process (Rodrik 2003).

By 1990, there was a firm conviction among Argentine elites that, after the end of the Cold War, market-driven development tied to international financial tendencies would act as the motor of economic growth, so long as the country adjusted to the international process. This assumption also complemented the interests of domestic groups, for whom such reforms would permit access to those resources necessary to improve their competitive capacity in what was considered to be unstoppable neoliberal economic globalisation (Kosacoff 1999).

One of the major institutional steps towards the hegemonic convergence of the domestic and the international was given by the promulgation, on 27 March 1991, of the Convertibility Law (23.928). This, together with the Emergency Law and the State Reform Law, represented a set of integrated and complementary measures establishing the institutional pillars of the new neoliberal–conservative regime. All of this complemented a set of measures addressed to anchoring and institutionally bridging the domestic and the international: fixing the peso to the dollar, referred to as the peso–dollar parity; guaranteeing the free convertibility of the peso to any foreign currency; a prohibition on the emission of currency without genuine reserves; and the independence of the Central Bank.

The strategy was accompanied by the freedom of the Executive Power to dispose of the privatisation of any state assets, its control of the Supreme Court of Justice and the Congress, the openness of the economy to international trade, and the untrammelled remittance of profits and repatriation of foreign investments (Fanelli and Machinea 1994; Pou 2000). Briefly, the Convertibility Plan made the national currency management into an exogenous variable, beyond the control of national government, a system known as a 'currency board', emulating the monetary devices of the British gold standard period used for trade with countries of high currency risk (Rapoport and Cervo 2002; Hanke 2002; Damill *et al.* 2005). However, despite the rigidity of the currency board, the Menem administration had a way out in case of system failure, namely, the use of public bonds and their collocation in international capital markets, to sustain monetary reserves (Law 23.928/article 4).

In this scenario, the political system as a whole, and political parties within it, came to play a chief role as agents of change of the Argentine process, revealing the loss of the historical identity and social commitment in favour of global ones.

The project met with little resistance, because of the absence of social leadership and organisation, which had vanished during the dictatorship. In the period from 1991 to 1994, the process of detachment of the political system from its historical identities and social bases, initiated during the democratic transition of 1980s, reached its peak.

The stage shows a final alignment of the principal Argentine political forces with tendencies set in train by the new neoliberal–conservative *transformismo*. The process has been identified usually as a progressive transformation from a political system dominated by two parties during the late 1980s, into the Menemist political hegemony of the 1990s (Di Tella 1998; Mainwaring and Sully 1995; Garcia Delgado 1994). As political parties defected to the neoliberal–conservative alliance, they turned themselves into electoral machines run according to market principles, bringing about a profound process of social and status differentiation at their bases. Through the agency of political parties, the state acted to transform the basis of the political system, guided by a new world view of development. It was a market-driven process, characterised by a break between the present and the past, and strong support for the new Menemist reforms and policies internationally endorsed.

The process of economic transfer was anchored through financial devices in which the state and the IFIs politically insured domestic and international markets. Combined with direct support by the political system, this made for a fast privatisation process. In the period from 1990 to 1994 alone, revenues for privatisations of Argentine state assets reached US$25,563 million (Basualdo 2001: 69; Azpiazu 2002). Hence, electricity, oil and gas (production and distribution), telecommunications, transport, ports and public banks were privatised, passing into the hands of Spanish, French, US and Chilean investors with an active role in the process of MDBs. After the critiques about the transparencies of the process, the electric energy privatisation was regionally and internationally regarded as the exemplary and accelerated process as a result of the coordinated efforts between the government and the IDB. In the midst of the perceived magical transition towards stability and growth in 1991, the USA fell into recession, triggering an outward flow of capital from global capital markets toward the so-called emerging economies, accompanied by the massive support for the IFIs.

Consequently some social and economic indicators, inflation above all, showed a notable improvement. However, the dynamics between growth and employment-generation began to exhibit an increasing gap which was not immediately apparent because the inflow of capital expanded the monetary base and credit triggering massive increases in consumption (Damill *et al.* 2005: 6). In short, up to 1994, the economy exhibited a period of growth in which internal consumption and credit were dynamic factors, but with a growing balance-of-payments deficit and rising poverty and informal sectors (Frenkel and Gonzalez Rozada 2002; Damill *et al.* 2005; Rapoport 2002).

In other words, the economic situation began to deteriorate as a consequence of a growing twofold inconsistency inherent within the neoliberal–conservative model. The first was the over-exposure of the domestic field to global changes, since the financing of development was now reorganised around privatisation, capital inflows and the repayment of external debt (Basualdo 2001; Weisbrot and Baker 2002; Frenkel and Ros 2004). The second was that since accumulation was based on domestic purchasing power anchored to an international currency, economically, there was an increase in manufactured imports and capital inflows weakening local production (impacting on the balance of payments). The result was that, socially, the new consumer boom and price stability gave rise to the popular wisdom among middle and upper classes that, given its access to international services – finance, tourism, and education – and to consumer products, the country had become part of the new globalised world (Frenkel 2004). This in turn increased the common feeling, reinforced by the government, that without convertibility the country would slide back into the abyss of chaos (Rock 2002).

Nonetheless, despite the consumption boom of the period 1991–94, employment generation was affected negatively by the economic restructuring, bringing about a growing loss of jobs in the domestic industrial sector, as these experienced a rise in costs compared to the decade before, since wages were now measured in dollars (Damill *et al.* 2005: 7; Frenkel and Ros 2004). Deterioration in income distribution constituted the main factor behind the continued growth of poverty and indigence during subsequent years, all eclipsed by the phenomenon of consumption and popular access to credit.

The political economy of privatisation

The privatisation of the Argentine public utilities represented the central fact in the process of consolidation of the convertibility regime and the main source of financing of development based on the transference of state assets to the private sector. The process was led by the political order and characterised by the consolidation of monopoly markets, acquisition of sub-valued public assets acquired with debt bonds, state guarantees in the transference abroad of extraordinary profits, weak regulation and supervision, and concentration of capital favouring domestic, regional and international economic actors. In a nutshell, the consolidation of the transformist political order through privatisations made viable an unprecedented advance of capital over labour (Basualdo 2001; Azpiazu 2002; Etchemendy 2005).

The process fostered the emergence of a new international and regional–domestic business community whose major discrepancies were about the extent of transfers and who should keep the final control of the different state assets. However, it was the political order rather than the businesses who took these definitions, which varied according to the public utility transferred and the role expected from each of the domestic and international actors involved. At domestic level, the central beneficiaries were mainly those actors favoured by the neoliberal transformations initiated at the end of the 1970s, who now remained at the centre of the privatisation process supported by the government and being key players in the neoliberal coalition (Basualdo 2001; Etchemendy 2005).

The public policy implemented was politically determined, in the sense that the goal was to benefit specific groups of firms and favoured determined foreign relations within each sector via direct adjudication and compensatory policies in order to gain international support, guarantee debt restructuring, restructure fiscal spending and strengthen coalition support (Azpiazu 2002; Etchemendy 2005). Compensatory strategies constituted a distinctive feature of the Argentine *transformismo* and its domestic–international intergoverned process on the basis of the absorbent and persuasive capacities of the political order to integrate or co-opt opposition forces. Examples and empirical evidence of compensatory policies are widespread and can be found in different areas targeting a broad range of actors such as domestic and international business, labour unions, provincial governments, the Church and intellectual sectors. In the case of business, for instance, firms were favoured by targeted privatisations, special tariff regimes, or indirect subsidies. Labour unions, in turn, benefited from side payments, participation in the control, administration of pension funds or ownership programmes in privatised companies (Azpiazu 2002; Etchemendy 2005).

The formulation of the privatisation programme delineated a legal framework in which foreign capital would play a key role in association with specific domestic economic groups, configuring a domestic–international business community. As the major purpose of privatisation was debt reduction, the participation of IFIs in its design, institutional engineering, and organisation were significant, although varying according to the government objectives defined by the financial or political importance of each sector. Thus, the major returns from privatisations were obtained from the areas of energy, oil, gas and communications. There, the major funds disbursed were in energy and extractive enterprises, absorbing 69 per cent of the total, followed by transport and communication with 24 per cent, while the national sector constituted 93 per cent and provincial government 7 per cent of the operations (Kulfas 1999).

Table 4.4 presents the relations between the sectors of major contribution, in terms of privatisation revenues for the country, and the percentage under control of foreign and national companies. As can be seen from the table, an average of 66 per cent of these sectors passed to the control of foreign private hands, with the significant cases of electricity and communications wherein foreign ownership reaching 73 and 70 per cent respectively.

In a context of exchange rate appreciation, general tariff deregulation and the pressing need to swap debt for privatisation to reduce financial external exposition and gain international support, the regime in coordinated fashion with IFIs compensated groups of domestic firms in the strategic sectors of oil extraction, petrochemicals, autos and steel through different means. One way to do that was through more or less direct awarding of public services. Another form was by slowing down deregulation and allowing the participation of their business people in the design of the deregulation policies affecting them. A further method was to allow them access to the privatisation of specific public utilities, i.e. energy.

The reason that the government favoured these domestic groups lies in the structural and dominant characteristics of these groups. In fact, these were firms that had operated in mixed sectors, i.e. sectors with private and state participation, representing in the past core ISI areas of development and who had played a key role at the outset of the process and were now strategic actors in the coalition pro

Table 4.4 Foreign and national ownership for privatised sector, 1990–98 (percentage)

	Foreign[a]	National[a]	Percentage of total
Electric energy	73	27	28
Oil and gas	60	40	26.6
Communications	70	30	19.9
Gas	63	37	13.5
Transport	63	37	4.5
Petrochemical	66	34	2.5
Others	n/a	n/a	5
TOTAL			100

Source: Based on Kulfas (1999: 10).

Note
a Percentages estimated from the total of the sector.

reform (Azpiazu 2002; Etchemendy 2005: 69). Another important feature of these processes is that, as a result of the government support, these firms became widely diversified as they accessed sectors sometimes alien to their core and historical activities (e.g. electric energy, water, transport and gas).

Given the political economic aims of privatisations, the participation of IFIs represented a key factor for their success. Government and multilateral institutions acted in coordinated fashion through the whole stage, although the extent of the IFIs participation varied according to the strategic importance each sector for the regime, which in turn, produced a sort of division of labour of multilateral institution participation in the privatisations. In this regard, it is possible to observe strong cooperation among the central executive, Ministry of Economy, Public Works and Services with a key role for the World Bank and minor participation of the IDB, in the privatisation of core sectors (e.g. oil, gas and communications). In other sectors, however, privatisations emerge less politically controlled, with the central executive unit not overseeing or coordinating the process in favour of specific private groups (e.g. electric energy). In this context, ministries and multilateral institutions assumed a major role and within these ministries were established special privatisation committees under the control of technical personnel from MDBs and the Ministry of Economy as well as private sector financial advisors and consultants (GAO 1996: 6).

Within this framework, the privatisation of electric energy public utilities in Argentina represents a significant case to study regarding the political economic role of the IDB in the consolidation of the convertibility regime, for three reasons. The first is because this was a key event necessary for the government's success in gaining external credibility for the process of debt reduction and international reinsertion. The second is because this was the most important case in which the IDB intervened during the privatisation stage. The final reason for its relevance is because the case was regarded, then and even today, as a sound example of a positive privatisation given its less politicised and technical-led process than others. Chapter 5 examines the case in depth and the role of the IDB in the process.

Rising tensions and contradictions

By the end of 1994, the period of economic growth came to an end and a new stage – 1995–98 – commenced, characterised by significant structural changes and the increasing domestic and international weaknesses of convertibility as a development strategy. Once the political economy of privatisation tailed off, the organisation of the financing of development shifted towards a massive process of transfer of domestic assets into foreign hands. This course was marked by their conversion into financial assets, all facilitated by the convertibility regime and motivated by the better external position of foreign capital. A key factor in this stage, with deep impact on the sustainability of external financing of development, was the process of privatising social security and its negative impact on fiscal spending and financing of development (Kosacoff 1999; Kulfas 2001; Basualdo 2001: 78; Azpiazu 2002; Weisbrot and Baker 2002).

In addition, another structural change seems to have played an important role in the configuration of the new open regionalism in South America, as most of the new foreign branches favoured by regional conditions became bases for companies to export to the rest of Mercosur (Kosacoff 1999; Kulfas 2001). As the period 1990-94 signalled the consolidation of the neoliberal–conservative hegemony based on the configuration of a community of business and political sectors, this new stage characterised the dissolution, first structural and then institutional, of the cohesion of the international–domestic pro reform coalitions.

Accordingly, in the period from 1994 to 1999, the purchasing by foreign companies and their merger with domestic ones acquired a central role in the financing of the development strategy, amounting in the period to US$37.7 billion (see Figure 4.1). Among the major targets for investment were those privatised or concessionary companies concentrated in such sectors as electricity, gas, water, transport and telecommunications, in which international investors were guaranteed hard-currency returns (Kulfas 1999; Kosacoff 2000; Chudnovsky and Lopez 2000; Basualdo 2003). During this period of mergers and acquisitions of export platforms to penetrate South American markets, a particularly outstanding role was played by US, Spanish, Chilean and British companies such as Repsol, Exxel Group, Coto, Disco, Bank Bilbao Vizcaya, HSBC, Bank of Nova Scotia, Danone, Nabisco, Nestle, Grand Metropolitan, Luksic, Etex and Solvay (Kulfas 1999: 14–15).

To this deep process of transfer of domestic private assets into foreign hands corresponded a complementary process of capital outflows which reached a peak in the period 1995–97, as illustrated by Figure 4.3. A close look at Figure 4.3 also shows how, in parallel to the growing process of mergers and acquisitions of domestic companies, capital outflows grew from US$5.2 billion in 1993 to $16.0 billion in 1997 before dropping to $6.1 billion in 1999. This fact depicts the dynamics of the organisation of the financing of development during the period and shows continuity with the 1990–94 privatisation process (Kulfas 2001).

As the convertibility system worked in a similar way to the old gold standard used by conservative governments in Argentina before 1930, the Menem administration argued that since every peso equalled a dollar, the system would

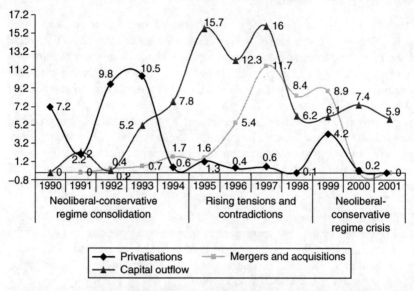

Figure 4.3 Argentina, evolution of the financing of development by privatisations, mergers and acquisitions, and outflow of capital, 1991–2001 (US$ billions). (Based on Basualdo 2003: 22.)

necessarily attract capital flows creating a sound credit system. However, as the dollar appreciated against other currencies, so Argentine exports became less competitive. Favoured by international interest rates, the system worked well, and was in addition supported by privatisation receipts.

However, when unfavourably influenced by external conditions, the balance of payments and foreign trade imbalances worsened, the rate of interest on debts grew in response to deepening financial crisis, and unemployment increased, so magnifying the increasingly recessive and exclusionary character of convertibility as a system. In addition, and as a result of the escalation of the international financial crisis (beginning with the US Federal Reserve Board's decision to raise interest rates in February 1994, followed by the crises of Mexico, Thailand and Russia) there were other external financial impacts on the model. Interest payments on the external debt increased from US$2.5 billion in 1991 to $9.5 billion in 2000, or from 1.2 to 3.4 per cent of GDP.

Worsening the situation further, in 1994 the government began a deep process of privatisation of the social security system, first at national and soon at provincial level, with the whole financial and institutional support of the IMF, World Bank and the IDB. The privatisation of social security was for the Argentine administration a strategic need. After the crisis of 1995, the government realised painfully the mounting pressures from international capital markets, and the short-term signals of creditworthiness as the economy became more and more globalised. Given the country's scarcity of capital, volatility created by the neoliberal reforms and the increasing dependence of high liquidity, private capital flows generated a deep vulnerability to external financial market shocks.

The Menem administration recognised this in 1995, accelerating the design and application of structural reform in social security to reduce external vulnerability in the long term and, at the same time, maintain investor confidence and widen the base of its coalition support. The reform of the system, implemented in alliance with the IFIs, aggravated the problem it was supposed to solve and added new ones, including the accentuation of gender-based and economic inequalities and the erosion of solidarity, with significant attendant social consequences (Barrientos 2004; Mesa-Lago 2004). Briefly, the social reform must be highlighted above all for its direct impact on the unfolding of the financial crisis and regime decline.

The transformation of the social security system of Argentina initiated in 1994, as with other similar reforms in the region, found its inspiration in the reforms put into effect by the Chilean dictatorship in 1981. The centrepieces of this model, applied later across the region, were the Second Generation Reforms, promoted and co-financed by the IMF, the World Bank and the IDB, which in the case of pension system reforms followed the Chilean experience (961/OC-AR, IDB 1996). The main restraints upon the country's adoption of welfare liberalisation were the negative impact of the fiscal deficit, the need to generate a domestic capital market and the formalisation of employee contributions to the system (Lousteau 2003: 127). The political economic dimension of the privatisation of social security in Argentina was indissolubly bound to a critical stage in the Argentine *transformismo* and its convertibility regime: that is, the reorganisation of the economic actors at its base and the need for financial resources and income to be transferred to the private sector pending an economic recovery.

The electoral campaign of 1995 marked the rise of tension and contradictions at the very base of the convertibility regime. As for the rest of the Menem administration, the period showed closer relations at the top level between the country's officials and the IDB's officials, even sometimes moving from one side to the other. However, despite the powerful institutional and discursive devices set in motion together with multilateral institutions, the negative impact of the structural changes was greater than expected, particularly affecting the source of production of the material life of the people: namely, employment and public welfare. Workers' salaries had sharply declined after 1976; following a partial recovery in 1985 they resumed their fall in 1994. This reveals who the losers were during this process. That can be observed in the performance of the variable of unemployment and underemployment as Figure 4.4 illustrates, which escalated from 6 per cent in 1979 up to 34 per cent in 1997. The particular effect of convertibility can be seen in its steep rise during the period 1994–98.

However, the Menem administration not only reformed the economy but redrew the political system and map of Argentina. By 1995, the hegemony had already shown its capacity to control the powerful armed forces and disarticulate any opposition by splitting the historical trade unions and integrating the opposition. Towards the military forces, the Menem administration adopted a complex policy

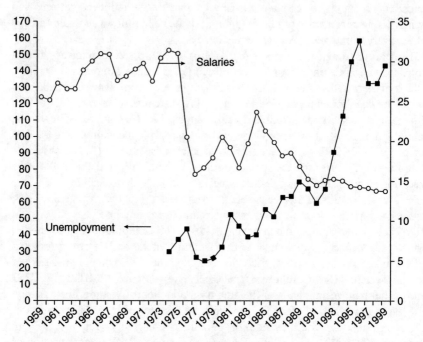

Figure 4.4 Evolution of salaries and unemployment in Argentina, 1959–99. Salary
1976 = 100, unemployment and underemployment as percentage of economically active population. (Based on Basualdo 2001: 76.)

of transformation based on 'national reconciliation and forgiveness', upgrading
their professional standards, and involving the armed forces in UN/US 'peace-
keeping' operations in Croatia, Somalia, Cyprus, Kuwait, Haiti and Angola.

Towards the labour unions, the Menem administration was aided by a split
in the powerful CGT union confederation, between unions favouring and those
opposed to the neoliberal–conservative transformation, leading to the formation
and rise of the Central de los Trabajadores Argentinos (CTA) (Rock 2002: 75;
Levitsky 2003). Facing this, the administration opted for a clear policy towards
organised labour, rewarding those leaders and organisations endorsing privatisations and reforms, and practising every sort of exclusion against those who did
not, the CTA in particular. These opposition unions would later play a central role
in the highway barricades organised by the *piqueteros* during 2002 completely
outside the formal political system.

As a matter of fact, the only political expression of dissent crystallised in 1995
in the so-called 'Alianza', constituted by the Frente Grande and the PAIS party,
both of which were inhibited by a superficial diagnosis that increasing social deterioration resulted exclusively from the actions of financial speculators, that the
governing party was the root of corruption and that its electoral defeat would
re-establish a new social alliance (Basualdo 2001: 80). Despite the Alianza, the

powerful Menem administration had no real contender; furthermore, it had transformed the Argentine political system. Now, rather than approaching people through social organisations, the new political machinery approached them as individuals, householders and consumers through media and local political operators (Levitsky 2003).

With the control of the Congress and the majority of provincial governments, and the acknowledgement and support of the international community, the Menem administration carried out three strategic changes to confront the domestic and external tensions raised by the convertibility regime. The first, on July 1996, was the replacement of the powerful Minister of Economy, Domingo Cavallo, by Roque Fernandez and the designation of a loyal Menemist, Pedro Pou, to the Central Bank, whose issuance of public bonds in capital markets would guarantee the control of financial deficits in the face of increasing external shocks. The second was the reformulation of the National Constitution in order to allow the government both to change the system of Federal Coparticipation to reduce public spending, as demanded by IFIs, and to gain a new period of government. With that in hand, the government now was in a position to initiate a historical pension reform addressed at strengthening the private organisation of the financing of development and reduce the influence of an allegedly inefficient corporatist state system in social provision (Basualdo 2001; Levitsky 2003).

Such moves soon triggered a series of political clashes between the government party and the opposition, and as a result, social animosity grew and the government faced increasing denunciation for its corruption. In short, opposition to the neoliberal–conservative order was rising, although characterised by its social heterogeneity and lack of organisation. In fact, the opposition was fixated by its moral discourse against the Menem administration, with an overemphasis on the fight against corruption and the prosecution of officials, instead of articulating wider social proposals as alternatives to the existent model.

Crisis of convertibility and fall of the Alliance administration

During the last period of convertibility from 1998 to 2001, the structural process led to an increasing deterioration in the fiscal sector triggered by the social security reform and increasing debt payments, and the emergence of two differentiated proposals to deal with the regime recognised inherent failures.

Table 4.5 presents the impact on national and provincial accounts of the privatisation of the pension system and external debt in the period 1994–2001. This table is quite revealing concerning the influence of the social reform transition cost and interest debt payments on the fiscal situation. As we can see, the public debt accumulated in the period was US$68.7 billion and the transference of sources to AFJPs (private pension funds administrators) represented $26.3 billion in public transfers, $11.1 billion in interest, and $35.8 billion in direct fiscal cost. The transition cost was about $47 billion, representing 68 per cent of the public debt.

According to the evidence, to finance the transition, the state supported by IFIs repeatedly sought to finance the deficit by placing more public debt in capital

Table 4.5 Argentina: impact on public debt of social security privatisation and interest payments for external debt, 1994–2001 (US$ millions)

	1994	1995	1996	1997	1998	1999	2000	2001	Accumulated
Public debt	4,513	5,781	6,012	7,828	8,049	10,106	12,117	14,282	68,688
Transference of sources to AFJPs	784	2,328	2,855	3,603	4,126	4,350	4,308	4,014	26,369
Interest	73	288	585	954	1,377	1,903	2,457	3,528	11,164
Total fiscal cost:	*802*	*2,509*	*3,294*	*4,376*	*5,291*	*6,016*	*6,510*	*7,043*	*35,842*
(1) Total fiscal cost as % of GDP	0.3	1.0	1.2	1.5	1.8	2.1	2.3	2.6	
(2) Interest payment for external debt as % of GDP	1.22	1.58	1.69	1.96	2.23	2.90	3.40		
Total (1) + (2) as % of GDP:	*1.25*	*2.58*	*2.89*	*3.46*	*3.03*	*5.0*	*5.7*		

Sources: Based on Martin Lousteau (2003: 121–146), Weisbrot and Baker (2002), and Economic Information, Ministry of Economy, Argentine Government.

markets ($31 billion), with an important participation by the Retirement and Pension Fund Administrators (AFJPs). Worsening the situation, interest debt payments steadily increased during the period due to the spread of the international financial crises. Consequently, due to the spread in emerging economies' risk premiums, the cost of these debt liabilities became more onerous than expected, raising serious doubts about the ability of the government to sustain the convertibility regime and honour international debts (Weisbrot and Baker 2002; Lousteau 2003: 121–146).

In political economic terms, the process was accompanied by a differentiation in the pro-market coalition sustaining the convertibility regime. The first project was associated with the interests of a foreign coalition – foreign banks, subsidiaries of foreign companies, foreign companies in control of public services – seeking to deepen convertibility through the full dollarisation of the economy. This would provide assurance that revenues would keep their value in dollars and allow foreign investors to retain their strategic export platform in the Mercosur market. The second coalition was formed by domestic and foreign interests whose objective was the abandonment of convertibility through a sharp devaluation. This proposal was hugely supported by the traditional domestic exporters of commodities since it implied a massive transference of resources to them (Basualdo 2001: 86, 2003: 29).

Both coalitions sought to maintain the hegemonic order via a political system that absorbed popular demands and defused growing social discontent. As their differences intensified, accompanied by a worsening in the social situation with serious limitations on the scope of the delivery of welfare, the tensions and contradictions of convertibility and of the conservative order began to be reflected in the national debate. Notably, since democratic institutions were limited in terms of social representation, global integration was producing poverty and social exclusion, international partnership was not leading to growth, and local governments were weak and unable to contain social discontent. Briefly, this growing debate began to express the Argentine search for a long-term, balanced and fair view of development.

It is within this context, aggravated by a global mode of financial accumulation that produced continuous financial crises, that the Argentine crisis must be understood: as the end of convertibility both as a model of financial accumulation and as a political regime detached from society. The permeability of the Alliance to the competing interest coalitions led first to the new administration supporting Machinea as minister of economy, an economist strongly bound to domestic industrial groups such as Techint, as well as to other members of the cabinet. However, supporters of the domestic option failed to block the adoption of the orthodox approach as represented by Lopez Murphy, an orthodox economist bound to the US CATO institute, which argued for more state adjustments, targeting in addition the benefits received by members of the neoliberal regime. Finally, and as a result of the failure of Murphy's plan, control of the national economy was acceded to Domingo Cavallo, whose economic measures again sought to favour domestic interests, although not the social sectors affected by convertibility.

However, through its industrial bias the measures triggered positive expectations, despite the incorporation of demands from financial interests for public spending to be reduced. Cavallo's first change was to tie the peso to a basket of strong currencies, opening the door for an indirect devaluation accompanied by a floating exchange rate. However, and with the risk premium rising, the restrictions imposed by the external situation forced a renegotiation of external debt to IFIs. New public bonds with massive interest rates to be serviced by the public sector were issued, demanding in turn a new reduction of public wages, further aggravating the social situation in the country. Finally, after a period of tense negotiations with the IFIs characterised by their intransigence concerning the need for more adjustment in order to keep the confidence of investors, foreign companies and holders of Argentine public debt, the IFIs withdrew their support, denying loans which had been agreed to finance a public deficit enlarged by the increasing costs of servicing debt.

In the context of fixed exchange rates, the continuous drain of public accounts to service debt with growing interest rates, and with the economic situation causing overwhelming social discontent, the collapse of negotiations with the IMF amplified the deterioration in the economic and social situation of the country, and produced two results. The first was to produce uncertainties in capital markets about the viability of the exchange rate, pushing up still further the country risk premium. The second was that by cutting primary spending the government finally triggered a bank run and a generalised social and political crisis (Weisbrot and Baker 2002; Frenkel 2003; Damill *et al.* 2005; O'Donnell 2001; Lozano 2001).

In short, the crisis in 2001 revealed the result of the long process, conducted under neoliberal–conservative hegemony, of the country's global integration, a process which involved the transference of capital abroad and a redefinition of Argentina's social structure. These processes came to an end, as the domestic adjustment to the global conditions caused tensions to rise and were socially contested, causing the political and financial systems that had sustained the process since the democratic transition to collapse. Within this long process, the dynamic of the IFI–government partnership, which evolved from direct association, to accompanying and finally distancing of IFIs from government in a complex relation brought about by the pursued strategy of globalisation, is significant.

Throughout the decline of the convertibility regime, the two differentiated coalitions of interests attempted to appropriate and reorient to their particular interests the social demands, and transformed and assumed them as their own. The new Alliance administration oscillated between one and the other, trapped in a moralist discourse but with a similar growth strategy to the Menemists. Indeed, it followed the same strategy, but was accompanied by an attempt to revive the old historical Argentine alignment with Mediterranean Europe instead of the USA and the Bretton Woods institutions. On the other side, the Bretton Woods institutions backed the dollarisation project, incorporating the idea within their crisis remedy discourse, justifying the role of IFIs in the last period.

The multilateral proposals came to repeat the same credo of the previous fifteen years, with the addition of dollarisation. According to this, the country collapsed because of excess public spending, and more adjustment, trade and financial openness and efficiency welfare delivery were needed, a diagnosis still held in Washington institutions despite the evidence to the contrary (Mussa 2002; Loser 2006). However, beyond this, the differential dynamics of the government–IDB partnership are noteworthy. In order to understand this, the next chapter will analyse how the role and development function of the Inter-American Development Bank converged with the stages of consolidation and the decline and crisis of the Argentine *transformismo*.

Conclusion

This chapter has given an account of the key stages of Argentina's political economy in the light of the critical political economy of South America developed in Chapter 2, and has highlighted the main tendencies and forces in a historical structural–agency dynamic which has defined every stage from 1940 to 2001. In particular, the chapter has analysed the complex dynamics of Argentina's political economy in the liberalisation process in the 1990s, in the context of the changing US hemispheric (and later global) hegemony. The purpose of the current chapter was first, to discover to what extent a new IPE of South America can tell us something new about the dynamics between economics and politics and between the domestic and the international as elements shaping the political economy of Argentina during these key stages of its development. Second, the chapter aimed to investigate the extent to which the changing organisation of the financing of development at each stage was associated with, or subordinated to, these complex and inseparable dynamics. Finally, it showed how, in particular, the neoliberal reforms in the 1990s find their explanation in regional tendencies taking place since the 1970s, which ended, in the middle of growing tension and contradictions, in a sharp decline leading to the collapse of convertibility in 2001.

As seen in the survey of the South American political economy given in Chapter 2, here again it is likely to find a pattern of development within Argentina which is similar to the region. That is, the rise, consolidation, attempts at reassertion, and decline of US hegemony; and the impact later of the rise and consolidation of global hegemony and global governance. The chapter highlights the extent to which Peronism, as a historical social phenomenon, represented a response to both the conservative–liberal founders of Argentina and to US hegemony in the region; and how after its downfall, there was a convergence between a domestic coalition and the hemispheric hegemony, which then assumed the form of hegemonic deadlock and ended in the hegemonic coercive reaction with the dictatorship in the 1970s.

The hegemonic deadlock marks, accordingly, the period of the internationalisation of production in Argentina, the so-called developmentalist stage, like other South American countries now shaped by the Cold War and military–civil political orders. This stage ended with the coercive reaction of the conservative coalition through the dictatorship, which, in turn, signalled a new stage that culminated in 2001 with the rise of the Argentine *transformismo* and the collapse of the neoliberal–conservative coalition. Significantly, the new hegemony was characterised by an element absent in previous stages of development, that is government–IFI alliance or the state–IFI complex as the force driving of a state-led form of globalisation anchored in finance and neoliberal guidelines.

In summary, it has been shown how the complex dynamics between hemispheric, international and domestic events shaped the political economy of the financing of development, throughout the changing hegemonies and until the collapse of convertibility in 2001. Accordingly, the continuity and evolution of the structural conditions shaping changes in Argentina's political system has been revealed, a continuity that began before the advent of the Washington Consensus. The investigation has also highlighted how the rise of the Argentine *transformismo* and its consolidation during the Menem administration with the active involvement of IFIs, provided the basis for the convertibility development strategy and its continuity during the De La Rua administration. Following this, the analysis showed the political economic process that led to a sharp deterioration of the convertibility regime and the government–IFIs partnership undermining the neoliberal organisation of the financing of development and leading into the crisis.

Accordingly, the chapter has sought to outline the configurations of social forces, state forms and political orders defining the domestic and international bounds between the Washington Consensus and the convertibility regime. As shown, it was an intergoverned process led by an IFI–state complex characterised by a particular form of pro-reform coalition, the international and domestic business community. In this regard, we highlighted two central stages of development of the convertibility regime showing two deep changes in this intergoverned process and role of IFIs: the consolidation of the regime defined by debt–equity swaps for privatisations of public utilities; and its decline and collapse characterised by the privatisation of social security and international financial bailouts to sustain the regime. These two stages will represent the central frameworks of the next two empirical chapters to study in depth the political economy of the changing IDB's role in the consolidation and decline of the convertibility regime.

5 The IDB's role in the internationalisation of Argentine public electricity utilities

Introduction

So far in this book, we have explored the political economy of the Inter-American Development Bank and of Argentina by focusing on the historical social processes shaping the role of the IDB in Latin America's development by deploying a version of the new IPE approach. This chapter takes a more empirical approach, illustrating the IDB's complex role within the consolidation stage of the convertibility regime. In so doing, the chapter analyses the Bank's function and its interventions in the process of externalising the financing of development carried out by the government–IFI partnership, as examined in Chapter 4. This stage was based on the strategy of globalisation of public utilities through the swap of external debt for equity in privatised firms, configuring a whole set of international–domestic private partnerships vital for sustaining the convertibility regime. Accordingly, the chapter highlights the IDB's role in the debt swap for public electricity utilities, officially recognised by the Bank as its most important intervention during the period of consolidation of the convertibility regime in the country (Tussie 1994: 125–129). It is important to bear in mind that the debt swap for public electricity utilities did not define in itself the consolidation of the regime, but it represents, as a complex process, a relevant case study capable of testing the main concepts of this version of the new IPE approach.

However, the relevance of the case study goes beyond this as, even today, the Argentine electricity privatisation is still regarded as one of the most substantial and successful reforms based on the Chilean and British market models within the framework of the Washington Consensus. The argument of this chapter is that the market-based transformation was indeed successful in terms of its agency, but in terms of its political economy it laid the basis for future limitations and bottlenecks.

In the early 1990s, Argentina became one of the world's leaders in the introduction of the neoliberal model under the patronage of the IFIs, with the IDB playing an active role. Notably, as leading scholars recognise, what was at first a universal formula subordinated to the notion of the efficiency of external financing became, a decade later, the centre of regional and domestic controversies concerning the capacity of the energy market and foreign companies to fuel growth, guarantee fair social access, support regional integration and diminish damage to the environment (Millan *et al*. 2001; Millan and von der Fehr 2003; Birdsall and Rojas-Suarez 2004).

Thus the case of the swap of debt for electricity privatisation and the market model introduced in Argentina necessarily refers to the IDB's intervention in the process in a coordinated fashion with the rest of the MDBs and in partnership with the Argentine government. The case is significant in two ways. First, because it provides a useful window onto the political economic dynamics of the IDB's development function in its interplay with a specific strategy of development such as the Convertibility Plan based on the globalisation of country financing of development and international–domestic partnerships and support. The second reason is that the study of this stage, i.e. the consolidation of the convertibility regime, can inform us about the conditions, configurations of forces, and international and regional–domestic dynamics of power accompanying the IDB's interventions defined, subordinated and coordinated with the major IFIs.

This chapter will argue that the complex and elusive nature of the IDB in the process of consolidation of the convertibility regime, as marked by the swap of debt for public utility privatisations, as in the case of the electricity sector, can be understood by focusing on its developmental capabilities. These are the IDB's capacity to adapt, frame, justify and legitimise specific political economic projects subordinated to and aligned with particular global financial guidelines of development. The first section analyses the IDB's role in the process of Argentina's debt swap for privatisation of public utilities – a process signalling the shift in the country's financing of development to external sources featuring a significant role for the IDB. The second section focuses on the IDB's ability to support and justify reforms of the electricity sector by achieving a consensus through a pro-market dialogue with professional and public opinion in the region, as expressed in the IDB's documents and programmes. The third section examines the political economic outcomes of privatisation in the light of the model-legitimising strategies deployed by the IDB–government partnership. Finally, the chapter ends with a short conclusion summarising the main findings.

Privatisation and external financing of public energy utilities

Any attempt to integrally comprehend the IDB's role in pro-market reforms of Argentina's electricity sector must locate these reforms within the regional framework of the globalisation of public utilities and state reforms pursued under the direction of the major IFIs in the early 1990s. This point is vital, as there is a vast array of literature highlighting the perils brought about by the pursuit of global integration and external financing through an overemphasis on financial liberalisation as centred on the privatisation of public utilities (Rodrik 2003; Stiglitz 2002; Birdsall and Rojas-Suarez 2004).

The IDB's interventions in the electricity public sector privatisation in the period were marked by three central elements. First was the adaptation of the hegemonic tendency in energy for development by the WB and the IDB, that is, the emulation of the tendencies and strategies followed by industrialised countries, in particular in the USA. The second was the role of the Bank in the process of framing the energy policies within the postulates of the Washington Consensus. The third was the introduction of the model of pro-market transformation at a regional and national level as a condition for gaining access to external official support and financial instruments in the complex process of swapping debt for privatisations within the framework of the Brady Plan.

The study of the IDB's intervention in the light of these tendencies clearly shows a complex role played by the Bank characterised by its capacity to frame, build consensus and support the pro-market coalition involved in the consolidation of the convertibility project. This intervention was subordinated to the objective of capital expansion promoted by the global financial architecture in coordinated fashion with the Menem administration, presenting it as a mainstream policy guideline and the only alternative for the transformation of the sector.

This transformational capability, present in all RDBs and MDBs, characterised by the amalgamation of the power of ideas and finances, refers directly to the capacity of transformation of the global economy through assimilation and absorption of domestic economies (Taylor 2005: 126). Two institutional mechanisms lay at its centre: its vaunted technical expertise, which provides the Bank with a rationale independent from its borrowing members; and its – self-proclaimed – political autonomy from governments, which facilitates a depoliticised monitoring and advice function, and which enables it to coerce governments through the exercise of conditions (Rodrik 1995). All elements are present and traceable in the case of Argentina's electricity sector reforms in the early 1990s.

Debt–equity swap and electricity privatisation

As seen in Chapter 3, the introduction of the neoliberal model for electric energy in the region was tied to the US–IFIs' compensatory policies for allied governments, as in the case of the Chilean dictatorship, or as a condition for access to external financing through the debt swap programme of the Brady Plan (Stiglitz 2002; Millan 2006: 60). Conditions and compensation, even when there were different policies, represented two inseparable elements of the same transformational strategy, something particularly clear in the case of electricity privatisation. Accordingly, a country might agree or disagree with the condition – privatisation – set for access to external financing and access to capital markets, but if it did agree it had to follow the multilateral guidelines.

As the implementation of the model demanded that governments meet important changes with significant domestic costs, its transformative policies became a vital function of the RDBs. To fuel the process, the powers of a regional institution such as the IDB were extended, providing the Bank with a more active role in regional development than it had ever had before. In short, the Bank's external financial support could now strengthen domestic legitimacy and fuel pro-reform coalition support (Benavides 2003; EIA 1997; Murillo 2001, 2002; Herz *et al.* 2005).

To gain access to external financing was the central objective of electric energy privatisation, in which debt swaps and privatisation were complementary political economic elements. Even though the Argentine electricity privatisation was led by specific political motivations as mentioned earlier, it constituted another significant example of the structural process through which the country's financing of development became anchored to external sources based on the internationalisation of public utilities. As a top economist of the IDB stated:

> Whether privatisations were right or wrong depends on who is speaking... but the truth is that by then there was a successful model to follow, already tested... Besides, there was a shared diagnosis; the Bank possessed a sound strategy and all the financial resources necessary to turn the historical outsourcing that the region needed to produce through privatisations, state reforms and market competition into genuine growth.
>
> (Anonymous interview 27/04/2004)

As a result, in 1992 the IDB came to play an active role in the programmes of debt or debt service reduction (DDSR). DDSR was established as an institutional condition for country access to the Bank's fast-disbursement programme, whose operations were restricted to deepen coordination with the World Bank (GN-1686-7, IDB 1991a). The IDB's major debt-related operations in the 1990s were executed in Argentina in which co-ordination between the IDB, the World Bank and the IMF contributed to the restructuring of long-term commercial Argentine debt of US$20.9 billion, i.e. half of the country's publicly guaranteed debt. The participation of the IDB in coordination with the major IFIs was central, since on its own the Bank would have been jeopardised by such a high financial exposure. However, the financial risk accompanying the debt restructuring was tempered by Argentina's own massive debt conversion/privatisation programme with the active participation of the IDB and the World Bank in the internationalisation of public utilities (Tussie 1994: 129–130).

As shown in Chapter 4, in the 1990s external financing as the main source of financing for national development became the central feature of the convertibility regime and of development strategy. Actually, the alignment of, and interdependence between, the convertibility regime and the Brady Plan were of such structural magnitude that by anchoring national development finance to international markets, with the active support of IFIs, the structure of Argentine financing consolidated a long-term shift. However, the change brought into being another element that would play a chief role in the crisis of the system. Thus, in producing this structural shift in finance, the Argentine *transformismo* became dependent upon the ability of the regime to sustain itself with external financing. The structural shift was a governed, interdependent political process, through which the country's financing of development came to be tied to the dynamics of international capital markets and multilateral support, and the globalisation of the economy to the generation of domestic–international and regional partnerships within which the WB and the IDB played a significant role.

Figure 5.1 illustrates the relation between the main sources of financing of development for each stage and lending from the IDB and the WB (MDB lending)

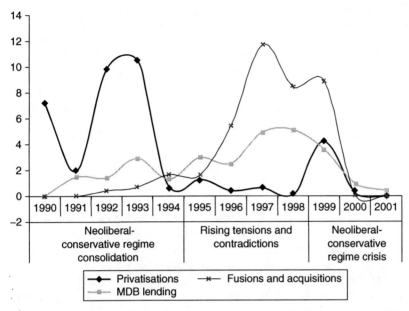

Figure 5.1 Argentina, external financing by main sources, 1990s (US$ billions). (Based on Basualdo 2003, and World Bank and IDB reports.)

through the period. This figure is highly pertinent since, first, it shows that MDB lending followed a similar pattern to the main sources of development financing – i.e. privatisations, mergers and acquisitions (M&A). Second, it is relevant because the IDB's actions during the period were subordinated to and conducted in collaboration with the IMF in Washington. In this sense, the evidence shows the complementarity in terms of targets and policies between those IDB instruments controlled by the major financial institutions – the IMF and the World Bank – and those over which the IDB together with borrower countries retained autonomy through investment loans and technical support (RE-299, IDB 2004a: 15). As can seen from the figure, multilateral lending grew steadily almost until 1998, following the abrupt drop between the period of privatisations and M&A, explained by the IDB's participation in the global financial bail-out of the country in the aftermath of the Mexican crisis. In addition, it is striking that multilateral lending as a countercyclical source of financing began to fall steadily after 1998–99, together with the debilitation of the M&A inflow. This is just at the time when international capital markets, the major sources of Argentine development finance, abruptly began to dry up, an issue studied in Chapter 6.

As seen here and in other chapters, it is plausible to assert that the IDB's participation, rather than being simply a financial and quantitative one, appears to be mostly linked to the Bank's political economic capacity to support the country's access to external financing. In this sense, the IDB's participation was more active in terms of generating consensus around the reforms implemented as central elements of its development role. In an assessment carried out by the Institute of Development Studies of the University of Sussex, Griffith-Jones (1994: vii) points out:

> The IDB contributed to the ... return to credit-worthiness. This has been done via two lines of actions. One was via an 'exercise in optimism' spread extensively via IDB special conferences, speeches of senior management. The second line ... was to support and encourage changes ... that helped attract foreign private flows ... [T]he IDB ... developed a special focus, by concentrating on particular sectors ... and within sectors, that it knows intimately, such as energy.

Sector transformation

One of the striking characteristics of the electric energy privatisation in Argentina was the rapidity of its transformation. There are two major interpretations concerning the reason for this. For some, it was part of a process of transformation characterised by the absence of a clear conviction about the importance of pro-market reforms. In this sense, the process of transformation is seen as driven by the necessity of the government to gain external official support in order to access capital markets and, at the same time, to patronise domestic business conglomerates (Gerchunoff and Canovas 1996; Schamis 1998; Murillo 2001; Pollitt 2004). Others argue that, even though these elements mentioned are present, they explain only the characteristics of its agency which must be related to its structural factors. In this vein, the transformation was associated with and part of the major process of debt swaps for privatisations defining the need of the Argentine *transformismo* to solidify its strategy on global integration. In this regard, the privatisation was addressed to giving both an external and a domestic signal about the government's will to transform a deteriorated sector, hitherto a historical symbol of Argentine statism and protectionism (Nochteff 1998, 2001; Basualdo 2003). However, from a political economic point of view, the most important characteristic rests on the configuration of forces accompanying the process and the flexibility of the neoliberal model to adapt to the domestic needs of different political economic projects in the region, as pointed out in Chapter 3.

A significant fact of electricity privatisation is that even in those countries that implemented similar energy reforms under the neoliberal model with the intervention of the IDB, political and economic outcomes varied widely, ranging as seen in Chapter 3 from a broad presence of foreign companies – e.g. in Bolivia – to the use of privatisation to create domestic support – e.g. in Chile. In the case of Argentina, the process presents two significant and interrelated characteristics. The first feature is that the process of pro-market reforms and the IDB's participation was coupled to the long-run economic restructuring process taking place since the 1970s, led by the Argentine *transformismo* in alliance with IFIs (Basualdo 2001). The second characteristic is that the outcome of electricity reforms suggests a particular form of globalisation of public utilities in which the IDB seems to play a significant role, supporting the creation of a middle option between major foreign control and domestic private control. This is central in our case, as the process gave rise to domestic–regional and domestic–international partnerships which monopolised, in particular, electricity generation and distribution in major urban areas. As a result, the transformation of the sector was accompanied by the consolidation of powerful regional and international pro-reform coalitions. In addition, there was a noticeable structural shift from a domestic-oriented energy sector towards a regional-oriented energy market with importance consequences for the future development of the country (EIA 1997; Millan 1999; Herz *et al.* 2005).

The electricity sector in Argentina, prior to the reforms in 1992–93, was characterised by the dominance of public-owned companies at both the federal and provincial levels. Public enterprises were vertically integrated and controlled their share of power generation, transmission and distribution in the major regional centres of the country. The biggest provinces operated their own electricity companies together with local cooperatives, and they became the first target of the process led by the IFI–government alliance. Attraction of investment capital, promotion of competition and the withdrawal of the state from the sector were the main objectives, in pursuit of which major efforts were addressed to making the old public companies financially attractive by updating tariffs, downsizing structures and reducing property risks (Bouille *et al.* 2001; Millan 1999; Herz *et al.* 2005). At end of the 1980s, before the introduction of the market model and the reorientation of the sector towards regional gas-based energy trade, Argentina had gas reserves for 35 years; by 2006 those reserves barely reached 8 years.

By the mid-1990s, Argentina had become the strategic provider of its own and Bolivian gas and electricity to Chile, Uruguay and Brazil (Millan 1999; Herz *et al.* 2005). The change came about as a result of three different factors: the prominence of gas in the country's energy matrix; the strategy followed by its administration; and the influential role of the IDB and World Bank in the configuration of the open regionalism. Thus, in the early 1990s, private investments were concentrated into gas-based electric energy and hydropower, with no major problems being evident. However, in the second half of the 1990s, the sector began to experience a critical process of market concentration, later followed by continuous interruptions in the provision of services (Maldonado and Palma 2004). As a result, by the end of 2001, serious structural limitations began to emerge in the reforms led by the government's partnership with the WB and IDB, as newly privatised companies neither expanded investments nor introduced more technology and services despite big profits, important state concessions, and public discontent with services and tariffs (Bouille *et al.* 2001: 14; Millan 2003; Calderon and Serven 2004; Herz *et al.* 2005).

Supporting and justifying electricity privatisation

A central element of the IDB's political economic role in the electricity reforms was its ability to support, justify and legitimise Argentina's electricity privatisation by achieving hegemony for a particular set of ideas or model of reforms which

defined the options available for the sector. Justification and legitimisation constituted central social processes, by means of which the Bank exercised its main
hegemonic function, namely, the generation of a consensus around specific economic guidelines. This hegemonic function was mostly expressed in the framing
of policy options, thereby circumscribing actions (Cox 1992: 179; Taylor 2005).
Lending, technical support and the central ideas at the base of the project become
inseparable and subordinate elements of the same hegemonic process.

Since the Bank's capabilities represent an amalgamation of material and ideological capacities, its capabilities typically manifested themselves in the ideas
underlying the reform model and in the process which accompanied its justification and legitimisation. This is relevant, as the identification of these ideas and
processes could permit us to trace both the international–domestic consensus
about the necessary conditions under which private sector participation should
take place and the areas in which the IDB punched above its financial leverage.
In addition, this would help us to trace the Bank's interventions addressed to the
defence and legitimisation of the political economic project of the government–
IFIs concerning the sector. The concern about the IDB's capacity to intervene
and promote development in borrowing countries is not a new issue and it has
been aware of this power, which can be traced extensively in its official reports in
different forms. An example can be found in the Energy Sector Strategy document that states:

> The Bank can draw on a variety of experiences, instruments, policies, and
> fields of activity to orchestrate a set of complementary activities and make
> optimal use of its institutional advantage . . . [T]he Bank is an influential
> regional player with a proven ability to convene conferences, meetings, and
> other forums for discussing important issues and reaching consensus . . . [It]
> also has a network of offices throughout the region that allows it to take
> advantage of its experience in the energy sector to adapt its services to the
> new circumstances.
>
> (IDB 2001a: 15)

The design of Argentina's electric energy privatisation represented a process
through which the IDB–government partnership turned a particular reform option –
fragmentation, privatisation of the sector and competition – into a unique, universal
and legitimate policy option. The Bank's blueprint for the privatisation of the sector – based on the Chilean and British experiences – was largely developed via
technocratic and consensual means, in which the multilateral model came to be
adopted and adapted in the early 1990s to the strategic needs of the Argentine
transformismo. The results of this investigation suggest that the Bank's capability
is composed of a combination of different sources. Noticeably, it is through them
the hegemonic view is gradually codified and concretised via interventions, negotiations, conditionalities and the making of concessions up to the arrival at a consensus enabling 'paramount sectional interests . . . to be displayed as the common
interest' (Taylor 2005: 127).

Intervening in reforms and privatisation

The IDB's intervention in Argentina's electric energy privatisation took place within the framework of an ongoing strategy of internationalisation of public utilities and financial globalisation of the Argentine economy, driven by the IFI–Menem administration partnership. By this time, the cooperative dynamics between the government and the IFIs reflected a deep alliance founded on shared interests and ideas concerning changes in the central guidelines of development, fostered by powerful domestic and regional phalanxes of social forces arrayed behind market-led development. Within this, the design of the electric energy privatisation took place throughout two interrelated processes. The first is the shift toward pro-market policies and international alignment that the Menem administration embraced as the only option for development for the country, something hitherto unthinkable for a Peronist administration (Palermo 1994: 314; Levitsky 2003: 150). The second is the process by which the IDB, in tandem with IFI support, shaped this domestic option into a particular model of privatisation and presented it together with the World Bank as a universal technical alternative. Unsurprisingly, both processes in which the government and the IDB appeared guided by a blind faith in the efficiency of unregulated markets and the view that the state's role should be narrowed to a minimal intervention in the process.

The privatisation of the national electricity industry can be explained by five central facts which also explain the IDB's involvement in the process. First is the fact that the sector was in a critical state after two decades of dictatorial and democratic governments, external shocks and repeated attempts to restructure it under market rules. Consequently, by the end of the 1980s, the profound deterioration of the sector was officially described by the Wholesale Electricity Market Management Company (CAMMESA) as:

> Energy crisis, administrative deterioration...Conditions of inefficiency, gigantism, bureaucracy, lack of control, lack of professionalism in its management, politicisation and incapacity of its management contributing to an energy crisis of great magnitude.
>
> (CAMMESA, www.cammesa. com/inicio.nsf/marcomem)

Second, the government was sending a signal to the IFIs and capital markets that it was committed to the new global postulates of development. This was a central element, since the recent privatisations had been criticised for their lack of transparency, and the government needed to improve its external image in the midst of a major swap of public debt under the Brady Plan (Nochteff 2001; Murillo 2001). Third, the administration had an urgent need to access external financing in order to improve the fiscal situation and sustain the transformation. Fourth, it was a signal that a Peronist administration was able to follow pro-market principles by privatising what was, for Peronist traditionalists, an icon: the public electricity sector (Basualdo 2003). Last but not least, electricity privatisation would be a trouble-free pledge in Menem's foreign policy aimed at winning European support for reforms (Escude and Cisneros 2000). These five facts represent interrelated elements which explain the importance of the technical control of the process in the hands of the staff of the Ministry of Economy and the IDB, and the particular conditions under which the Bank entered into the process.

In 1991, Argentina's urgent need for fresh funds to drive the changes demanded by the convertibility strategy opened the way for the intervention of the IDB in the country's reforms. The Bank concentrated on 'fast-disbursing loans' (highly policy-based), coordinating with and tied to the IMF and World Bank's surveillance, within a framework of consensus and cooperative relations between the administration and the IFIs (Tussie 1994: 124). Thus, in 1992, Washington and Argentina commissioned the IDB to deliver financial support 'as soon as the Convertibility Plan was under way' (682/OC-AR, IDB 1992), in order to accompany economic reforms. Accordingly, three perceived central problems were targeted: the reduction of the fiscal deficit, federal reforms and the privatisation of public assets. In this scenario the participation of the IDB in the reforms rapidly became wider than that of the World Bank. State and provincial reforms and the privatisation of electric energy became inseparable aspects addressed by the Bank's intervention by then (see Appendix C).

Two of the IDB's programmes targeted electricity privatisation: the Provincial Electric Program (863/OC-AR, IDB 1991b) and the Reform of National Electric Power Utilities (682/OC-AR, IDB 1992). Both loans included support for the development of institutional capabilities in the form of non-refundable components addressed to hire consultants, carry out financial evaluation concerning the viability of the reform, and so forth. Both programmes, in turn, were tied to two core programmes for state reform in association with the World Bank: the Public Sector Reform (633/OC-AR, IDB 1991c) and the Provinces Development Program (619/OC-AR, IDB 1991d). The IDB's justification of electric energy privatisation is here expressed as a depoliticised and technocratic approach shared with the banks and the Ministry of Economy, dominating their discourse concerning the economic roots of Argentina's misfortunes over the past decades, as is clearly stated in an official Bank document:

> The deterioration of the economy is mainly attributed to the unchecked growth and resulting inefficiency of the public sector. The expansion of the public sector, and the erosion of fiscal discipline gave rise to chronic fiscal deficits . . . [leading] to inflation, high interest rates, loss of private sector confidence . . . and the inability to meet high external obligations.
>
> (633/OC-AR, IDB 1991c: 1.2)

The text expresses the supremacy of neoclassical postulates in the Bank and the implicit belief that states, due to politics, were by nature incapable of fiscal responsibility and attending to external financial obligations. However, the official document goes beyond this, defining the roots and the targets of reforms in the public sector:

The overall public sector deficit is...at the centre of Argentina's... economic difficulties...[It] originates from...(i) the Central Government itself; (ii) the social security system; (iii) the public sector enterprises; (iv) the provincial governments; and (v) the Central Bank (net) losses...Argentina must deal with all these sources [by generating] primary surplus sufficient to meet its debt obligations and to increase domestic saving; essential elements that will...enhance the investment outlook.

(633/OC-AR, IDB 1991c: 1.3)

The statement is quite revealing as it shows two important normative elements to which the IDB's conception was subordinated. First is the idea that the root of the problem was the structure of the national state in itself. Second is the concept that the country's growth depended purely or chiefly upon external market elements such as investors' rational perceptions about the country's capacity to honour its external debt. Analysing the participation of IFIs in Argentina's transformation, Rodrik summarises this multilateral perspective as follows:

Viewed from this perspective...Economic growth requires foreign capital. Foreign capital requires removing sovereign risk. And removing sovereign risk requires a commitment not to play games with other people's money...[The government's] hope was that [it] would be rewarded with a sharp reduction in 'Argentine risk', leading to large amounts of capital inflows and rapid economic growth.

(2003: 17)

In sum, it emerges that the central objective behind reforms and privatisation, for the IDB and the government, was not so much the transformation of the out-dated structure of public services but the fostering of international financial credibility. This was the central element in the globalisation of the financing of development under the government–IFI alliance.

Shaping and justifying privatisation

The design, justification and implementation of the electricity privatisation model was carried out in a coordinated fashion by the staff of the Secretary of Energy at the Ministry of Economy, the major MDBs, and a small group of financial, legal and technical consultants (Murillo 2001; Bouille *et al.* 2001). Key figures in the process and later in the defence of the reform were Carlos Bastos, former Secretary of Energy, and Agustin Leon Tapia, a Chilean civil-electricity engineer with a meteoric career in the industry, among other consultants. Also playing a prominent role were Harold Smartt, IDB Regional Operation Department; Jaime Millan, a chief energy economist from the IDB; Jaime Sujoy, an economist at the Bank and a key figure in the IDB's department of regional operations; Ignacio Perez-Arriaga, a Spanish-born MIT professor in electricity engineering; and the

UK financial consultants KPMG and Merz and MacLellan, which played a central role in the financial reorganisation of the state companies before privatisation.

The IDB accompanied and supported, by and large, the leadership of Bastos even when, at an initial stage, some of the Bank's technical staff were sceptical about the final outcome of the process. The WB and the IDB consolidated the institutional and political power of Bastos by according a higher status to the Under Secretary of Energy over other actors, including provincial governments. The agreement provided Bastos' team with independence from the public sector, enabling it to supervise provincial entities and private companies benefiting from the loans, and to develop a powerful financially and legally autonomous parallel public structure. Among the conditions set by the IDB for the disbursement of funds for reforms to the government, the Bank also demanded the creation of the Central Execution Unit (CEU) in the department of the Under Secretary:

> provided with personal, financial autonomy...and which has the following legal instruments: 1) the agreement of guarantee that has to be subscribed between the Under Secretary and Provinces...2) the agreement of loan that will be signed between the Under Secretary and the electrical entities...[the CEU will take] all necessary measures...so that tariffs of electricity service yield income and profitability enough to cover the expenses of services [for new private owners].
>
> (863/SF-AR, IDB 1991: Appendix I, A; Appendix III)

Having created the organisational structure, the Bank concentrated its efforts on two fronts. First, it targeted the financial reorganisation of public enterprises in preparation for their privatisation (Bouille *et al.* 2001: 14). Second, it focused on the transfer of experience, by bringing key figures from the Chilean and the British processes into developing the technical and private links of the new CEU. This included the later hiring by the Argentine government of Leon Tapia, a former engineer of the Chilean public electricity company, former financial manager of Endesa-Chile, and an IDB consultant with important participation in other privatisation processes in the region – i.e. in Bolivia and Ecuador. The Bank's opinion of the process was summarised in a statement by a well-placed staff economist:

> The privatisation of electricity energy in Argentina was good, despite some issues on how contracts were adjudicated...nowhere else will you find a better example of exhaustion of the old model based on state control and subsidies than in the Argentine case...With Cavallo there was an excellent dynamic and Bastos was an ambitious professional who understood that a privately owned and competitive sector was the only chance for the industry...We brought the Chilean experience and contacts, and helped Bastos to know more about the British process as well as to get the right people for the team.
>
> (Anonymous interview 20/04/2004)

A central role of the IDB in the electricity privatisation was justification of and legitimisation of the reforms. The process of justification took place through the political strategy of depoliticising the electricity issue and economising the alternative model imposed by the IFI–government partnership. Strikingly, what later came to be justified as the introduction of an economically, technically, environmentally and socially viable model for the sector diverged considerably from what this investigation finds to have been the original justification (Millan 2006).

Depoliticisation or the draining of any overt political dimension from the issue, and economisation of the issue and its presentation as a technical proposal are inseparable parts of the Bank's institutional strategy in the process. Both elements materialised via technical institutional means jointly for the WB, IDB and the government. The process was based on the presentation of the model as a technical solution to development, and on the continued repetition of two factual claims turned into normative principles: first, the inability of the old state monopoly to meet the new technological demands of development; second, the inherent financial incapacity of the state to manage the electricity industry, in contrast to the dynamism of pure markets (Millan 1999; RE-251, IDB 2001c; Millan and von der Fehr 2003; Littlechild and Skerk 2004). According to a leading scholar in the subject:

> The strategy employed . . . was to present alternatives as unworkable, radical reforms as inevitable, and the state owned companies as enterprises with low credibility and prestige.
>
> (Bouille *et al.* 2001: 12)

The factual claims concerning the incapacity of the old model, which emerged in the IDB–government discourse, were bounded by two central elements. One was the normative principle that the state should withdraw from the sector in order to avoid further economic problems for the country; another was the necessity for the IDB to work within and support the framework of privatisation reforms already defined by the World Bank and IMF. This is expressed clearly in the IDB's document for the reform of national electric power utilities:

> The principal objective of the reforms is to reduce the public sector deficit by means of large cuts in government spending . . . [I]n accordance with the government's strategy, the Bank will consider operations designed to encourage private-sector participation in the economy.
>
> (682/OC-AR, IDB 1992: 1.7–1.8)

Within this overall objective, the justification of electricity privatisation emerges in the IDB's documentation through the description of four problems at the roots of the troubled national public companies, subordinated as they were to the performance of public finances. The distinctive feature of these factual claims is that they were grounded on financial arguments, with scant reference to their political, economic and environmental context or technical origin. The first was that national companies' rate levels 'have long been too low to cover their needs' (ibid.: 3.6). The second was that decisions about rates had been repeatedly frozen for social reasons and were centrally fixed by the arbitrary authority of national and provincial governments, weakening the sector's performance. In the same vein, the result was that the companies had been overstaffed with employees and over-protected by law and collective union rights, deeply affecting profitability (ibid.: 3.24). Finally, since electricity revenues had been historically high and used to cover current public spending, the sector had continued to borrow. As a result, the sector had become increasingly unable to 'meet the interest payment on the debt they have incurred', falling back 'on the guarantees granted by the national government and resign[ing] themselves to a situation of permanent delinquency *vis-à-vis* the financial system and their own government' (ibid.: 3.15).

This economised understanding of the national sector, present in practically all the official documents, appears grounded in an empirical description of the con-junctural circumstances of the three major national companies – Hidronor, AyEE and SEGBA. Noticeably, this economised diagnosis was then extended to all elec-tric energy companies in the country and identified as a representing a structural financial problem at the core of the diagnosis on which the IDB–government's jus-tification of privatisation was premised. Furthermore, these empirical descriptions came to be the centrepieces of an argument justifying and technically demonstrat-ing why 'the traditional model of supply based on State monopolies and indiscri-minate consumer subsidies had run its course' (IDB 2001a: 1). More strikingly still, examination of the IDB's official documentation during the period does not reveal any background research on the national electricity sector or any studies of international experiences which justify why fragmentation and private control was the only way to restructure the sector. Indeed, most of the references in the official documentation refer to performance of market transformation in developed coun-tries and in particular to the US, British and Chilean electricity sector. What appears instead is a depoliticised and economised framing of the policy options which are far more preoccupied with justifying the government's commitments to the IFIs than to giving attention to a structural issue of development. Two of the IDB's specialists in the sector, Jaime Millan and Nils-Henrik von der Fehr, arrive at the same conclusion:

> The hope was that introducing private capital and unleashing market forces in electricity markets would produce a more commercial, efficient, and customer-sensitive power sector that was less politicised ... [P]rivatization ... was viewed as an excellent way to fill empty coffers. [And] multilateral funding sources, thrilled with Chile's success in attracting new private invest-ment to meet growing power demand, became more reluctant to finance an 'unrepentant' public sector.
>
> (2003: 1–2)

The approach these IDB specialists criticise is no other than the World Bank model for the privatisation of the public electricity utilities in the region, which the IDB had to adopt, adapt and put in effect under the surveillance of the WB in the

1990s. The model defined several necessary steps for privatisation: parliamentary approval; establishment of an independent privatisation commission; preparation and approval of legislation and decrees guaranteeing the protection of the private sector; contracting technical, legal and financial consultants; definition of separate business units; labour-restructuring and voluntary retirement schemes; preparation of bidding documents and transfer contracts; prequalification of potential bidders; issuance of calls to tender; evaluation of bids; awards; company and asset awards; disposal of minority share holdings; and organisation of employee stock ownership programs (EIA 1997: 81).

Beyond the emphasis on transference to the private sector, the IDB's technical framing and justification shifted later in the 1990s towards address more regulatory issues, from its early emphasis on tariffs and public spending towards the role of the state, efficiency incentives and institutional weaknesses. The model, however, expresses the exclusionary consensus between the Bank, the regional pro-market network and the government that 'the state was no longer capable of carrying out the tasks of energy planning, investment and management' (Bouille *et al.* 2001: 10). As in all first-generation reforms, the negative definition is officially dominant, the Bank calling on 'the state to withdraw completely from the electricity and gas industry . . . [and concern itself with] its ability to attract private investment'. The central argument was that efforts should be concentrated on making these assets more attractive to investors in order 'to reduce investment risks' (Bouille *et al.* 2001: 4).

These views were not just an isolated multilateral discourse generated by the IDB and other multilateral institutions. In fact, this approach was also present and rooted in the government's view of the electricity reforms. Rather than reflecting a convergence in policy options between government and IFIs, it mirrored the dominant vision of the IFI–Argentine *transformismo* partnership. The government was deeply committed to a strategy that the Menem administration did not doubt even when confronting its own party members opposing the reforms, presenting not only a defence of privatisation but also an entire pro-market approach to Argentina's history, until then unthinkable for Peronism:

> Why accuse me of [being a] liberal? . . . . They are statists . . . a mentality that Peron himself had discarded in 1954, when he put in motion the process of oil deregulation and condemned, by and large, because of inefficiency and deficiency, the state enterprises . . . . Up to 1952 we used to live almost without working . . . Frondizi was the only one who assumed an attitude of change . . . [and] Rapanelli did not animate himself to put into motion our proposal of market liberalisation.
>
> (Cited by Palermo 1994: 314–315)

Justification of the reforms was inscribed within the hegemonic discourse addressed to redefining collective values via negatively resignifying the past and equating progress with pro-market reforms and multilateral support. The process was grounded on continuous invocations of a dark statist past, favoured by a clear leadership of public opinion and by the absence of significant resistance among political actors within and outside the official political party (Palermo 1994: 315). The framework of rupture between the past and the new present was a central feature of the government–IFI alliance, in which the Bank was mainly concerned with framing policy options, circumscribing actions and legitimising reforms, thereby aligning itself with the convertibility regime.

Fragmentation and competition

Another central issue around the electricity privatisation was the role of the state and the transformation of the federal structure, which later in the 1990s would become explicitly defined as one of the pillars of the IDB's model for and justification of regional electricity liberalisation (Millan 2006). Strikingly, a short survey of the Bank's official documentation in the early 1990s reveals no mention of the role and structure of the Argentine state in the sector, which is only negatively and indirectly addressed via its economic and technical aspects. Analyses of the political roots of the process are missing from the official justification of the process. One of the central political issues, given its strategic financial, economic and social role, was conspicuously absent: the political struggle over the control of the electricity industry by provincial states. Politically, the control of electricity provision had represented for the provinces a powerful resource bolstering their relative political independence in face of the overwhelming power of the national state (Bouille *et al.* 2001: 10; Etchemendy 2005).

   Public electricity enterprises had historically been factors in the political conflict between national government and the provinces. This represents a political element and a striking fact underlying the reforms and the active participation of the IDB, which is that the reforms began not at a national but at a provincial level. In this regard, the multilateral justification based on the Chilean and British model coincided with a central political objective sought by the Menem administration: to reorganise and transform the federal political landscape. Investigation of this reveals how the IDB's role in the reforms involved the exercise of another hegemonic function exercised jointly with the government in support of the political economic project of the Argentine *transformismo*, namely the Bank's capacity to support the hegemonic co-option and absorption of opposition forces by reinforcing the Menem administration's compensation strategies for provinces and for unionised workers. In this process, hegemonic co-option, compensation tactics and segmentation of the industry seem clearly aligned behind national political objectives. Some hints can be found in the opinion of an important member of the Bank's staff:

> With Cavallo and his staff the relation was excellent and the Bank worked well while he was there. . . . He had two problems. First, to adjust inflation, which he did with the convertibility, and after, to dominate those who most wasted money, i.e. the provinces. . . . There the Bank acted through different means, mostly seeking to support reforms via reorganising the fiscal situation of provinces and privatising, as in the electricity case. . . . The rule was simple,

if provinces carried out fiscal reforms, the nation would open the door to international sources to finance investments, as simple as that . . .. There would be
financial support, but in exchange for reforms . . . Cavallo . . . had firm control,
and the institutions in Washington backed him.

(Anonymous interview 27/04/2004)

It is interesting to see that, beyond recognising the political control of the Ministry
of Economy over the process, the multilateral justification takes a pointedly different form, with a focus on two normative concepts – fragmentation and regulation –
derived from the theory of market incentives. Summarising the IDB's official
discourse, Millan and von der Fehr state:

It was reasoned that effective competition could be achieved if the scale of the
individual enterprise were reduced, thereby increasing the number of independent players. To the extent that direct competition could not be relied
upon, market competition could be facilitated indirectly by reducing or eliminating entry barriers . . .. In this way, markets would 'get the prices right',
thereby providing incentives for efficiency and optimal system expansion.

(2003: 3)

Millan, the chief energy economist at the Bank and initially a reluctant IDB officer
involved in the introduction of unregulated pure market reforms, extended this
view and deepened the official justification of the reforms in the early 1990s,
stating in 2006:

[R]eforms intended to strengthen scarce incentives for efficiency, mobilise
financial resources, and release the state from heavy finance charges, without
forgetting to attend to the needs of poorest . . . [P]romote the participation of the
private sector . . . while at the same time dealing with the restructuring of the sector, separating it vertically and horizontally . . .. An independent regulator would
protect investors from opportunist interventions of governments and would
defend interests of consumers from possible abuses from providers of service.

(2006: 35)

The separation, vertical and horizontal, of the sector was justified under the
technical consensus that there were two prerequisites for the creation of a competitive market. The first was to separate the potentially competitive (and therefore
attractive to investors) segments of the markets from those that constitute a natural
monopoly – the 'unbundling of the productive chain' (Bouille *et al.* 2001: 6). This
concept was tied to the idea that markets are driven by the rational expectations of
economic actors, an article of faith which is the starting point for all neoclassical
economic approaches (Foley 2002, 2003). The second prerequisite was the adoption of a regulatory principle that 'generators could not act as distributors or
participate in [energy] transmission simultaneously' (Bouille *et al.* 2001: 6; Herz
et al. 2005). In a nutshell, the greater the segmentation of the productive chain,

vertical and horizontal, the more possibilities of involving market players; hence segmentation and market regulation became the normative assumptions underlying the Bank's strategies for the region.

However, as important as the role of these normative concepts is in the defence and justification of privatisation, it is also the case that such concepts reflected, as does all such discourse, the scenario of the political action or the road map of the process. The IDB–government model, in defining what the reforms should and should not be, also mirrored the limits and the means of legitimisation of those actors within the scenario. It is important to bear in mind that, at the heart of the process, there was a central political element: the federal structure and its central actor, that is, the provinces within which the Bank was aligned with the national project. The IDB–government discourse and actions again appear complementary, as the provinces represented both obstacles in the way of a trade-oriented national energy market, and chief political actors for the Argentine *transformismo*. In this regard, Bastos' team is a paradigmatic example of the reforms. Created and backed as a parallel state by the government and IDB, Bastos' team had the financial autonomy to administer the Bank and national funds, the legal power to impose reforms, and the direct political support of the Menem administration through its regional political operators to push provinces into the process.

The IDB's justification, by invoking the claim of necessity, of fragmentation and competition as devices promoting economic efficiency, and the creation of an independent regulator separating the state from this activity, clearly went beyond a single justification and appeared, as well, to contribute to legitimising the political economy of the electric energy privatisation. Fragmentation of the sector and its regulation were perhaps unquestionable normative assumptions underlying the sectoral model. However, translated into reality, these might result in political outcomes contrary to those expected, or at least to those claimed by the official promotion.

Transforming and legitimising the electricity sector

Bastos' team was in charge of the design, main decisions and execution of the process of electricity privatisation. The working group and consultants, with the continuous support of the IDB and the WB, had the overarching 'objective to undertake preparations for the unbundling and sale of the federal electricity companies, and to work out the new legal and market framework for the sector' (Bouille *et al.* 2001: 11). The official discourse maintained that the power sector was close to collapse, a message which was amplified by the government's use of the mass media to present a dichotomy between the abyss and privatisation. An outstanding characteristic of the process was that no-one out of the IFI–government team took part in discussions regarding this strategic developmental issue, while many of those with the capacity to oppose privatisations were co-opted and/or compensated and assimilated within the convertibility strategy.

In January 1992, the Electricity Law was approved, establishing a legal structure for the restructuring and privatisation of the sector. That same year Argentina and the USA signed the Bilateral Investment Treaty, giving US companies the right to invest in the country under terms as favourable as those accorded to Argentine firms. The process featured a public auction, 'in which bidders were in a position to fix the desired level of profitability upon entry' (Bouille *et al.* 2001: 6). The WB, IDB and the private sector modified tariffs that were adjusted before the auction and prices were simply fixed with eight-year pricing contracts in place, in order to guarantee the profitability of companies and reduce private investment risk. Summing up the privatisation of the sector as whole, foreign and domestic companies paid US$330 million in cash and issued $1,160 billion in debt bonds to the Argentine state for the electricity enterprises. That means that the new owners paid (on average) for 22.13 per cent of the companies with real disbursements, while 77 per cent of the purchase was executed through bonds (APJAE 2006: 8).

The transformation of the sector consisted of vertical and horizontal unbundling and separation of the generation, transmission and distribution functions. The regulation criteria were based on prohibiting companies from taking responsibility for more than one function simultaneously, although there was no regulation regarding investment for expansion. The wholesale market would be regulated by competition under the surveillance of the Whole Electricity Market Management Company (CAMMESA). In turn, the retail market was divided between a regulated segment and a segment subject to competition among suppliers. The regulated segment guaranteed a monopoly to the distributor who was granted the concession. Concession contracts specified the obligation of the concession holders only in terms of the technical and commercial quality of services (EIA 1997: 65; Murillo 2001; Bouille *et al.* 2001: 6), although without any reference to expansion or to new investments in infrastructure and technology. Generating stations were divided into over twenty separate generating companies. Transmission was allocated to a new company, Transener. The profitable distribution line of the state SEGBA was divided into three companies, each with 99-year leases (EIA 1997).

The general supervision of the Argentine electricity industry passed into the hands of the National Electricity Regulator (ENRE is the Spanish acronym), the new private–public independent regulator. On the other hand, the federal government – the executive branch – retained the power to deal with all activities involving international and inter-provincial trade and electricity distribution within the Buenos Aires conurbation – 43 per cent of the country's demand for electricity. The responsibilities of the central administration also included the control of power generation channelled through the wholesale market and of the high-voltage electricity transmission network, while the provinces' role was reduced to the control of distribution within their jurisdictions. The maximum national enterprise of the sector remained in Comahue – the strategic subregion slightly to the south of the national centre close to the Chilean border – also under the influence of the national government. Comahue was strategic in the energy trade with Chile given its large reserves of gas and the introduction of new CCGT technology of gas-based electricity production. By the mid-1990s Comahue had become the central source supplying Chilean demand for energy (Bouille *et al.* 2001: 7; Littlechild and Skerk 2004).

The first three federal electricity companies to be privatised were Segba, Ayee and Hidronor, which produced 80 per cent of the nation's supply of electricity and had the greatest number of customers. In April 1992, part of Segba was sold to Chilean companies, and in May, the rest to US companies. In 1993, a new governmental decree was approved, removing any remaining restrictions on foreign investments, and permitting 100 per cent foreign ownership of Argentine firms and full repatriation of profits and capital to the home country of foreign investors. Figure 5.2 illustrates the initial stage of the restructuring of the sector and the main private beneficiaries of the reform. Strikingly, beyond the positive results in diversification of ownership in power generation and transmission, there was a concentration of electricity distribution, the major sources of income, in the hands of three companies – Edenor, Edesur, and Adelap.

The process of the privatisation of public electricity led by the WB, IDB–government complex established a clear role and division of labour between the two biggest participating multilateral banks. The WB, initially the strongest donor, remained in charge of in-house improvements to public companies and dealing with the national government, while the IDB's functions were wider and were addressed to the reorganisation of the national and provincial areas of control, taking an active role working in partnership with Bastos' team at provincial level and 'guaranteeing the conditions of the private sector' (Bouille *et al.* 2001; Littlechild and Skerk 2004).

In both cases, the WB and IDB's functions were concentrated on guaranteeing the conditions for the participation of the private sector. The IDB and World Bank

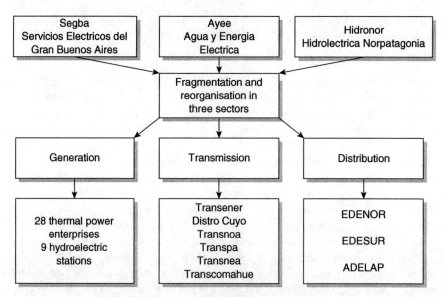

Figure 5.2 Argentina, federal electricity structure privatisation, 1991–94. (Based on reports from Energy Information Administration (EIA) 2006.)

played a central role in the inspiration and initial implementation of electricity privatisations, though later the World Bank would reduce substantially its leverage.
After this the IDB financed mainly the strengthening of law and regulations as
well as technical and business regional exchange. They supplied the sector with
funds for preparing public companies for the change and supported the government when it faced severe fiscal shortfalls as the new macroeconomic plan was
not yet consolidated. The IDB and World Bank were particularly concerned with
improving the operational and managerial performance of Segba, Hidronor and
AyEE. Funds were also allocated for the payment of consultants and support staff
under the Secretary of Energy in charge of the restructuring (Bouille *et al.* 2001).

Compensating provinces

In the early 1990s, the internationally and domestically endorsed convertibility
strategy and Menem's political powers had made it politically illogical or impossible for the provincial governments to stand outside the hegemonic process of
transformation and its policies. Indeed, to be a part of this was a political opportunity and a way of survival. Whether by necessity, conviction or coercion, all the
major provinces became targets of the strategy and sooner or later aligned themselves with the regime. The process of absorption and co-option of the provinces
constituted a central element in the success of the Argentine *transformismo* in the
first half of the 1990s (Eaton 2005: 89), and a central component of the electricity
privatisation. In these years, for a provincial governor to defy Menem's reform
entailed high political costs, whereas a less risky and more effective response for
the governors was to sign onto the pacts while simultaneously lobbying for side
payments or negotiate different national compensations.

Side payments were central instruments of compensation of the national administration. These included a wide range of instruments from National Treasury
funds to access to multilateral funds under the tight control of the executive branch
and the Ministry of Economy. The strategy lasted while the national government
enjoyed the support of the IFIs and while convertibility delivered macroeconomic
stability, creating favourable conditions to push for further reforms and compensate provinces adopting them. But multilateral financial assistance was tied to
reforms and once assistance was removed, later in the 1990s, the system showed
its intrinsic weakness, in particular after the dismantling of the federal structure.
These emergent weaknesses were the result of years of pro-market transformation
in public services, social welfare and national support to the provinces subordinated to the IFI–government partnership and good affairs.

Provinces were ambivalent about the privatisation, because 'provinces were
losing an important source of income and share of tax revenues, given the ongoing
federal fiscal reforms being carried out in compliance with international commitments to the IFIs' (cited by Eaton 2005: 99). Thus the transformation of the electricity sector required a major use of compensatory instruments to discipline the
provinces. Actions by the IDB at a provincial level to secure the financing of electricity privatisation represented merely a part of a much broader process of the

fiscal reorganisation of the provinces (619/OC-AR, IDB 1991d). The program was directed towards strengthening the institutional, financial and operational capabilities of the provincial entities administering public electricity services prior to privatisation (863/SF-AR, IDB 1991b). The inclusion and transformation of the federal structure was carried out through compensation strategies whereby pro-reform provinces were compensated financially and rewarded politically. Compensation became a key element in a strategy of co-opting and absorbing major provincial political spaces by the Argentine *transformismo* (Basualdo 2001; Etchemendy 2005; Murillo 2001; Levitsky 2003). This is clearly expressed by a former member of a provincial government:

> Provincially, everyone knew that there was only one way to survive politically. That was to accept the reforms, otherwise they over-ruled you with their national powers.... They give money and access to multilateral institutions in exchange for reforms. If you agreed with Bastos, you opened the door and got support.... He had the support of Cavallo, Menem and there were powerful national operators such as Bauza, Mazon and Manzano behind them, who could close or open access to strategic positions in the Justice Party, the Congress, and the state at national and provincial level. So you had to choose, to be with Rome or against Rome.
>
> (Anonymous interview 28/08/2004)

The use by the national government of compensation strategies in the electricity privatisation, as well as in other public areas, also involved the participation of its multilateral partners, who institutionalised these practices via international agreements with the national government. This can be seen in the official document agreed between the government and the IDB for the provincial reforms of 1991:

> One of the most important risks for the execution of the program [can be the] resistance of provincial governments in relation to institutional autonomy...
> To overcome the risk... the operation has been subordinated to the efforts in terms of reforms provincial governments carry out... [Thus] the participation of provincial entities is conditional... on [the fact] that the... province has been declared eligible for participating in the Program of Financial Reorganisation and Economic Development.
>
> (619/OC-AR, IDB 1991d: 1.12–1.13)

The objective of the above-mentioned IDB programme, coordinated with the WB and under the control of the national Ministry of Economy, was to execute national reforms and subordinate the provincial entities to the national authority. In official words, 'to transform the provincial governments from generators of public deficits to generators of surplus... [And to be eligible, provinces] must satisfy certain criteria agreed on with the Federal Government...' (ibid.).

The criteria for such agreements were the implementation of reforms demanded nationally and the acceptance of the compensatory measures. For instance,

619/OC-AR was above all a compensatory instrument in exchange for reforms, to which the IDB's investment programme for electricity sector reforms was tied and subordinated. The authority of the Bank and the Washington institutions is clearly defined in the Program of Financial Reorganisation and Economic Development (619/OC-AR), which states:

> [Once defined by the beneficiaries] the information provided by the CEU [will] be forwarded to the Bank's headquarters for approval. The review to be made in Washington will be done in coordination with the World Bank and a written record will be made of any aspects requiring special attention.
>
> (Ibid.: 3.60)

619/OC-AR (IDB 1991d) had three central components which reveal the political aims behind the IDB's support and its relationship with the national privatisation strategy. First was to strengthen the Central Execution Unit (CEU) in the Ministry of Economy. Second, to develop institutional capacities – more technical staff – involved in reforms at provincial level. Third, to maintain the functioning of existing public service systems (ibid.: 4). In sum, it seems fair to infer that the programme, rather than being a fiscal reform in itself, was oriented more towards developing, at a provincial level, parallel areas aligned with the national strategy as a way to facilitate reforms and avoid bureaucratic and political obstacles. The institutional design coupled to the strategy suggests the creation of a parallel state, comprising areas subordinated to the IFI–government complex, thus extending the convertibility regime's powers of co-option and assimilation.

Selecting private participation

One of the remarkable features of the multilateral capability of the framing options of development and justification of political projects has been the inherent flexibility of its instruments and discourses, enabling it to adjust to different pro-market strategies of globalisation. As well as designing and defining a model of fragmentation and regulation for the sector, the multilateral institutions and the IDB participated in the definition of selection criteria and supervised the process, and in so doing, they legitimised the assignation of contracts and selection of beneficiaries. Argentina, in this regard, represents a paradigmatic case in the region of how the WB and IDB legitimised a politically pre-defined plan for private participation and supported the government in co-opting opponents.

As seen in Chapter 4, Argentina's strategy of the globalisation of public utilities featured two elements. First was the favouring and generating of domestic–international partnerships to control strategic areas of development. The second was the replacement – at a federal and provincial level – of state monopolies with private enterprises, concentrating the most profitable parts in their hands. This process was driven by the IFI–government partnership, which created privileged positions and rents for important domestic and international strategic allies (Nochteff 1998; Schvarzer 1998; Murillo 2001; Schamis 1998). Selection and concentration of private companies and legitimisation of the transformation of the electricity sector appear as the chief outcomes of the Bank's role within the government–IFI partnership.

The electricity privatisation displayed a rather selective and politically oriented character in the assignment of contracts. An examination of the outcomes of the process reveals three key political directions. First is that the central actors in the process were the main actors in the hegemonic order initiated under the dictatorship, such as the major industry-based groups. Second, a significant portion of favoured foreign companies were of European and South American origin, encouraging the integration of domestic–regional and international, pro-reform coalitions. Finally, together with the private sector, mainstream union leaders were at the top of the list of beneficiaries (Kulfas 1999, 2001; Murillo 2001; Azpiazu and Basualdo 2002; Etchemendy 2005). This pattern of selectivity and transformation is not exclusive to the Argentine experience, but can be traced in the different and varied experiences of Chile, Colombia, Peru and Bolivia (EIA 1997). Established industrial players, foreign companies and dominant unions were the principal beneficiaries of the reform coalition both in the Argentine *transformismo* and in the rest of the region. They were favoured by government policies, were compensated with weak regulations and privileged conditions of access, and were actively involved in the drafting of legal frameworks jointly with the WB and IDB in order to foster private sector participation in the reforms (Etchemendy 2005).

Table 5.1 shows the participation of the major Argentine economic conglomerates in the process of privatisation of the sector. As can be seen from the table, Perez Companc, Techint, Astra (Repsol), CEI Citicorp Holdings, Loma Negra, and Soldati are present. In addition, it is worth noticing that all of these conglomerates had been traditional state suppliers and major debtors in the late 1970s and 1980s, and in all cases had participated in association with transnational companies and investment funds (Murillo 2001; Azpiazu and Basualdo 2002). All these companies used to monopolise the major activities in the domestic sector during the dictatorship and under the transformation in the 1990s, they came to take

Table 5.1 Participation of the major Argentine economic groups in the process of privatisation by sector in the 1990s[a]

Sector	Perez Companc	Techint	Astra (Repsol)	CEI Citicorp Holdings	Loma Negra	Soldati
Electricity (distribution)	×	×	×	×	×	
Electricity (generation)	×	×		×		×
Electricity (transport)	×					×

Source: Azpiazu and Basualdo (2002: 14).

Note
a Includes major participation of conglomerates in privatisation, although note that an important part of these were late transfers through mergers or acquisitions.

control of sectors alien to them, such as electricity and other sectors, and all these industry-based national groups were compensated for changes in the structure resulting from liberalisation process (Etchemendy 2005: 67).

The second orientation in the political economy of electricity privatisation is the evident concentration of private ownership in the hands of specific foreign companies, wherein the European and Chilean presence is significant. For instance, Electricité de France acquired 80 per cent of the new Edenor; Endesa, the powerful Spanish multinational, took over 72 per cent of Edesur. Enersis, the Chilean multinational group, acquired stakes in both Edenor and Edesur. And finally, AES Corporation, a US company, took majority control of Adelap. In most of the cases, the foreign beneficiaries emerged in association with powerful domestic conglomerates such as: the associations between Endesa and the domestic group Astra in control of Edenor; the alliance between Enersis, controlling 58 per cent, and Perez Companc in Edesur; and AES Corp and the Soldati group in the case of Adelap. It is noteworthy that European and Chilean multinationals acquired the companies which dominated national electricity distribution, while US firms took control only of minor companies in generation (EIA 1997; Verbitsky 2003). This is the case with AES, a company controlled by former senior officials in the US government and the World Bank. AES was criticised for its role in the California energy crisis of 2001 (Hall 2004, 2005).

Foreign companies and investors sought to invest in the privatisation of Argentina's electricity industry for strategic reasons. There were growth opportunities in which the Argentine sector had been forecast to expand at an average annual rate of 8 per cent during the period 1994–2000. Thus Argentina represented a rather promising scenario and laboratory for testing how to operate in a deregulated market, as the regional tendency showed. It was a golden opportunity in particular for those actively engaged in the control and expansion of the regional natural gas market. Investing in Argentina, therefore, was significant for those companies seeking to position themselves to subsequently expand into investment in the electricity industries of other countries in the region. Last but not least, the IFI–government partnership offered an optimal umbrella for those foreign investors able to enter into associations and deals with domestic business conglomerates (EIA 1997).

It is worth noticing, in the assignment of the contracts, the scant participation of US multinationals, given their much-trumpeted experience in the sector, in contrast to MNCs from Chile, Spain and France. The US participation was reduced to a set of small companies and mainly financial entities seeking to take financial positions (EIA 1997). This is explained by the fact that beyond its strong participation in the WB and IDB, the experienced US private sector was reluctant to acquire major shares. Actually, the presence of US firms appeared to be associated with the strategy of gaining financial position for further privatisations in the region and experience in the sector. Accordingly, it is important to notice the concentration of asset ownerships, wherein a great part of the public electricity sector passed into the hands of financial consortia, composed of several Argentine companies allied with international and regional groups. Hence the participation of US transnationals was concentrated in the financial administration of the assets but they soon abandoned their stakes in public energy enterprises (GAO 1996). In the words of a broker from Wall Street:

> The reason why the powerful US electricity companies did not participate in the process was rather simple. Public enterprises were cheap but there were too many commitments of the government with the Europeans... Everyone in Wall Street knew that it was a political deal of the Argentine government with the multilateral banks helping to make huge business... There is no other way of explaining the absence of US companies and the low profile and limited expertise of many companies acquiring the major Argentine electricity companies.
>
> (Anonymous interview 17/05/2004)

Despite the low barriers to participation in the privatisation and the value of Argentina's debt bonds – 70 per cent below nominal price – instead of widening private foreign participation, the process led to the assignment of contracts to actors with specific links to the national government's foreign allies, a fact that is better understood in the framework of Argentina's globalisation strategy. This is the case with the Spanish multinational Endesa, whose participation was not only strong in Argentina but also in Chile under the dictatorship. The involvement of Endesa in the reforms had been officially promoted by the Menem and Gonzalez administrations in the light of Argentina's renewed relations with Spain. For the Argentine administration, Spain was the gateway to vast European funds. The Argentine administration did not spare any effort in offering a profitable, safe and long-term beneficial relationship for Spanish investors and companies such as Endesa (Escude and Cisneros 2000; Gonzalez 2006).

Another important case is that of Electricité de France, which displays similar characteristics of acting under the umbrella of a state–state relationship, with governments being the major lobbying agents (Escude and Cisneros 2000). Finally, there is the case of Chilean multinational Enersis with stakes in Edenor and Edesur, whose participation in the Argentine privatisation cannot be precisely justified by its profile and expertise in the sector. Enersis represents a classical example of a company that is a state creation, which was aimed at reinforcing and broadening Pinochet's political coalition by rewarding supporters (Murillo 2001). The favoured participation of Enersis and its acquisitions in Argentina appear to be mainly related to the links between the coalitions of Pinochet's and Menem's supporters.

Co-opting and absorbing labour

The final element in the political economy of electricity privatisation was the co-option and absorption of the labour movement through compensatory measures implemented and legitimised by the government–IFI complex, in which the IDB also assumed a role. Compensatory policies were mainly addressed to the union leadership and to workers in the formal sector, generating a deep division between labour movement insiders and outsiders (Rock 2002). These strategies were facilitated by a bureaucratised union leadership, which, seeing that reforms were unavoidable, opted for the preservation of corporatist power and legitimised the electricity privatisation in exchange for corporatist, political and financial compensation. In Argentina, as in most parts of the region – especially Chile – control of pension funds and worker shareholdings represented the main policies designed to co-opt employees into the process and reduce trade union resistance (Basualdo 2001; Levitsky 2003; Etchemendy 2005; Hall 2005).

However, even though compensation was central in the privatisation, this was complemented and reinforced by other national reforms such as the fragmentation of the productive chain of the sector, and was also facilitated and accompanied by reforms aimed at deregulating the labour market. Collective bargaining agreements covering electricity workers were replaced by separate negotiations within each company. Union membership became divided and private companies were allowed to downsize more or less as much as they wanted, which in addition to layoffs and redundancies, were used to systematically reduce the workforce and labour costs and increase labour flexibility (Hall 2005). To achieve the transformation of labour in the electricity sector, the government–IFI complex, including the IDB, targeted the labour movement – and specially the union leadership – aiming to absorb it into the reformist coalition through four means identified by different scholars (Bouille *et al.* 2001; Hall 2005; APJAE 2006): protection of those union leaders aligned with the national strategy; granting unions privileged positions in the private pension fund market; granting workers a share of privatisation; and granting voluntary retirement.

The relation between the national administration and the labour unions finds its explanation within the framework of the consolidation of the Argentine *transformismo* and its absorption of the political system and the structural bases of major political forces such as the Justice Party (JP). Two decades of repression and the consolidation of bureaucracies within the unions, the discrediting of the electricity sector for its past, the economic transformations already underway and the lack of protection of labour rights – all these permitted the national administration, in a short space of time, to assimilate those aligned with reforms and isolate and marginalise those presenting any opposition. According to Murillo (2002), this must be understood in the context of unions seeking to protect their organisations at a time when their capacity to fight in the industrial and political arenas was shrinking. As the JP had been intensively deunionised, it was relatively easy for the Menem administration, compared with other reforms, to control and compensate the bureaucratic leaders of what once were the most combative unions in the country (Rock 1987; Brennan 1995).

In the early 1990s the government began to design and implement the privatisation of the pension system (see Chapter 6). In the course of this process the government, under pressure from union leaders, amended the bill and accepted the idea that labour unions could create their own pension funds and associate with private actors to compete in the market, as in the Chilean model. In the case of the electricity union, a handful of its leaders came to control FUTURA (Spanish acronym AFJPs), a private pension fund administrator. By 2000, most of the unions had sold their stakes in the pension market and only FUTURA retained some relation with its original union.

The electricity workers' union was also compensated during the privatisation with a percentage of the share stock of the new privatised companies, echoing Pinochet's experience of popular capitalism in which the IDB also played an active role. The Employee Share Ownership Program (ESOP), created by the national government, institutionalised the compensation of workers in the sector. The central characteristic of the national programme was that government and loyal union leaders negotiated the percentage of stocks to include in the ESOP, and the government consented to the unions taking over the programme in almost every privatised company, despite the absence of any mention of this in the decree (Etchemendy 2005; APJAE 2006).

Finally, the early and voluntary retirement of employees, co-financed by the IDB, WB and the national government, was addressed to downsizing even more the structure of the newly privatised companies. It is almost impossible to trace the extent to which the IDB took a role in this process, since the contributions of the Bank appear merely as support for macroeconomic reforms, although some interviewees agree that this role was rather significant. These payments, equivalent to the amount of salaries up to the date of retirement, were much higher than those due under normal circumstances. Most of the employees opting for the scheme used the funds to become self-employed and establish small businesses such as taxicabs, delivery services and small shops – many of which did not last beyond the short or medium term. Former employees soon came to swell the increasing ranks of the unemployed or to integrate themselves into the great mass of informal employment, both reflecting the regressive redistributive tendency accompanying the reforms (Frenkel and Gonzalez Rozada 2002). According to some specialists, the total number of people made redundant, retired or otherwise pushed out of the sector reached 350,000 by 1998 (Bouille *et al*. 2001: 24).

Conclusion

The purpose of the foregoing analysis was to understand the political economic function of the IDB within the process of liberalisation led by the Argentine *transformismo* in partnership with the IFIs during the 1990s. This investigation has shown that the Bank was not a major player but was nevertheless an active participant in the process of reforms acting under the guidelines and policies set by the IFI–government partnership. In addition, the investigation has attempted to comprehend the nature of the IDB's role and interventions by analysing a selected political economic event fundamental to the consolidation of the convertibility regime: namely, the case of debt swap for the privatisation of the electricity sector.

Returning to the central argument posed at the beginning of this study – that, tied to the policy framework of the Washington institutions–government partnership, the Bank played an important hegemonic political economic role in the country's electricity privatisation, this is graspable by examining the four chief elements inherent to its political economic function. It is now plausible to state that, to an important extent, the IDB, in its association with the WB and the government, worked by strengthening capital and supporting international and regional capitalist expansion in a clear alignment of its financial instruments, conditions and approaches with Washington institutions. Nonetheless, an important caveat needs to be noted in this regard, namely that the conclusion reached is strictly limited to the actions and partnership of the IDB with the Argentine government, and this cannot be extended to other regional cases given the specificities of the IDB's interventions in the region, as seen in Chapter 4. Briefly, this study has shown that the Bank's role and policies in a major member country were structurally conditioned by the hemispheric character of the institution and its participation within the global financial governance.

The first section was devoted entirely to the study of the Bank's ability to adapt and endorse global hegemonic tendencies in regional and domestic guidelines of development, and to the study of the outcomes of efforts to privatise electricity generation, transmission and distribution in the region. This study examined the institutional power of the IDB to construct a hegemonic option of development, a model of reforms for member countries. The chapter showed how the IDB adopted the neoliberal model of pro-market reforms for the electricity sector defined by the World Bank, adapted it and incorporated it into its regional strategy; and how this tendency was institutionally transformed, becoming the model for electricity in the region. The central finding of this chapter is that the Bank's capacity of adaptation was operationalised through two technically based institutional means, defined as the IDB's power to economise and depoliticise the issue and to transform this into a sort of rational and universal option of development.

The second section followed with an analysis of the Bank's capacity to introduce the pro-market option of development for electricity, and to limit the government's reform options in accordance with the hegemonic model and its agency, the IFI–government alliance. The study demonstrated how the Bank's ability to justify neoliberal reforms was expressed through its introduction and design of policy options derived from a particular reform model comprising the following essential elements: the critique of public ownership, the economic and financial nature of reforms, the fragmentation of the sector to provide the basis for market competition, the separation of the state from the sector and the creation of an independent regulator, and, wherever viable, the transference of the sector into private hands.

Following the analysis based on the premise that multilateral institutions frame ideological and policy options and, in so doing, circumscribe actions and legitimise scenarios, the third section analysed the translation of the market model into the political economy of the transformation of the electricity sector. This section focused upon an examination of the relationship between the model and the strategic orientation of the convertibility regime as chief elements of the hegemonic transformative character of the IDB–government association. Central to this study was the identification of two tactics inherent in the process of hegemonic transformation: co-option and absorption via legitimisation and compensation of the major actors involved – the provinces and the labour unions. Finally, the section explored the IDB's role in selecting and legitimising the participation of the domestic and international private sector. In this regard, it is important to notice that even though the Bank did not perform a direct role in the assignment of privatised assets, it did play a central role in the construction of its framework and in the legitimisation of the process.

6   The IDB's development role in the decline of the convertibility regime

Introduction

So far, this book has shown that the historical development function of the IDB has not been immutable. As part of the structure of the region's political economy, the Bank's role has changed throughout time as emerging structures and new problems of development have confronted the regional institution with new challenges. In the early 1990s, as seen in Chapter 4, the IDB's development role was dominated by the objective of global economic integration subordinated to global financial guidelines, with the Bank's financial and technical functions integrated and directed towards supporting, defending and legitimising state reform and the privatisation of public utilities. However, since the mid-1990s the dynamic between the evolution of global financial markets and the convertibility regime's decline prompted a new shift in the IDB's role, characterised by an increasing divorce between its technical and financial development functions. In this process, characterised by the increasing dominance of finance in the development mandate, the IDB's financial role of promoting global economic integration increasingly overshadowed its technical mandate of domestic development.

This fact is underlined by the Bank's official assessment as a stage wherein 'programming entered a period of confusion . . . and later, in the crisis period ceased to be consistent with the Bank's mission . . . at a time when there was no alternative but to provide liquidity' to the country (RE-299, IDB 2004a: iv). This opens a useful window on the political economic nature of the IDB, revealing the shift in its development function, from a legitimising role in the consolidation of the political economic project of the convertibility regime towards inconsistent and sometimes contradictory interventions aimed at supporting the regime's survival. The shift of the Bank's development function is defined by a divorce between the international and domestic interests that had cemented the pro-reform coalition during the consolidation of the convertibility regime. However, with the splintering of this coalition and the decline of the convertibility, the IDB faced the institutional challenge of both preserving international guidelines and foreign interest demands and at the same time, supporting the domestic pro-reform coalition, political and intellectual allies.

This chapter argues that the IDB's changing and inconsistent interventions during the period were the consequence of the financialisation of its development mandate. This fact must be explained by considering the larger context of the pressures imposed upon the IDB by two elemental forces: the growing power of global capital markets in the financing of development, and the rising tensions within, and steady decline of, the convertibility regime resulting from the structural reforms that the IDB had helped put into place. It is argued that this process led to a divorce between the different components at the core of the IDB's development function. This was manifested in the persistent and increasing contrast between those Bank interventions directed towards the promotion, support and legitimation of structural reforms, on the one hand, and the political stability necessary for the survival of the convertibility regime, on the other. These elements pulled in different directions, generating an inconsistency between the Bank's actions and its stated mission, aggravating the tension between the IDB as a bank and as an agent of development.

This chapter is arranged in three parts. First, it discusses the impact of the major shift towards market-based financing of development by multilateral development banks and the IDB. This process increased the power of financial actors in those countries pursuing market-oriented models of global integration, further increasing their external vulnerability, and triggered a redefinition of the IFIs' development role and in particular that of the IDB. Second, it analyses the Bank's role in the privatisation of social security, a key event impacting upon the IDB and associated with the emergence of tensions and contradictions which marked the decline of the convertibility regime. Third, it investigates the rising tensions and contradictions in the IDB's development mandate as global financial instability grew and the convertibility regime became more and more unsustainable. The final section highlights the lack of consistency in the IDB's policies for the country, even though it remained engaged – in contrast to the major IFIs, which distanced themselves from the country during the worse periods of the crisis.

Dominance of finance in the IDB's development mission

As shown in Chapter 4, the deep process of globalisation of Argentina's political economy in the 1990s obliged the leadership of the state–IFI partnership to co-opt, assimilate and integrate a vast array of forces, and to generate an international–domestic coalition without rupturing the existing domestic hegemonic structures expressed in the convertibility regime. This hegemonic *transformismo* defined, in turn, a complex and dynamic division of labour among the actors in this alliance, consolidating its hegemonic and transformative powers between 1989 and 1995. This scenario, as seen in preceding chapters, circumscribed the challenges of development and limited the IDB's ability to fulfil its development mandate, to shape a specific role based on its capacity to frame policy options, to deliver financial support, and to legitimise convertibility's political project in Argentina.

As seen in Chapter 3, from 1995 up to the crisis in 2001, a new set of international–domestic changes once again redefined the IFI–government relationship and the IDB's role within it. The process deepened the IDB's banking function *vis-à-vis* its development mission, the former becoming critical to the survival of the globalisation project and to continued capital expansion during the decay of convertibility. The IDB's role shifted in response to the growing tensions between the international financial architecture necessitating stability for capital expansion versus the domestic needs of development.

This shift, driven mainly by political factors, began in the mid-1990s with five major changes that shaped the political and economic landscape. One of these is what Drucker called the 'unseen revolution' (1976) of mass investment driven by OECD countries, with the financial explosion of pension and hedge funds and institutional investors – the new global power and source of development financing. Another factor was the Tequila crisis, an event directly related to the prevailing optimism in IFIs that, after liberalisation, capital flows would foster sustainable growth (Griffith-Jones 2003). However, it would be the same IFIs, which despite their over-optimism about financial globalisation, would succeed in halting the spill-over of the Tequila crisis via financial bail-outs. Another key event was the Argentine administration's decision to deepen structural reforms and global integration, as reflected in the replacement of Domingo Cavallo, the Economy Minister and ally of powerful industrial-based domestic groups, by Roque Fernandez, a Chicago-educated economist and friend of the financiers. Finally, the period of the Alliance administration, which pursued a politically and economically weak project and which was marked by its failure to sustain the convertibility regime, leading to its rupture with the major IFIs.

Financial rescue and countercyclical role

By 1995, the high ratio of short-term foreign debt to reserves triggered sudden outflows of capital from the so-called emergent economies, becoming a principal cause of 'contagion', the rapid spread of financial crises from one country to another. The first victims of the Tequila crisis in Argentina were the financial sector and social security, later spreading to the labour market (Rodrik and Velazco 1999; Radelet and Sachs 1988). Up to then, Argentina covered its fiscal deficit through revenue from privatisations, FDI, and – significantly – through portfolio investments, such that without major reforms and privatisations, the country could barely navigate a way through the crisis and sustain the convertibility regime (see Chapter 4).

The shared view in Buenos Aires and Washington was that the problem was essentially a temporary lack of liquidity (defined as a 'crisis of confidence') and that the solution demanded the deepening of reforms, particularly in public banking (to reduce moral hazard) and social security (to widen the sources of financing). This was the diagnosis of the Clinton administration, which was keen to support its regional ally, the Menem administration. In this regard, the Clinton government represented a continuity of the G.W. Bush's vision and initiatives for Latin America and helped to maintain and even increase the sense of friendship and alliance between the Argentina and the USA. However, the most important test of this relation came at the time of the Tequila crisis, when the Clinton administration reacted to the crisis by providing bilateral and multilateral support for the

Menem government. As a result, the Argentine government was firmly convinced that a long-term period of stable relations with the USA was beginning (Cavallo 2004b: 142–144).

However, not everyone shared this perspective, and within the IFIs, others understood it as the result of conjunctural international and regional conditions. The political nature of the IFIs' financial rescue of convertibility was expressed more crudely by an IDB staff member who was involved in the operation:

> If you have the Treasury Department pushing the Fund [IMF] and the World Bank, plus two of the major shareholders in the IDB supported by the European lenders all in favour of the rescue ... there is a rescue ... In 1995 reforms depended on the political survival of the Menem administration ... There was no room for any Mexico-style devaluation, the convertibility just had to be rescued.
>
> (Anonymous interview 05/2004)

As the evidence shows, the idea of a rescue was, over and above its economic importance, a political objective shared by the US and European governments and all the multilateral institutions, including the Bank. In addition, as mentioned earlier, 1995 was also an electoral year in Argentina; a defeat for the administration could have undermined convertibility, negatively impacting on US global interests. However, as Cavallo remarks, the Clinton administration reacted positively, playing a leading role in the bail-out of the country and exerting its leverage within the IFIs. Beyond that, it is worth noting that the bail-out was combined with specific conditions which sought to guarantee capital expansion, to avoid a Mexican way out (devaluation) and to promote a deep transformation of public banking and social security in order to deal with the vulnerability of convertibility to external conditions.

The Tequila crisis left several marks upon the country. The first was on the banking system, with 34 banks closed and many more expected to merge or be acquired by other institutions. The second was on social security reforms, as a result of a drop both in state revenues and the financing of the system. The final effect was a marked rise in unemployment. In March 1995, the Argentine government solicited an extension of existing agreements with the IMF, receiving US$5 billion in financial support from IFIs, providing the necessary liquidity to meet all its financial obligations, considered vital to re-establishing the confidence of investors in the convertibility regime. On the whole, the IDB contributed almost a quarter of the emergency loans: $750 million for the Program to Support Provincial Banks Privatisation (865/OC-AR, IDB 1995b), complemented by a $750 million loan from the World Bank, and $450 million to the Sector Program in Support of Fiscal Adjustment and Social Reform (871/OC-AR, IDB 1995c). As pointed out by a senior officer at the IDB:

> For an emergency loan you need the approval of the Fund [IMF], whose corporate governance is in the hands of the G-7 and where the IDB does not have

any power at all.... After the Tequila crisis, the international community understood that Argentina needed to consolidate the deepening of macroeconomic reforms, and of reforms to the banking sector and social security.

(Anonymous interview 05/2004)

The two above-mentioned loans and the opinion quoted express the essence of the countercyclical role played by IFIs and the lesser, although significant, position of the IDB in the plan for the financial rescue of the convertibility regime. The rescue operation added a new function to the IDB's role and greatly augmented its political power. While prioritising the provision of liquidity to sustain the convertibility regime, it demanded reforms specific to the banking sector and to social security.

In fact, these financial interventions largely represented a unique opportunity to introduce major structural reforms in the provincial and municipal banking system, aimed at reforming both the public provincial and financial sectors. The formula was simple: financing would be channelled to eligible provinces to cover short-term liquidity needs, until the provincial banks could be privatised. Consequently, financing would be used to pay back private deposits, repay short-term advances from the Argentine Central Bank, and cover costs associated with hiring advisors and consultants for privatisations (865/OC-AR, IDB 1995b: 1–2).

The official text agreed between the IDB and the government shows the dual nature of the new role given to and adopted by the IDB: to provide financial support for the deepening of reforms aimed at reinforcing the strategy for the globalisation of the country; to provide liquidity to the banking sector to allow the honouring of contracts founded on convertibility; and to reinforce investor confidence. With the bail-out in hand, the government reacted quickly, establishing the Trust Funds for provincial bank privatisation and private bank restructuring, this emergency loan being crucial for the rapid restoration of investor confidence.

However, these emergency loans and the Bank's countercyclical role were also understood as necessary for the promotion by the state of reforms to social expenditures, thus helping to reinforce macroeconomic stability. This was the role of the Sector Program in Support of Fiscal Adjustment and Social Reform (871/OC-AR, IDB 1995c), targeting, this time, core public spending on social programmes focusing on poor and vulnerable population groups (ibid.: 2). Accordingly, this programme focused on a set of specific targets: providing fast-disbursing resources for funding government measures aimed at maintaining the country's macroeconomic stability; ensuring adequate levels of public spending on programmes that delivered basic social services targeting low-income groups; and, in parallel, assisting in the implementation of major reforms in the social services, health, labour and education sectors (ibid.).

The programme referred to above is illustrative of the evolution of the IDB's changing function as it sought 'to maintain an integrated approach to social spending', keeping the link between macroeconomic reforms and focusing on minimising 'the social cost of fiscal adjustment' (ibid.: 1). The Sector Program in Support of Fiscal Adjustment and Social Reform (871/OC-AR, IDB 1995c) stands out among the IDB's interventions as it marked a growing comprehension and recognition by the Bank that the social impact of reforms were becoming more and more a central development issue for the convertibility regime. As claimed by a member of the IDB staff:

> [All] the problems of financial assistance were linked to more fiscal reforms... [And] without financial assistance there could be no reforms.... The model depended on external financing and was not generating its own financial resources or the trickledown effect as Cavallo always assumed.... But in 1995, Cavallo and the whole government started to realise that.
>
> (Anonymous interview 05/2004)

In summary, the international–domestic conditions within which the IDB's interventions took place led it to focus its institutional capabilities on lending as the central component of its development function, subordinating its role to buttressing fragile macroeconomic stability, conditional upon the execution of major reforms. In addition, the increasing financialisation of the IDB's development function appears to have been further impelled by domestic changes, with the Menem administration redefining its relations with the IFIs and MDBs as it entered a critical financial and political period in which its survival was at stake. However, even though the IDB's financial function became more and more subordinated to the policies of the major IFIs, the IDB, paradoxically, attempted to develop a separate and independent role by focusing more on development issues and political support.

Deepening banking mission

It is worth noting that even when global financial disruption prompted the emergence of the IDB's financial countercyclical role, it was a domestic change that deepened it. With the end of the consumption boom and economic growth in the third trimester of 1994, the community of international–domestic interests that had been consolidated by the convertibility regime began to break up, bringing new challenges and changes to the Argentine *transformismo* that impacted on the IDB's role. Menem's electoral victory and his success in dealing with the Tequila crisis, helped by the IFIs and the IDB, strengthened his administration and its conviction that it had a clear mandate to deepen reforms and global integration (Levitsky 2003: 182–183). However, with the erosion of union influence, the electoral defeat of the Bordonista coalition (the only opposition party by then), and the consolidation of the political order, the power and role of the provinces grew as these had largely contributed to these national successes. But with the recession badly affecting the regional economies and amid mounting unemployment, the federal political structure began to differentiate itself from the national administration, with growing demands on the government for large-scale compensation for those negatively affected by the reforms (ibid.: 177–181).

In 1995 the Menem administration therefore faced two strategic paradoxes which meant that it found itself in a race against time. The first was whether to strengthen its global or its domestic alliances; the second was how to reduce long-term external financial vulnerability without losing short-term external confidence. Its chosen option was to take more risks – increasing political leadership over development strategy in order to increase flexibility and improve its bargaining power, making this a priority over all technical considerations. The Menem administration's 'all or nothing' strategy impacted on the IDB's interventions in three ways (Palermo 1994: 322; Levitsky 2003): the replacement of Cavallo by the former president of Argentina's Central Bank, Roque Fernandez; the redefinition of relations with the IFIs; and the reformulation of the privatisation of social security. The significance of this strategic shift was recognised by Jose Bordon, currently Argentine ambassador to the United States and leader of the electoral coalition defeated in 1995, who stated:

> Already in 1994, I began to warn that it was desirable and necessary, by using the opportunity presented by the electoral victory, to use market mechanisms to gradually exit from convertibility. But certainly, multilateral organisations and industrialised countries backed the model ... they knew the risks .... The administration continued taking more risks, carrying out social reforms that worsened the already vulnerable economy.
>
> (Interview 05/2004)

Significantly, a similar opinion can be found in an official IDB country report (RE-299, IDB 2004a: iii, iv). In this assessment, the Office of Evaluation and Oversight of the Bank concluded that clearly none of the actors involved, domestically or internationally, wanted to take responsibility for changing the prevailing regime. The convertibility regime, in fact, had become untouchable in the country's development strategy; together with the rest of the IFIs the IDB assumed the sustainability of convertibility to be beyond question. The result of this was that the whole IFI–state complex was driven to focus on macroeconomic issues, which became dominant from 1996 onwards, reducing the IDB's interventions to its financial contribution and increasing the role of domestic politicians (RE-299, IDB 2004a: iii, iv).

Within this context, the government agency responsible for implementing the national strategy was deeply affected: Cavallo was sacked and replaced by the Chicago-educated economist Roque Fernandez, an economist more aligned with the orthodox approach of global governance and financial actors. The replacement of Cavallo was greeted as a victory for politicians leading the administration's technical staff controlling the reform process (Levitsky 2003). As a result of the politicisation of the strategy, the government reassigned the roles of the IFIs, assigning support for the national government and its debt obligations to the IMF and the WB, while the IDB was given the task of supporting domestic structural reforms, in particular at provincial level. The IDB's new role was summarised by a member of its staff as follows:

> Up to 1995, all interaction with Washington institutions was coordinated by Cavallo and his technical team at the Ministry of Economy ... In 1996 the

relations ... shifted from a technical to a political one ... For them, the IDB should play a counter-cyclical and a financial rescue role in the event of crisis and the natural source of financing should be the capital markets ... Then the process of reforms stops.

(Anonymous interview 05/2004)

This interpretation of the change is also confirmed by the IDB's official assessment, which regarded 'the increased participation by the *Jefatura de Gabinete* [Cabinet Chief] as a factor affecting the dialogue with the country', and was influenced by three elements. First, it considered that the Ministry of Economy 'assigned multilateral banks an anti-crisis role'. Second, it noted 'a lack of commitment regarding persevering with pending reforms'. Finally, it considered that the 'demand for investment initiatives lack[ed] a unified strategic institutional leadership' (OVE,-299, IDB 2004a: 14). These ideas were corroborated by the fact that both the Ministry of Interior and the Cabinet Chief were central components of the Menem administration, in political charge of building the domestic coalitions, and in particular the federal coalition, through either compensation or co-option (Levitsky 2003). In other words, the national government defined the Bank's role according to its domestic political strategy, which in turn politicised the IDB's development function.

The new division of labour among the IFIs, clearly defined by the government, removed the IDB from the debate around development issues confronting the convertibility regime. This is confirmed by a member of the IDB staff in the following statement:

All Washington institutions played a poor role ... or better to say a deplorable one – beginning with the Fund, which never made a real evaluation of the risks of convertibility. Their only concern was macroeconomic stability and the deepening of social reform in the midst of a drop in international prices, a fall in exports and mounting unemployment.

(Anonymous interview 05/2004)

Within this framework, the consequence was that the Bank lost its autonomy and delegated the responsibility for assessing the situation to the Fund, which also came to define the approval of sector operations and emergency loans with the IDB relegated to playing a secondary role. The shift is significant as it turned the discussion of development into a debate about macroeconomics and financial liquidity, involving only the government, the Fund and the industrialised countries (ibid.).

Legitimising contradictions

Given the course adopted by the government, the fiscal cost and the political control of the privatisation of the public pension system became particularly important for the Menem administration (Torres and Gerchunoff 1999; Weisbrot and Baker 2002; Rofman 2004; Basualdo 2003; Frenkel and Ros 2004). The pension system reform and its impact on the government's fiscal situation marked the beginning of a steady process of decline of the convertibility regime, reassigning a legitimising and financial role to the IDB which was particularly targeted towards state reform, to the detriment of its ability to frame policy and accomplish its development function. According to the Bank, during this stage 'programming entered into a period of confusion (1996–1998)', becoming a 'formal exercise, with very short-term validity, and which in any case was altered to accommodate the [government's] fiscal requirements' and its political demands (RE-299, IDB 2004a: iv). The importance of the period and of the social reform is succinctly expressed by Jose Bordon, who stated:

> The administration confused actions that aimed to maintain financial stability with a development programme, and the quality of institutions and policies with privatisation. They opted to privatise the pension system instead of flexibilising convertibility and assuming fiscal responsibility for avoiding more debt...In this scenario, the IDB's role was to support the government with loans and to legitimise its actions.
>
> (Interview 04/2004)

Beyond the perils for the convertibility regime of the timing of the social security reform, the dominant ideas or assumptions driving the process of privatisation would impact further upon its sustainability. Even though it is not plausible to assert that the reform was driven by the IFIs, there is no doubt that the criteria the Bank followed were aligned with the universal model which MDBs actively participated in defining (Torres and Gerchunoff 1999; Frenkel and Ros 2004; Rofman 2004; Barrientos 2004; Uthoff 2006). Accordingly, despite adapting to the political needs of the convertibility regime, the model of reforms embodied structural contradictions. These were, first of all, the assumption that Argentina, as with other countries in the region, could attract FDI through a developed capital market regardless of the instability and volatility introduced by this reform, in particular its dependence on short-term capital (Uthoff 2006). Second, Argentina was still a middle-income country, notwithstanding the vast sectors of the population who had fallen below the poverty line and the increase in unemployment which negatively impacted on contributions and coverage (Frenkel and Ros 2004). Third, it is the institutional weaknesses of the country's capacity to regulate and supervise a new set of financial actors and the direction of their investments (Torres and Gerchunoff 1999).

Sponsored by the WB and the IDB, the government initiated the analysis and the design of public pension reform in 1991, although it was not until 1993 that the government signed a commitment with the IMF to propel the reform through the Congress. The process had two clearly defined stages and it was only in the second stage that the IDB came onto the scene with its function of financially supporting and legitimising reforms determined by the national administration acting at a federal level. The first period was driven by Cavallo, who organised a team of experts recruited from the political system with the clear aim of adapting the Chilean model of electricity privatisation (in this, he was supported by the IMF, the WB and the IDB). The second stage was dominated by the reformulation of the proposal to take account of financial concerns and the political struggle between the government and labour unions and with the provinces. Despite the attempts to reorganise welfare according to liberal principles, the final outcome was the creation of a mixed system composed of public distributional pillars and a private sector managing individual capitalisation. In a nutshell, the outcome was a hybrid, a compromise, which rather than improving the old system, aggravated it by adding new financial problems which demanded major financial help from the IFIs and the IDB (Torres and Gerchunoff 1999; Rofman 2004; Barrientos 2004).

The reforms, as in the case of the privatisations, were pushed by the WB and the IDB, coordinated with the government, and financed through a transfer of income from state–labour structures to domestic–international financial actors. The two institutions contributed US$640 million, exhibiting a clear division of labour in which the WB supported government reforms at a national level and the IDB at a provincial level in order to transfer the provincial social security system to the national sphere. Signed with the Ministry of Economic Affairs and Public Works (MEyOSP) and the National Security Administration (ANSeS), the IDB's Provincial Social Security Sector Reform Program (961/OC-AR, IDB 1996) was based on contributions of $320 million from the IDB and $320 million from the World Bank.

This was a strategic programme given the fragile financial conditions of the country and the rapid deterioration of its social conditions. The central idea was that the programme would help to control provincial fiscal imbalances, considered part of the Argentine fiscal problem, and to consolidate a market-based social security system. The formula was that, pushed by private savings and investment with state and IFI support, employees would *en masse* join the new system of pension fund administrators (AFJPs). On the other hand, the Bank's financial con-tribution would help to balance provincial budgets by lessening the significance of the impact on provincial finances of deficits run by provincial retirement funds (CPPs). In addition, the IDB programme would support the strengthening of ANSeS administration and controls to prevent fraud and evasion within the conso-lidated system (961/OC-AR, IDB 1996). Assessing the Bank's role in this reform, a member of the IDB staff claimed:

> The pension reform is the first important case of how the relation between the Bank and the country became politicised.... The Bank both was and was not a participant, since it supported the policy formulation but didn't intervene in it...[The] performance of the IDB in the reform was mediocre.... No con-trol, no monitoring, no investigation into whether the main assumptions and estimates were correct.
>
> (Anonymous interview 05/2004)

In 1993, official Ministry of Economy projections foresaw a massive growth in contributions to the new system – based on the level of employment in each sector – well beyond what turned out in reality. It supposed an unemployment rate of 5 per cent and a moderate rate of evasion among autonomous workers and industry and services. Accordingly, after a short period draining its financing, the system was expected to reach fiscal equilibrium by 2002, but the fiscal deficit of the privatised provisional system was greater than had been calculated. Briefly, the liberalisation of welfare represented an extra cost to the public accounts, having a deep impact on an already unequal scheme of federal coparticipation and worsening Argentina's fiscal balance even more (Lousteau 2003). Speaking about the subject, an economist of the IDB staff stated:

> The fact that the Bank rests on its political management is an advantage... because in cases like this, the Bank does not have to take great financial risks.... The risk is political.... Technically, it is clear that the risk of the reforms were evident and seen by many, but there was a political decision to continue regardless, where the Fund drove the dynamic between the multilateral banks and the country.
>
> (Anonymous interview 05/2004)

As is corroborated by different specialists (Rodrik 2003; Frenkel and Ros 2004; Quijano 2004) and as we saw in Chapter 4, pension reform detonated the sharp decline of the convertibility regime. Consulted about the role of fiscal spending in this process, Eugenio Diaz Bonilla, Executive Director for Argentina and Haiti at the IDB, presents a different panorama, claiming that:

> At the root of the crisis there was no overspending; Argentine public spending was more or less stable as a percentage of GDP throughout the period. What began to rise were interest rates on the debt, alongside a drop in revenues with massive transfers to the financial sector.... The social reform was carried out on the basis of misleading assumptions, blaming everything on fiscal spending and in particular the provinces and unions.
>
> (Interview 05/ 2004)

It is worth noting that the transfer of public sources to AFJPs also had a significant impact on provincial fiscal accounts, as deficits resulting from privatisation in social security were also financed by deductions from provincial coparticipation, accumulating in the period to US$20 billion. Therefore, transfers to the private sector – AFJPs – not only affected national finances but also provincial finances, in a period of deep economic recession and growing unemployment. For the period 1995–2001, the fiscal deficit of the country represented 1.8 per cent of GDP, and that of the provinces 1.1 per cent of GDP. Without the transition costs and transfers to the private sector, these deficits would have been 1.0 per cent and zero for the country and the provinces respectively.

Losers and winners in the privatisation of the pension system

Despite concerted financial, fiscal and multilateral efforts to create incentives for the private sector, economic revival and the generation of employment did not happen. Instead, unemployment escalated and with it the number of workers in the informal sector, further worsening the financial predicament of the new pension system (Weisbrot and Baker 2002; Frenkel and Ros 2004; Quijano 2004). The real impact at a political and economic level was that the major economic beneficiaries of the social reform were the financial actors and a handful of loyal labour union leaders, whose interests were aligned with the reforms being promoted by the IFIs. While it cannot be argued that the IDB role drove the process, it is important to recognise that the Bank, in prioritising state reform to benefit investor confidence, in setting conditions for it and in financing it, legitimated a government strategy which was trapped by the contradictions that from then on emerged in the political economic scenario of the convertibility regime. As Jose Bordon stated:

> The Bank had to adjust itself to the political demands and fashionable ideas dominating the Washington scene ... as in the case of the social security reform .... [B]ecause the Bank was tied to the international financial structure ... [So] rather than carry out a role of investment and development, the Bank became a tool to finance financial stability, legitimising a regime in decay to the detriment of domestic interests.

(Interview 05/2004)

The pension reform, which consolidated the internationalisation of the financial system, redefined the political and economic landscape and, in addition, became a strategic source of finance for the convertibility. The growing power and presence of this new dimension of the pro-market coalition led to increasing differentiation of interests within the powerful industrial sector, a process reflected in the emergence, by the end of the 1990s, of opposing alternatives to convertibility (see Chapter 4).

Table 6.1 shows the list of top shareholders in the five largest Argentine AFJPs up to September 1998. As can be seen, the biggest AFJP was Siembra, owned by

Table 6.1 Top shareholders in the five largest Argentine AFJPs, September 1998

AFJP[a]	Largest owner	Percentage of equity	Second-largest owner	Percentage of equity
Siembra	Grupo Siembra	99.0	Citibank–US	1.0
Previnter	Bank of Boston AIG	90.0	Bansud	10.0
Consolidar	Banco Frances	53.9	Banco de Galicia	26.9
Origenes	Banco Provincia Buenos Aires	40.7	BSCH–Spain	39.8
Maxima	HSBC Banco Roberts	17.0	Banco Quilmes	17.0

Sources: Based on Argentine Government, Superintendence of AFJPs and Salomon Smith Barney (1998).

Note
a   Administratoras de Fondos de Jubilaciones y Pensiones.

Citibank with an important participation by the labour unions of the telecommunications, oil and gas industries. The second largest AFJP was Previnter, 90 per cent owned by the Bank of Boston and also associated with the same labour unions although with different financial associates. Clearly, Argentina's pro-regime labour unions became significant participants in the ownership of the AFJPs, and also of a broad range of financial firms including worker resorts and health care centres. Banks, insurers, labour unions and health-management companies formed most of the AFJPs, in which the IDB played an active role, following the failure of the WB–Cavallo–Schulthes project.

The significant participation of labour unions alongside other financial actors in the control and administration of the AFJPs led the IDB in 1999 to fund a joint Argentine/Chilean project to strengthen labour union participation and expand the experience to other labour organisations. The AFJP Future, for instance, came into the hands of the electricity labour union after the privatisation of the sector, while in 2002 municipal employers and social security workers unions came to control smaller pension administrations. The AFJP Claridad remained largely under the control of construction and sanitation workers. The four largest AFJPs – Consolidar, Maxima, Siembra, and Origenes – account for 69 per cent and are majority-owned by foreign companies – mainly Spanish, North American, German, Italian and British financial firms. The pattern of industry concentration in Argentina is remarkable. In 1994, there were 26 funds, falling to 18 at the beginning of 1998 and 15 after later mergers.

The privatisation of social security, and the accompanying set of economic measures promoted by the IFI and government to encourage growth, clearly constituted a major event whose first result was to benefit the domestic economic conglomerates. But they were also significant since they tied the participation of financial actors to fiscal performance and the national debt. According to the IDB '[t]he economy not only became heavily dependent upon capital flows, but was also sustained by debt' (RE-299, IDB 2004a: 4). This is evident in both the foreign participation and the investment focus of the AFJPs. Table 6.2 presents the allocation of AFJP assets by area of investment. As can be seen from the table, the

Table 6.2 AFJP asset allocation of private pension funds in Argentina (1994–98) (percentage)

	1994	1995	1996	1997	1998
Government securities	50	53	53	43	50
Mortgage bonds	0	0	0	0	0
Time deposits	28	25	14	24	21
Shares	2	6	19	21	18
Investment funds	5	2	2	5	7
Corporate bonds	6	9	8	3	3
Foreign securities	0	1	0	0	1

Source: Based on Superintendence of AFJPs, Argentine Government.

private domestic sector was not the main target for AFJP investments; instead it was government debt and foreign corporate equities. Very little was allocated to mortgages, real estate, or local development and venture capital.

Losing the hegemonic path

Between 1996 and 1998, the inconsistent role played by the IDB reflected the sharp decline of a model based on indebtedness and facing escalating external and domestic constraints. This process led the regional institution to act more as a bank than as a financial development institution, and also to assuming a much more pronounced political character. Within this framework, with the major IFIs demanding a major deepening of reforms and the convertibility regime subordinating its role to short-term political aims, the Bank's interventions rapidly began to lose the integral character that they had displayed up to the mid-1990s. The IDB began to perform two separate roles within the IDB–IFI complex: one was to stress macroeconomic stability through massive injections of funds in exchange for major reform commitments to guarantee investment confidence; the other was to support the political stability of the regime via increasing its investments and technical assistance. The increasing tension between the quest for macroeconomic stability and major reforms on the one hand, and the quest for political stability in the context of greater social unrest on the other, were the central elements giving rise to the inconsistencies of the IDB's role during this period.

As a result, by 1998, the IDB's role seemed to drift somewhere between the IMF–WB and the government, and became more subject to and dependent upon the political factors driving the convertibility regime. According to the official technical assessment '[t]he Bank's reaction' to the political economic changes was 'in the form of a positive response to the emergencies.... However, the inherent risks that this behaviour would have on future developments in the country's financial situation... were not assessed... [L]ending instruments were not well integrated' (RE-299, IDB 2004a: v). Providing a political perspective on this, a member of the IDB staff claimed:

> [R]egion's members have more autonomy over investments than sectoral loans, where lenders have a greater degree of control... Up to 1996, the dynamic between investment for development and reforms was integrated but since 1996, these began to diverge, reflecting the differing changes and perspectives of the players.
>
> (Anonymous interview 05/2004)

It is noticeable that in comparing the assignations of the Bank's sector and investment loans during the period, sector loans or support for structural reforms and macroeconomic stability surpass by a long way the IDB's investments in the country (US\$4,020 billion to \$1,423 billion – see Table 6.3 in the next section). These rough data provide a quantitative indication of the magnitude of the financialisation of the IDB's role, during a period characterised by an increasing dissociation

Table 6.3 IDB sector loans (PBLs) and investment loans by stage, 1991–2001 (US$ billions)

	Regime consolidation (1991–94)	Rising tensions (1995–98)	Regime decline and crisis (1999–2001)
Sector loans (subject to IFI governance)	1,375	4,020	1,400
Investment loans (subject to IDB–government association)	1,859	1,423	364
TOTAL:	*3,234*	*5,443*	*1,764*

Source: Based on IDB/OVE, RE-299 (IDB 2004a).

between structural reform and investment policy, with sector loans predominating over investment support. This fact was the outcome of the rescue packages assembled by the IFIs during the Tequila, Asian and Russian crises, and also revealed the priority of ensuring the country's financial stability over any other function.

This shows the dynamics underlying the increasing financialisation of the IDB's role, and the increasing inconsistency, alluded to in the official assessment, between sector loans (PBLs) and investment loans. Actually, as the Bank officially recognised,

> [a]fter 1996, the operations approved did not correspond to those programmed.... This led to a considerable portion of the resources not being used for the originally intended purposes ... [as a result] of a failure to take account of the heterogeneity in institutions at the sub-national level.
>
> (RE-299, IDB 2004a: vi)

Accordingly, sector loans presented positive results 'when they were tied to structural reforms and when the country was committed to these reforms. In contrast, outcomes fell short of expectations when the liquidity goal took precedence and the country was in a weak economic situation' (ibid.: ix). A similar situation, although somewhat more positive, is to be found with investment for development, wherein the actions achieved poor results in finance and mixed results in terms of labour market reforms.

The evolution of the IDB's promotion of structural reforms and its provision of investment during this period reflects the crucial role played by the IFIs in providing financial resources necessary for sustaining the financing of convertibility (see Chapter 4). This tendency appears to have been accompanied by a continued reorientation in the IDB's interventions towards promoting ever-deeper structural reforms, in line with the SGRs' ruling economic orthodoxy which in this period focused on financial liberalisation and labour flexibility (see Chapters 3 and 4). Examples of these guidelines include the privatisation of provincial banks (865/OC-AR, IDB 1995b), labour market deregulation (871/OC-AR, IDB 1995c), privatisation of provincial pension funds (961/OC-AR, IDB 1996), and emergency food aid (1118/OC-AR, IDB 1998d).

These actions, in turn, with the exception of the privatisation of provincial banks, were characterised by a deviation from the aims agreed between IFIs and the government, and a reorientation, in not a few cases, towards covering fiscal financial needs in the face of mounting restrictions on access to international capital markets resulting from the wave of financial crises (RE-299, IDB 2004a: 30, 35). On the other hand, investment loans subject to the IDB–government partnership began to steadily decrease in size during this period, revealing inconsistencies between their various objectives.

This was true, for instance, in the case of 'institutional strengthening', a component present in the majority of the Bank's programs but which delivered 'dubious benefits' (RE-299, IDB 2004a: 12). This component has been criticised for developing parallel structures to those of state bureaucracies, weakening their political position in order to facilitate reforms (Basualdo 2001). However, this component had rather positive results when applied in sectors with weak institutional structures, in particular in the health and municipal social areas (1164/OC-AR, IDB 1998e; 1111/OC-AR, IDB 1998c). A similar tendency can be observed in those actions addressed to promoting labour market flexibility, wherein it is not possible to see an empirical correlation between reforms and poverty alleviation (RE-299, IDB 2004a: 12). The technical considerations justifying this are clear in the following statement:

> Between 1996 and 1998 the bank started to develop an independent portfolio, channelling investments in a more improvised manner . . . . Most of disbursements were from non-programmed projects driven by the country fiscal problem . . . [T]he Bank opted for concentrating on deepening and consolidating the structural reforms and on making extensive reforms to the provinces and municipalities, mistakenly ignoring the growing indebtedness.
>
> (Anonymous interview 05/2004)

The inconsistency in IDB programming is widely present in the opinion obtained from interviews with members of the IDB's technical staff. Accordingly, the social agenda underlying these programmes was inconsistent with the nature of the real problems of Argentina's political economy. Programmes addressing development and structural reforms ceased, and attention came to be focused on social symptoms of change through programmes fragmentarily oriented to women, youth and indigenous groups. In this regard, the technical interpretation is that the IDB, rather than promoting structural reforms, began to finance poverty alleviation, diverting the IDB's real development mission (Anonymous interview 05/2004).

In 1997, the Argentine government assigned primary responsibility to the Cabinet Office (*Jefatura de Gabinete*) for conducting negotiations with the IDB, and designated the Ministry of Economics as the executor of its loans. During this period a total of eleven programmes were approved that were not planned at the time of the discussions with the Bank on its programme for the country. Seven of these programmes were operations with the private sector and other projects including regional finances, multisector loans and emergency job creation programmes. Most of these changes were prompted by the huge external financial crises of 1997 and 1998 in Asia and Russia (RE-246, IDB 2001b: 8), crises which triggered a new period in the IDB's role in the country. In addition, as part of the unfolding of a more independent role for the IFIs, the IDB began to make major use of technical instruments in order to strengthen its support for the country in areas of social policy. After 1996 the IDB organised seventeen studies, advisory services and conferences linked to the Bank's role in the country, whereas eight were OVE evaluations (RE-299, IDB 2004a: 16). The Bank published its first study on poverty and development in 1997, providing the Bank with a comprehensive picture of what was happening in the country.

The priorities set out in the IDB's country strategy were the allocation of 30 per cent of loans to reform of the state, 20 per cent to enhancing competitiveness in the private sector and 30 per cent for fighting poverty and raising living standards. However, given the escalating financial problems and the needs of the convertibility regime, the allocation of the Bank's support diverged markedly from what had been agreed with the country. Thus, state reform concentrated 55 per cent of the approved loans (nearly twice the programmed funding), while the private sector received only 15 per cent and poverty alleviation 30 per cent. The resulting diversion of the loans from the emergency Special Programme of Structural Adjustment and Strengthening of the Banking Sector amounted to US\$2.5 billion (RE-246, IDB 2001b: 8). Beyond that, and following on from its more independent agenda for the country, the IDB was notably able to propel fourteen projects in social areas, including social infrastructure: disadvantaged groups (1021/OC-AR, IDB 1997b), employability (1031/OC-AR, IDB 1997c), attention to at-risk children and adolescents (1111/OC-AR, IDB 1998c), of which 68 per cent was executed at the provincial level.

More than a bank

The dynamic of the IDB's role in Argentina in the period 1998–2001 shows the exhaustion of its financial function as an agent of transformation in support of global capital integration, and the rise of its political function amid escalating contradictions between global and domestic interests. The process was characterised by growing tensions between the international financial community's increasing reluctance to provide more liquidity to the model without major reforms or dollarisation to guarantee investor confidence, and restive domestic forces – demanding a devaluation of the national currency – which the fragmented and clientelistic political system was increasingly unable to contain. In turn, this dynamic became amplified by the dissolution of the domestic pro-reform coalition, accompanied by a rapid decomposition of the political system and the absence of a clear strategy and effective management from the new government faced by imminent crisis. The result was a split in the coalition supporting the convertibility regime as the different interests of its members led them to advance rival alternatives to replace the system. On the basis of the fieldwork, it has been shown that the Bank did not remain neutral within this process, but at the same time it did not abandon its political commitment to the country.

The process started with the IDB's shift from reducing its provision of liquidity towards exercising an increasingly political function as it sought to avert a complete rupture between the country and the major IFIs. Analysis of this process reveals the IDB's shift towards a role more and more involving its *political* body or regional corporate governance, since by 1998 there was a widespread international perception that the time of convertibility was running out (Meltzer 2004). After the emergency loan of 1998, financial support by the Bank, together with that of the major IFIs, experienced a sharp decline.

Table 6.3 presents a summary of the major net flows of the Bank to the country, in the form of investments and PBLs including emergency loans. As the table shows, between 1995 and 1998 there was a spike in financial support, reaching US$4 billion, signalling the financialisation of the IDB's role. The last period, 1999–2001, during which all the country's variables worsened, the IDB's financial support abruptly fell to $1.4 billion. The plunge in financial support accompanied the steady withdrawal of capital markets from the country and increasing disagreement between the IFIs and the government over how to implement major reforms demanded by the IFIs and the industrialised countries (see Chapter 4).

A member of the Bank's staff offered this interpretation of the decline in financial support:

> The process of reforms had already stopped in 1996, and nobody in the country was able to force through the necessary reforms or dismantle the convertibility…. Then the Asian and Russian crises came and country risk soared, producing a capital outflow. Finally, the Brazilian devaluation came as a body-blow, putting the country out of the game of capital markets.
>
> (Anonymous interview 05/2004)

Interpretation of the period 1998–2001 is still a matter of controversy. On the basis of the fieldwork, it has been shown that perceptions inside and outside the Bank are not uniform regarding the role played by the IDB. This is aggravated by the absence of official information, indeed the technical assessment stated, '[i]t has not been possible to verify the existence of documentation either consistently analyzing the crisis, or of alternative proposals discussed or agreed with the country' (RE-299, IDB 2001a: 9).

The IDB's decision to stand by the new administration despite the widespread perception of an imminent change in, or collapse of, the convertibility regime, presents lights and shadows in its relation with the country regarding its developmental nature and its role in the process. On the basis of the fieldwork, it is possible to identify three different, and perhaps complementary, opinions concerning the rationale of this decision, which highlights in each case a portion of the IDB's complex and mixed political nature.

The first is the technical interpretation, which is represented by the technical staff and with major ties to the hemispheric network consensus identified in Chapter 3. This stratum stresses the subordination of the IDB's development function to the promotion of reforms necessary for global economic integration of member countries under the IFIs' guidelines. This view highlights the unsuccessful countercyclical role of the IDB's financial intervention as a result of the inconsistency between a stable and predictable country development programme and financing during the financial emergency. Convertibility was inconsistent with the policies necessary for resolving the fiscal problem of the country, since the model was based on indebtedness and strongly dependent on external financing. This fact, in turn, was aggravated by the Bank's management of relations with the country, since the IDB did not assess properly the risks involved and instead prioritised the political objectives of the major IFIs over the technical consistency of its development function (several interviews 05/2004).

Concurring with and illustrating this interpretation, the IDB's technical assessment of the 1998–2001 period states:

> In this context, both the IDB and the World Bank supported the Fund's role of lender of last resort... And from that moment on, both banks subordinated much of their development-support role to the need to provide liquidity. After 1998, the chosen strategy was based on increased lending to maintain cash flows and thus guarantee the repayment of debts.
>
> (RE-299, IDB 2004a: 9)

However, this interpretation contrasts with the multilateral opinion of those who highlight more the pertinence of the Bank to the international financial architecture and its deficiencies. This perspective is expressed by the stratum of officials and economists bound to the IDB's regional operations and its dealings with member countries in the region; their opinions are more influenced by the political dynamics of borrower member countries. They consider that the central element in the limited impact of the IDB's financial intervention is defined by two central facts. First, given the size of Argentina, the international financial architecture did not measure up to the crisis. Second, domestic political instability reduced and limited the government's capacity to drive any change in favour of major reforms. Within this framework, the stance of the IDB was fair and it correctly stood by the government in order to counteract the effects of the international and domestic crisis in a coordinated fashion with the international financial architecture and with the support of the G7. From this perspective, both the IDB and the major IFIs came to realise that the convertibility was exhausted only after the Brazilian crisis but they remained confident that the government would introduce major fiscal reforms in order to avert the crisis (Anonymous interview 05/2004).

The third perspective shows the realpolitik approach expressed by its board and country officials at the core of the Bank's corporate governance. This perspective revolves around the role of the states in the bargaining process taking place within the decision making structure of the IDB. Its view evidences a clear distance from the traditional technical and conceptual discussions about the IDB's role in development and is determined by a realistic interpretation of the everyday political construction development. Accordingly, they stress that facts must be understood in the light of the directions of the US and European policies towards Argentina given its fragile economic and political condition (the US position, influenced by the Meltzer debate in Washington, finally prevailed). Reflecting this dominant political approach inside the institution, a former IDB official summarised:

> They and the Treasury Department decided what should be done with the emergency funds.... So long as the country worked with them, money was made available; and when it did, the IDB got on board.... The Bank is politically subject to them... [And] they saw that support for the country was ending up in private banks, which were making risk-free investments so the solution was to stop the financial help.

> (Anonymous interview 05/2004)

Last financial help

The financial function of the IDB reached its apogee in 1998, when the IDB approved a major emergency loan for the country, the largest loan in the Bank's history. Once again, this event featured the intervention of the major IFIs in support of convertibility, battered by international financial turbulence and by widespread social discontent with reforms, amid a complicated national electoral confrontation and an increasing debate about whether and how to abandon convertibility. The financial rescue granted to the Menem administration, for US$2.5 billion (1163/OC-AR, IDB 1998d) was co-financed by the World Bank and coordinated between the IMF and the Argentine government 'to deal with the consequences of the virtual cessation of capital inflows', and was driven by the necessity to maintain the confidence of capital markets (RE-246, IDB 2001b). The loan had an amortisation period of five years, a three-year grace period, and an interest rate of LIBOR plus 400 basis points, and included 112 undisclosed conditions, designed to discourage misuse of the loan and to promote reforms (1163/OC-AR, IDB 1998d; RE-299, IDB 2004a). In the opinion of an IDB staff member:

> The rescue package of 1998 was... accorded between the Fund and the government... on the basis of false assumptions. [Its authors] thought that the same formula that was applied during the Tequila crisis would work again.... That was a terrible mistake... because neither the size of the financial problem nor the weakened political capacity of the government would permit a good intervention.

> (Anonymous interview 05/2004)

The international crisis produced an increase in country risk and in interest rates, which translated into a sharp decline in economic activity, with a direct impact on employment and social conditions. During 1997 and 1998, Argentina's external debt increased by US$17 billion, its biggest jump since 1995, aggravating the country's fiscal burden, owing in particular to the need to finance pension system reform (see Chapter 4).

The outcome of this intervention has given rise to divergent interpretations of the relevance, and impact on development, of the IDB's financial function and capacities. In this regard, the evidence from the fieldwork shows a stark contrast and difference between the opinions of the IDB's technical staff, members of staff involved in country operations, and top officials or members of the board. Thus, IDB staff members interviewed considered 'the financial rescue of 1998 made things worse as the government was no longer committed to carrying out reforms to change the system' (Anonymous interview 05/2004). The rationale of this position is that the Argentine administration cooled its relation with the Bank and at the same time opted for an erroneous course of action. The Alliance administration gave the Bank the same countercyclical role as in 1995 and the Bank stood politically by the government despite the technical inconsistencies of its economic policy. Whether the IDB carried out this strategy out of political commitment to the country or for their own financial benefit is, according to the staff members, a matter of controversy, but the Bank received important revenues from this emergency loan and nobody in the institution reckoned that these financial instruments would generate further problems for the stability of the country (ibid.).

In contrast to this technical position, the opinion of economists and members of staff responsible for regional operations appears to be more positive. According to an economist at the Bank:

> The financial assistance was timely and the country benefited from it, because it eliminated fears about Argentina's financial situation and encouraged the resumption of capital flows....We decided to support the maintenance of macroeconomic stability and access to external financing.... In the short term, it would be expensive for the country, but only if it didn't carry out the reforms.
> (Anonymous interview May 2004)

Endorsing this political/institutional interpretation of the event, the interviews of the Bank's officials render a more realistic interpretation of the IDB's financial function. Accordingly, to understand the significance of such interventions it is necessary to place them within a larger framework of the alternatives to the convertibility and potential beneficiaries from these alternatives. In this sense, officials recognise that financial help was only released in exchange for major fiscal and social reforms, as a former official states:

> It was certain that emergency PBLs would have been better for the country, because an emergency loan is better than any other multilateral financial instrument but you have to do reforms. The PBLs go into the country's reserves, boosting liquidity without appearing in the deficit due to how the Fund measures primary surplus... an accounting trick.... The problem comes when you have to repay the loan and accomplish some conditions.
> (Anonymous interview 05/2004)

As the financial problems mounted, by early 1999 the IMF and the government were engaged in a prolonged debate concerning ways to cope with the increasing fiscal deficit in the current account. The debate on how to deal with the limitations of convertibility soon resulted in a technical proposal emanating from orthodox economist circles which achieved a broad consensus in the IFI–government complex: the dollarisation of the economy (see Chapter 4). In February 1999, Roque Fernandez officially presented the dollarisation proposal, attracting serious questioning from Brazil. One month later, Alan Greenspan, the chief of the Federal Reserve of the United States, rejected the idea, arguing that 'the Central Bank of the United States cannot manage the monetary and economic policy of other countries' (*La Nacion* 25–27/02/1999). In the same way Fernando De La Rua, leader of the opposition, protested that the project was 'hardly serious' and former president Raul Alfonsin termed it 'ridiculous' (*Clarín* 24–25/02/1999 and 28/02/1999).

Financial withdrawal and political engagement

During the period 1999–2001, the IDB's interventions in the country manifested growing tension within the IFI–government relationship concerning alternative ways to gradually dismantle the convertibility system. This stage was the outcome of two factors. First, a major escalation of Argentina's financial problems, given the coincidence of the maturities of bonds issued under the Brady Plan, the repayment of emergency loans and the steady growth of the pension system deficit, together putting the convertibility regime under a massive debt burden. The second factor was the long-unmet social needs, the profound absence of legitimacy of the political system, and institutional opposition led by the provinces and factions in Congress aligned with the Justice Party (Levitsky and Murillo 2003). These facts shaped the political economic scenario within which international and domestic actors sought to impose conditions and struggled to promote their alternatives to convertibility. Figure 6.1 portrays Argentina's performance in development financing through the 1990s. As we can see from the chart, MDB lending in the final stage of convertibility, including by the World Bank and the IDB, followed the same pattern as the withdrawal of the private capital markets. This fact is explained by the complex international–domestic scenario.

After the emergency loan of 1998, the IDB's role underwent a huge shift from a steady decline in its financial support to its increasing political agency, as the institution sought to avoid a rupture between the country and the system of global financial governance. Throughout this period, the Bank's financial function was clearly subordinated both to the prescriptions of the IMF and the political relations between IFIs and the government. The IDB targeted state reforms through three relatively small PBLs: US$400 million for Fiscal Balance and Social Management (1295/OC-AR, IDB 2000b); a $500 million loan for Financial Services (1324/OC-AR, IDB 2001d); and $500 million for the Federal Commitment to Growth and Fiscal Discipline (1341/OC-AR, IDB 2001e). This brief period of financial support was accompanied by a cooling in the relations between the IDB and the Alliance administration, as the new government gave priority to its relations with the international financial community. In this regard, the targets set for the PBLs provide some hints about the major concerns preoccupying the Bank: federal fiscal reform and reform of the social security and pension system (RE-299, IDB 2004a).

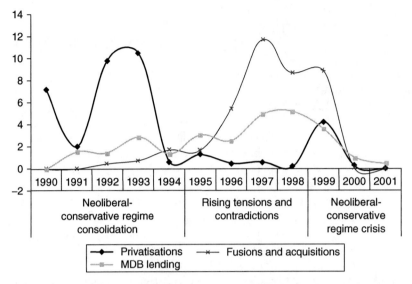

Figure 6.1 Argentina, capital inflow from privatisations, M&A, and MDB lending in the 1990s (US$ billions). (Based on Basualdo 2003, and several World Bank and IDB reports.)

Fieldwork has yielded similar interpretations of the underlying reasons for the role assumed by the IDB during this period, indicating that a radical change in the strategy of the country under Alliance administration led to a worsening in the relations with the Bank. Indeed, as seen in Chapter 4, the strategy of the Alliance administration mainly concerned relations with the IMF and sought support from the European countries in order to distance the new administration from Menem's close relation with the US administration. From the perspective of the IDB staff this was a strategic mistake and was accompanied by another central error, its unwillingness to dollarise the economy. In this scenario, accordingly, the last three PBLs received by the administration were no solution but instead created more fiscal and political problems at a domestic level, comprising two elements. First, in 1999 the capital markets had already said 'no' to any form of international financing until investors were guaranteed that no devaluation would happen and received a clear signal to this effect from Washington. The second element was that in Washington everyone was oriented to the protection of foreign investments in the expected eventuality of an exit from convertibility.

Within this framework, an interview with an IDB official reveals the dominant and pragmatic interpretation of the scenario. According to a former officer of the Bank:

> There wasn't just one factor at play in the crisis, and from that point of view the Bank did what it could.... Its financial instruments are subject to the major Washington institutions and to the G7.... The Bank began to take on

an enhanced political role under the leadership of Don Enrique Iglesias, beyond the opposition in Washington, driven by the conservatives, to the delivery of more rescue packages.

(Anonymous interview 06/2004)

As we can observe from this opinion the IDB's interventions began to shift towards a more political stance in relation to the country's relations with the system of international financial governance. Undeniably, the explanation for this rests on the political economic nature of its corporate governance: despite including borrowers, non-borrowers and the IMF, in times of financial crisis it seems to be slanted in favour of the latter, with its borrowing members atomised and marginalised. However, it is important to know that despite the distancing of the international financial community from the government there were two different diagnoses based on realistic assumptions about the best way to exit from convertibility. 'For the conservatives, [Argentina] was a basket-case with no other solution except default and dollarization.... For the Europeans a devaluation, given their investments, was not appropriate... and for the region, there should be no collateral damage' (Anonymous interview 05/2004).

Unsurprisingly, a similarly realistic interpretation can be found in the opinions of the former government officials, who emphasise the isolation of the government and its conflictive relations with the major IFIs regarding the future of the convertibility. This is possibly one of the most sensitive issues, as it refers to the IDB's development function and its interventions in regional member countries in times of crisis and financial turbulence. However, given the institutional implications of the issue, former officials recognise the IDB's support but regard it mostly as having been symbolic and of scant relevance and impact owing to the location of the political tensions (government–IMF relations). The interpretation is that the Bank was impeded from acting in any formal way externally by the bonds between the IDB and the IFIs and internally by the financial and political implications of any intervention. According to a former member of the administration 'the country was already on its own... and in financial and political default with the world major financial actors' (Anonymous interview 06/2004).

On the other hand, IDB staff members and former officials stress that, due to the institutional importance of the region's members, the Bank supported the country even in the face of major conflict with the World Bank and the IMF, putting the institution itself at risk. In this regard, the dominant view of the IDB staff and officials highlights its political intervention. Accordingly, even assuming the pursuit of institutional survival was the driving factor, the Bank was compelled to support the country for key financial and political reasons: 'there was a firm desire in the directorate to seek ways in which the crisis would not affect other regional members of the Bank' (Anonymous interview 06/2004). Consistent with this argument, another factor is that as the Bank's portfolio is composed mainly of regional assets, the impact of the Argentine crisis necessarily would affect the Bank's spreads. The political argument is that 'Argentina is one of its bigger members' and so any IDB action would impact internally upon the institution (ibid.).

In sum, as financial support from the IFIs abruptly declined, together with the withdrawal of the capital markets, IDB support shifted steadily towards a deeper political engagement aimed at averting a final rupture of the country's relations with the global financial governance. As the fieldwork shows, this process was led directly by the IDB's president, Enrique Iglesias, and the Board of Directors, who managed to maintain their support for the country while it teetered on the edge of the crisis.

Conclusion

This chapter has given an account of the rise and decline of the financialisation of the IDB's role in Argentina in the period 1995 to 2001 and of the underlying reasons for it. Returning to the question posed at the beginning of the chapter, it is now plausible to state that by tracing the international–domestic and structural–agential dynamics and factors, an integral comprehension of the elements shaping the dynamic of the IDB's development role can be gained. The analysis suggests that, after the mid-1990s, the IDB entered into a period of tension and gradual dissociation from its development function, as a result of the changes in international finances and the emergent contradictions in and decline of the convertibility regime.

Two logical findings emerge from this chapter. First, given convertibility, which is a particular strategy of globalisation, the contradictions between the financing of reforms on the one hand and investments in development on the other became acute and disrupted the IDB's interventions, generating inconsistencies with its mandate to promote global economic integration. Second, the transformative effect of its financial function as a factor facilitating economic expansion and global integration became exhausted, because of escalating domestic needs and the fragmentation and decomposition of the political order.

The study has gone some way towards enhancing our understanding of the political economic nature of the IDB. It has shown how transitions, changes and crisis in international–domestic finances can bring to the fore one or other of the three major dimensions of this regional multilateral institution. These three traceable dimensions are the technical, financial and political sides of the organisation. This concept reinforces the idea suggested in other chapters that the political economic nature of the IDB is expressed in its dual role as a regional bank and as an agency of development, two functions brought together at its apex by a political corporate governance. In times of global and domestic stability, these three institutional dimensions are expressed in the integrity of its role and in the congruence of its technical and financial development functions. In times of turbulence and crisis, as in the last stage of the period in Argentina, this integrity gives way to the dominance of its financial dimension and major political tensions with its recipient countries.

7   Conclusion

Introduction

The contention of this study was that the blind adoption of the economistic fallacy mislead the development mission of the IDB. Moreover, that this was a major factor behind the financial crises of the 1990s in which international and regional multilateral institutions played a central part or were even, in some cases, the origin of them. To investigate that, we deployed a heterodox and critical framework and methodology that delivered tangible insights confronted with the study of specific cases. In this research, it shed light on the changing political economic nature of the Inter-American Development Bank, against the backdrop of the internationalisation of production and globalisation of the financing of development within the wider relations between globalisation, regionalism and multilateralism. Accordingly, it has shown the structural and agency factors shaping the IDB's mission and interventions in development at a regional and domestic level. In so doing, it has also revealed the factors behind the creation, rise and consolidation of this powerful regional institution, and the extent to which its policy has responded to the opportunities and constraints set by South American development.

Academically, this book presents the investigation of the political economy of the world's leading RDB, the Inter-American Development Bank. Far beyond the dominant approaches of the so-called North American school in International Political Economy, we applied a heterodox version of the critical PE of development (Cohen 2008). It explores the changing nature of its development mission and the subordinated character of its interventions in the region to the global neo-liberal financial projects of development and major actors of development. Briefly, it has been shown how the logic of the neo-liberal project, its dual governance and instruments driving the Bank played a role in the fall of the convertibility regime by promoting its neoliberal reforms and supporting the government. Indeed, the political economic nature of the Bank could not take it to a different place, beyond its regional commitments, proving that rather than a Latin American bank, the IDB is structurally and agentially conditioned to the dynamic of the global neo-liberal financial governance of development. The nature of the Bank is its financial and political survival which demands promotion of open regionalism and tends to split in times of international crisis, prioritising survival and global financial governance.

This book has sought to unveil the dynamics of development shaping the Bank's actions by deploying a critical approach to comprehend the complex international–domestic and state–social forces and dynamics behind this regional developmental actor and its global–regional nature of governance, instruments and approaches of development. In this regard, it has explored and identified the specific conditions of neo-liberal globalisation and hegemony, and the international–domestic configurations of forces that have historically accompanied the Bank's successful or failed interventions in domestic development. To trace that, the investigation critically explored its role in the consolidation, decline and crisis of the Argentine convertibility regime, one of the most applauded political projects in the region by the international financial community and led by a democracy in the 1990s. At the same time, it has sought to develop and operationalise a theoretical framework capable of addressing these research issues as a contribution to scholarship in new IPE. This concluding chapter serves to review the extent to which these ends have been met.

The sections present an overview of the research findings and the general contribution that this book has made to the study of the political economy of Regional Development Banks.

Findings

The purpose of the current study was to address three sets of research questions in relation to the changing political economic nature of the IDB. The first question has been regarding the extent to which a new IPE can inform and understand the political economic nature of RDBs. As seen, it has a complex political economic nature defined by world, and increasingly regional, political orders linking globalisation, regionalism and multilateralism in particular ways. The second question has been concerned with the developmental significance of the IDB's roles and interventions in regional and domestic development, especially in relation to the political economic projects promoted by its technical, financial, and political interventions. Finally, it has been about the extent to which the theoretical framework used was further refined by this investigation. The following details the findings of each chapter, except Chapter 1, which is dealt with separately in the next section.

As the study of contemporary hegemony, multilateral institutions, regions and *transformismo* demands a direct critical reflection on the basis of the changes in historical contexts of development, Chapter 2 began with a historical and critical review of the long-run historical process of the political economy of the Americas and Latin America shaping the creation, rise and consolidation of the IDB. In particular, attention was given to the process shaping and defining the IDB's development mission and its role in development financing and in shaping welfare outcomes. Drawing on a version of Coxian historical materialism, the chapter argued that the political economic nature of the IDB has been hemispheric rather than Latin American, and defined by two major historical processes, production and financial globalisation. These processes were driven by US regional leadership and its security and economic policy concerns towards the region, defining two unwritten but clear historical development mandates for the regional institution. The first of these shaped the Bank's role from its inception to the debt crisis in the 1980s, and was directed to the promotion of hemispheric integration into the US hegemony through US FDI expansion, financial aid for governments loyal in the fight against the communist menace, and to provide intellectual leadership for the so-called *developmentalism*. The second process, from the end of the 1980s to the end of the 1990s, defined by financial globalisation, was directed to the restructuring and preparation of the region for market-driven integration into the global economy, radically shifting regional financing of development and welfare along neoliberal and liberal lines.

On the basis of these re-readings, the chapter went on to identify four major historical stages and clarified the main structural elements that have shaped the IDB's development mandate and its interventions in regional development. The first stage identified has been the consolidation of US hegemony in the Americas and the transformation of the Pan American Union into the Inter-American system – two elements which defined the state character and US-led orientation of the major regional multilateral institutions. The period analysed has seen the process of hemispherisation of the state and the regional reaction to it. The period marked the IDB's take-off as a cooperative agency of development under the tight control of the USA. Accordingly, the analysis highlights not only the state-led character of the IDB but also the complexity of its Bank–state relations. The third phase described has been that of the decline of the USA and the end of the Bretton Woods system. According to the analysis the stage was accompanied by the regional reaction in the form of dictatorships and the internationalisation of production and financing of development that marked the IDB's active developmentalist role. The final stage identified was that of the debt crisis period, marking the historical change in the IDB, from being an agency of development to being a RDB, with the USA acting to reassert its economic hegemony in the region through the Washington Consensus and new 'open regionalism'.

This process of change signalled the new development mandate of the institution, that is, the promotion of global economic integration, through the IDB's new powers over the region's economies. These were initially manifested in its capacity to promote globalisation and the marketisation of public utilities, and after social security reform, by the framing of policy alternatives, contributing to increasing the capacity of absorption of political orders and the exertion of domestic influence. Briefly, these capacities of absorption and exertion of domestic influence constituted the central elements at the very base of the IDB's power-balance legitimisation effect that supported specific political economic projects aligned with the global guidelines of development. The chapter ended by presenting the specific research issue of this investigation to be developed in subsequent chapters: (1) To what extent can a new IPE of the IDB tell us something different about the political economic nature of RDBs? (2) How can we grasp the political economic nature of IDB and what are the main capabilities defining their development role in different regional political configurations? (3) Are the IDB's development mission and role defined by political, technical or financial elements? (4) What were the results of interventions in regional and domestic development?

Chapter 3 moved on to investigate the role of the IDB in the process of neoliberal reforms, promoted by the IFI–state complex managing the global economy and pursued by South American countries during the 1990s. Instead of abstracting the IDB from its context and examining it in the light of its internal mechanisms and its institutional and programming efficiency, the chapter focused on identifying the links between its financial, technical and political policies and their specificities. These links were grasped by focusing, instead, on the social dynamics and development strategies followed by countries in the region under the sponsorship and leadership of the major IFIs and developed states. The approach was central as it allowed us to grasp the differential nature of the IDB's interventions in relation to the major IFIs.

The chapter grasped the IDB's multilateral nature by assessing its quantitative and qualitative influence in development within its framework of open regionalism. It did so by appealing to and operationalising the notion of hegemony and the need to recognise the indissolubility of the relations between the domestic and the international and between economics and politics in order to uncover the Bank's nature. It argued that the IDB's political economic nature rests on the complex bank–state character that defines its power-balance legitimisation effect. This power is expressed in the IDB's capacity to generate consensus, across the region and in recipient countries, around the demands of the global economy, through an ideological process and through its emphasis on strategic areas of development and in particular areas of development financing.

The chapter moved on to identify the complex and dynamic relations between the IDB and recipient states, locating the ideological, political and economic connections between the development strategies pursued through the Bank's lending targets and policies and their impact on development. Finally, the chapter analysed the IDB's role in each stage of regional development, showing how its development mission within the global financial guidelines changed in tandem with the rise, consolidation and decline of pro-market reform in the region. Central results here include, first, the enthusiastic role played by the institution in the promotion and legitimisation of neoliberal reforms; second, its reaction to the financial turbulence and social troubles brought about by those reforms; and, finally, the IDB's distancing from pure market-driven reforms, shifting the institution towards its major political regional commitments (although without abandoning existing paradigms of development).

In Chapter 4, the other side of our case study was investigated. It studied the political economy of Argentina's development, in the light of the political economy of South America developed in Chapter 2, and in particular the liberalisation process in the 1990s, in the context of changing US hemispheric and global hegemony. The purpose of the chapter was, first, to analyse how the dynamics between economics and politics and the international and the domestic shaped the Argentine political economy in the light of the major stages of South American development. Second, it aimed to investigate how these dynamics defined the political economy of development, its financing and outcomes.

The investigation found the common elements between the Argentine and regional patterns of development, especially in relation to the rise, consolidation, reassertion and decline of US hegemony in the region; and later in the closely related process of the global governance. It highlighted the counter-hegemonic domestic responses manifested in the rise and fall of Peronism, the convergence between domestic and hemispheric hegemonies, and the period of deadlock ending with coercive reaction in the form of the dictatorship in the 1970s.

It was shown that the period of coercive reaction accompanied the end of the Bretton Woods system and the rise of another historical phenomenon that would last for three decades, *transformismo* and its neoliberal–conservative coalition. Noticeably, the new hegemony was characterised by an element absent in previous stages of development, that is, the government–IFI alliance, or 'state–IFI complex', as the driving force of a state-led form of globalisation anchored on finance and on neoliberal guidelines.

The central findings of the chapter revealed, first, the continuity and evolution of the structural conditions shaping development strategies since the 1970s, via the dictatorship and converging a decade later with the Washington Consensus. Second, it revealed that these structural conditions were extended throughout the De La Rua administration. The third finding is the intergoverned strategy and process of global economic integration, pursued through the country anchoring its development financing on volatile external sources and the absorption of the political domestic order. Finally, it is the capacity of the Argentine *transformismo* to co-opt and absorb opposition alternatives and actors at the economic, ideological, labour and political levels.

Chapter 5 took a more empirical approach, investigating the IDB's role within the stage of consolidation of the convertibility regime, in conformity with its development mandate of promoting global financial integration. The chapter investigated the political economic function of the IDB within the process, led by the government and IFIs, of marketisation of public utilities, focusing upon the case of the debt swap for the privatisation of the electricity sector. The case study was relevant for two reasons. First, it showed how the Bank–government partnership promoted, strengthened and legitimised a political economic project directed to regional capitalist expansion and the building up of international and especially regional–domestic private partnerships as a way of propelling globalisation. Second, the case study showed that, in a period of highly international–domestic governed development, the political, technical and financial aspects of the IDB's powers remained integrated and coordinated, and facilitating capital expansion independently of social development.

The chapter identified the complex manifestations of the power-balance legitimisation capacity of the IDB in domestic development in its use of a blend of technical, financial and policy instruments. The first IDB power identified was its capacity to endorse global hegemonic tendencies and adapt them into regional and domestic guidelines of development. The investigation examined the Bank's institutional power to frame development policy options through technical-based means oriented to depoliticising and economising developmental issues and transforming them into rational and universal options of development.

The chapter followed with a study of the introduction of pro-market models of development for electricity, and the complex political operation that presented this as the only rational alternative for the country and for the transformation of the sector. The analysis then moved on to focus upon the relationship between the introduced model and the strategic orientation of the convertibility regime, the chief elements of the hegemonic transformative character of the Bank–government partnership during the period. Accordingly, in the processes of co-option and absorption via legitimisation and compensation of the major actors involved, two central elements and tactics of the Argentine *transformismo* were recognised: the labour unions and the provinces, and the process of selecting domestic and international private actors as participants.

In Chapter 6, attention was turned to the IDB's changing role since the mid-1990s and its interventions in the decline of the convertibility regime. As we have seen, the stage was characterised by two tendencies. First, an increasing dominance of finance within the IDB's development mandate, generating a subordination of technical and political imperatives to international investors' concerns regarding the growing tensions in the country; second, the growing inconsistency, and sometimes contradiction, in the Bank's interventions.

The chapter argued that this shift in the IDB's development mandate, namely, the financialisation of its development mission, expressed the power of capital markets and industrialised states upon the model of development financing that the Bank itself had helped to put in place. The chapter highlighted how the IDB's role and interventions were caught in the middle of the growing tensions between global mandates and the domestic imperative of the survival of the Argentine *transformismo*. Its deep analysis was based on the information obtained from interviews of top personnel at the IDB, Washington think-tanks and former officials of the Argentine government. The chapter therefore focused on the IDB's interventions in the privatisation of social security and its impact on development financing, the impact of the international financial crisis upon public accounts, and the financial and political relations between the Bank and the government during the critical last period of the convertibility regime leading up to the crisis in 2001.

The conclusion was that given the contradictions between the financing of reforms, policy framing, and the legitimisation effect of the IDB and IFIs' interventions, the Bank's development mandate became disrupted and its financial function exhausted because of escalating domestic needs, social security privatisation, and the fragmentation and decomposition of the political order. The chapter showed how, given the global and regional nature of the Bank, structural changes in global finance and domestic development impelled the dominance of one of the three major dimensions of the IDB's development capabilities (financial, technical or political ones).

In sum, this work has added a number of significant explanations to our understanding of the changing nature of the IDB's political economy. Utilising and developing a version of the new IPE theoretical framework, the investigation has shown how the economic–political and international–domestic political and economic dynamics defined the structure–agency of the IDB's power-balance legitimisation role in development via its political, financial and technical capacities. In this manner, the thesis has demonstrated the ways in which the domestic, hemispheric and global reconfigurations of the political economy of development, in particular development financing, have shaped the nature of the IDB and its interventions in intra-regional politics and the strategic choices taken by its corporate governance. In the next section our attention will turn to the contribution of this investigation to the new IPE, particularly in respect of the theoretical framework developed in Chapter 1 and deployed in subsequent chapters.

Theoretical contribution

The theoretical discussion put forward in Chapter 1 performed two central functions. First, it furnished us with the dominant approaches to the political economy of RDBs, contrasting these with the perspective of the new IPE adopted here. Second, and more importantly, it set out the more specific theoretical and conceptual terrain upon which research into the questions posed was then undertaken. This was of central importance, as we followed a methodological approach addressed to refine the theoretical framework through the discovery of the dynamics of the process achieved through the investigation of the questions posed. For this purpose, we turned in Chapter 1 to Cox's method of historical structures as a way to introduce the new IPE approach to five issues of development under globalisation – the state, *transformismo*, international institutions, regionalism and multilateralism, and the new IPE of RDBs.

The state

In the process of elaborating a critical approach to our research subject, particular attention was paid to the concept of the state, or the emerging or prevalent forms of political authority – international, regional and domestic forms of the state–society complex – which historically have expressed specific balances of social forces in different times and places. These entities became the material of our analysis, aimed at understanding the developmental connections between power in the state, power in production and power in the region. And equally important, they provided us with a picture of a particular configuration of forces and interrelations in the economic, political and social realms, and served as a framework able to deal with the traditional theoretical separation between politics and economics, bringing the international, regional and domestic realms into an understanding of the political economy of RDBs.

A central theoretical point here was that, historically, the hegemony created by the different balances of social forces have exceeded mere domestic boundaries and that, furthermore, these have been regionally and internationally moulded, in particular in the last few decades by the internationalisation of the state. It was argued that the internationalisation of the state is never complete and is constantly contested by domestic and regional counter-tendencies. This is central to understanding why the internationalisation of production and globalisation of finance might assume different forms in different regions and in turn define different contexts and development missions for the RDBs.

The first and central point to make in relation to this political economic approach is that, as a method of description, it does indeed grasp the specificity of development in the Americas and particularly in South America. The critical re-readings presented in Chapters 2, 3 and 4 would certainly seem to confirm two central arguments of this investigation. First, the Latin America *developmentalist* stage, lasting between the 1940s and 1980s, was determined by a particular form of internationalisation of production dominated by US security concerns. It is this framework of the Cold War which further fostered antidemocratic regimes aligned with the hegemony and which defined the IDB's development mission as a regional cooperative agency for development aid, dominated by a developmentalist approach and directing its support mainly to countries loyal to the hegemony. The case study was illustrated by the processes leading to the creation, rise and consolidation of the IDB as the major regional multilateral institution in Latin America, and the determination, by the hemispheric hegemony, of its approaches and policies.

Second, the new stage of international change starting in the 1970s was accompanied by a hegemonic shift from security to financial concerns, increasingly giving rise to a new form of political authority at the international, regional and domestic levels. This new form of development regime finds significant similarities with the historical materialist notion of passive revolution and in particular the configuration of power named *transformismo* – the political power to frame alternative policies and co-opt and absorb opposition forces in development. Our case study, the Argentine *transformismo*, seems clearly to confirm the argument, given its domestic, regional and international character assumed in the 1990s through the convertibility regime.

In this regard, the investigation paid particular attention to and gave a detailed analysis of international–domestic and market-oriented state reform in strategic sectors of development such as electric energy, social security and federal reform in Argentina in which the IDB played a role. The direct lessons that can be extracted from these are important. First is that contrary to the economistic idea that by commodifying developmental sectors such as energy, social security and labour forces, countries have a strategy for economic efficiency and sustainability in developmental terms, the reality of past decades presents another prospect. After decades of this classic belief, the renewed importance of energy, protected domestic consumption, domestic use of commodities, and the protection of labour forces seem to be vital to keep domestic stability and sustainability of any development strategy. The strategic issue after decades of neoliberal failures does not seem to be persisting in the attempt to be part of the global economy but rather that of the region. Another central lesson is that state reforms promoted by this type of regional bank have been barely technically founded and consistent or based on the historical knowledge and expertise of these institutions in the regions. Briefly, they were ideologically and politically driven rather than based on their knowledge of the region. In this vein, the investigation revealed the political economic nature of some of this process labelled as successful (e.g. the Chilean case of neoliberal reforms and Argentine electricity privatisation) and their links and roles of social actors which emerged during times of dictatorship, and their past relations and links with democratic orders. The final lesson is that any kind of state reform requires specific political conditions and produce specific political setting reinforcing or fragmenting the national order in particular under neoliberal guidelines of development. In Argentina's case this is marked by the consolidation and decline of *transformismo*. The nature of the reforms lay at the very basis of the political decomposition of the regime, namely the rupture of its commitments with the domestic and its subordination to the global financial governance of development.

International institutions

In Chapter 1 it was argued that the notion of *transformismo* might aid comprehension of the hegemonic form of the current global order and the intertwined historical dynamics of the inseparable international–domestic relationship. The international order was defined as institutionally and socially mediated, wherein the state does not juxtapose but integrates, whether harmoniously or in conflict, into an inseparable complex.

This concept proved to be useful in capturing the nature of the intergoverned domestic–international processes of development and their specificities throughout different stages of the political economy of the Americas, of South America and in particular of Argentina during the past century. It was seen that intergoverned domestic–international and regional processes of interdependence can be found throughout all the stages and places in the region, and have shown, in South America, a marked presence since the 1980s. Intergoverned domestic–regional interaction appeared as a central characteristic of the strategies of globalisation, pursued by the various countries, mirroring in turn different power relations through diverse forms of cooperation or conflict between domestic political alliances.

Drawing on insights provided by a variety of research conducted into the Americas' political economy and their re-reading in the light of the new IPE approach, Chapters 2 and 4 present the major features of the region and of Argentina's intergoverned processes of development. On this basis, the study has attempted to understand the issue of development in regional and domestic complexes by placing them in an empirical context, within a more integral approach than that provided by traditional economic or political science perspectives.

Chapter 2, for instance, rather than resting upon a dichotomous separation between the political and the economic and between international and domestic perspectives of Latin American development, instead provided an account based on the extent to which the hegemonic dynamics between the USA and the region's governments gave way to different and segmented domestic political orders and development strategies in the region. The resulting analysis proved relevant to understanding the relations and interactions between different country strategies of development financing, domestic political orders, the IDB's mission and development outcomes. Particularly important in this regard was to appreciate the different development paths followed by major (Brazil, Mexico, Argentina), medium (Colombia, Chile) and small states (Bolivia, Peru) within the internationalisation of production and globalisation of financing of the development stages studied.

The other chief contribution of this section was the notion that all intergoverned domestic–regional processes of development are anchored in the IFI–state complex, since the former remain tied to the political structures and agency that originated them and sustained them, as was proved in the case of the IDB. The case study was presented in Chapters 2 and 3, through the analysis of the relations within the IDB's corporate governance among the USA and borrower members from its creation until the globalisation period. The analysis found that the IDB–state relationship clearly provides a power-distributional effect upon regional and domestic development, thus framing development alternatives, favouring the interests of specific actors or coalitions, and legitimising political economic projects aligned with the management of the global economy. The development power of RDBs, and in our case the IDB, is defined by their capacity to frame policy alternatives, assimilate opposing positions, justify and defend a particular political economic project, and legitimise those transformations along the guidelines of development set by the management of the global economy. The central issue of a future research agenda on RDBs, therefore, should focus on the extent by anchoring their structure of governance on regional forces under similar development projects, so that the dynamic of these institutions could really foster development with social justice.

Regionalism, multilateralism and RDBs

In contrast to the traditional dispute between unilateral and multilateral views of regionalism, Chapter 1 approached the relations between regionalism and multilateralism in the overall context of changing hegemony, defining their coexistence and sometimes their conflict. We argued that, so far as this investigation was concerned, regionalism has been more associated with so-called open regionalism, a manifestation of economic globalisation and prevailing forms of hegemony shaping the role of RDBs and the IDB.

We also extend the critiques to the studies on the political economic nature of RDBs and in particular, the IDB, that have focused on their multilateral nature and its role within the framework of open regionalism (Birdsall and Rojas 2004; Sagasti 2002; Bezanson *et al.* 2000; Bulmer-Thomas 1996; Tussie 1995; 2003). The base of the observations was the economistic and empiricist character of these perspectives, most of the time, hiding a naïve or depoliticised interpretation of the regional realities of development. The work of Sagasti and Bezanson clearly reflects this, and a similar position can be found in the works of Birdsall and Rojas. At this stage, it is important to recognise, beyond any critique, that the work of Diana Tussie remains the most important academic endeavour to approach in wider terms the political economy of the IDB, and its major weakness, in that her research could not get beyond the institutional control.

The chapter contended that formally organised regions have been defined by different dominant formal region-wide organisational and inter-state frameworks. Accordingly, even though RDBs function under the IFIs' global guidelines, structurally they vary, since they are defined by different RDB–state configurations and state–society complexes in each region. The concept was vital as it proved to be capable of dealing with both the specificities and the multilateral character of the IDB. In this regard, Chapter 3 presented a detailed account and analysis of state relations in the structure and agency of the IDB, its tensions and the shifts in its development mandate during the internationalisation of production and the globalisation of South America's development financing stage.

The concept was optimal, as it seems to apprehend the political economic nature of the IDB and its historical and geographical context in two ways: first, by capturing the different mixes and balances of ideas and forces shaping its development mission and interventions given its specific region; second, by comprehending the main dimensions of its structure (financial, technical and political) as well as the complexity and real political economic character of its instruments of development, the concept has allowed us to grasp the nature of its role.

Accordingly, the first characteristic that defined the IDB is its location within the region of the Americas and in the presence of the USA. That has been central, first because Latin America has been configured in relation to the changing forms of US authority, second for its self-reconfiguration as a region, with the consequent absorption of Mexico into the North American region and the rise of South America. The second feature is the participation of borrower members in the corporate governance of the Bank, which rather than making the IDB a sub-regional bank makes it a hemispheric institution tied to the USA.

In accord with this perspective, this investigation found that comprehension of RDBs, within the context of the relationships between globalisation, regionalism and multilateralism, should integrate three elements: first, their consensual and technocratic character as well as their relative autonomy from governments; second, their relation with the state structures that gave them origin; third, the presence of the region's countries in their corporate governance. To deal with the problem, it was argued that RDBs play a vital role in the hegemony, ensuring the continuance of a particular political economic project through the mediating, consensus-forming and legitimising functions that they perform. Chapters 3, 5 and 6 empirically illustrated these arguments in detail.

For instance, Chapter 3 provided a clear example of the IDB's policy-framing capacity via the investigation of its role in the debt swap for privatisations and in particular in the privatisation of electric energy public utilities in Argentina. The chapter showed that it is through framing, negotiations, conditions, and assimilating opposing domestic positions that they build consensus among governmental and corporate powers for the management of the regional economies. States, international organisations, economic actors and specific forms of knowledge exercise power and frame the development mission of these regional bodies and the IDB in particular. The IDB historically has reflected the power relations prevailing within its scenarios and dominant values. The Bank has played a complex and varied role in the region, which seems to have been defined by the particular amalgam of material and ideological resources which far overflow their own institutional boundaries, through political, technical and financial channels, instruments, and regional networks accessing domestic areas and actors.

The investigation proved the existence of three dimensions of the IDB's development role, reflecting the complex political economic nature of this regional body of development: the political, technical and financial dimensions that are traceable in their organisational mandates, constitutions and strategies. The political dimension comprises their relationships with the USA, the major IFIs and borrowing members in Latin America, allowing them to participate directly in intergoverned strategies of global integration adopted by the member countries. The technical dimension is defined by the central consensual devices through which the IDB has contributed to the hegemonic consensual role, depoliticising specific ideas of development, and operationalising them into rules, procedures and programmes. The financial dimension encompassed its capacity both to channel official and private resources to support a political economic project, and to provide access to capital markets through assessing creditworthiness and officially endorsing country strategies and policies. At the top of the IDB lies its complex corporate governance, which has been widely regarded as its main strategic advantage. The IDB's corporate governance displays a dual political economic nature, or an integrated interdependence, defined by both the IDB–IFI relationship and the relationship between the IDB and borrowing state members.

It should be clear that this book has not attempted to provide a full account of the hemispheric dynamic of development but instead has sought empirical answers to questions derived from the contributions of new IPE, in order to refine a set of concepts and contribute answers to a small set of inquiries into development at regional level. In fact, the book has sought to place its study of the IDB inside the broader analysis of the political economy of globalisation, regionalism and multilateralism as developed by the new IPE.

Appendix A

Methodological notes

Operationalising the RDBs' development role

The RDBs' development mandate is considered to be the central element driving their interventions, functions and roles in development. Development mandates are the centrepiece of the RDBs' constitution regulating its interventions, in addition to the national constitution regulating the life of a country. However, RDBs as well as countries are challenged by the historical changes in their external and internal scenarios, demanding major or minor adjustments of their constitutions to the new realities, from which it is possible to accept the existence of variations in their governing mandates.

The development mandate determines the institutional life of RDBs such as the IDB; but, as regional actors promoting development, their development function can be subject to readjustments, reorientations, or reinterpretations in order to support the needs of its borrowing and non-borrowing members. The research on the IDB's development role thus presented a twofold methodological problem for this investigation. First, it demanded a definition of the IDB itself, which could be congruent or not with the official understanding of it, with further consequences for data collection. Second, the definition needs to be traducible into the methodological approach in order to understand and assess the existence or otherwise of variances in the IDB's role.

To deal with this issue, we opted to take consideration of, and also to stand some distance from, the traditional official understanding of its role, dominated by a financial quantitative and technical-oriented interpretation, defined as the summary of its programmes and the coherence, consistency, and efficacy of their internal aims (RE-299, IDB 2004a). Instead of this financial and technical descriptive approach, the investigation opted to consider the IDB's intervention programmes as indicators of the directionality of its strategies for the region and member countries, based on the major guidelines set by the institution for them (see Chapters 3, 4 and 5). This methodological option rendered two benefits. First, it identified the development targets of the Bank's interventions – state, private sector, and welfare – together with the major conceptual guidelines and diagnosis underlying its design and instrumentation. Second, it avoided the positivist technical discourse in defining the collection of consistent data.

However, given the fact that the IDB, as with all multilateral institutions, is composed of different actors with greater or lesser control over its major instruments of interventions, the investigation proceeded to make another division, this time between those instruments whose corporate governance and guidelines were subordinated to the power of the major IFIs – the IMF and World Bank – and those determined by the IDB itself and the member country receiving the intervention.

With these elements, we elaborated a conceptual framework that could grasp qualitative variations in development function, their origin and their impact on different scenarios by analysing interventions in specific target areas of development throughout every stage of the consolidation and decline of the convertibility regime. Therefore, variations in the domestic or international scenario should necessarily be accompanied by variations or shifts in target areas of development with a greater or lesser presence of the IDB's instruments – the PBLs and investment programmes (see Chapters 5 and 6). Once the variations had been grasped, the logical next step was to find out how it was instrumented, how it was legitimised and who benefited from these interventions.

Methodology

Methodologically, this investigation is composed of two bodies of analysis. The aim of the first part is to develop a general theoretical framework capable of addressing fully the research questions outlined above, while the second empirically explores the cases in the light of research into the questions posed. This stage of the investigation utilises a 'new' IPE approach in order to delineate those aspects of the global and regional political economy most pertinent to this study of the RDBs' changing development mission and role. The delineation of the elements of the global and regional political economy serves two specific purposes. First, it provides the necessary theoretical context for investigating issues of the hegemony, *transformismo*, state, international institutions, and the RDBs' political economic nature and development mission. Second, it serves the general purpose of placing the agency-oriented mainstream approaches of development inside the perspective of a particular historical context, Latin America.

The empirical part of this book is based on a quantitative and qualitative analysis of primary and secondary data gathered in the United Kingdom, the United States and Argentina. The study relies specifically on field research conducted in Washington, New York and Buenos Aires in 2004. The central purpose of this was to obtain information not available in the UK and, in particular, to conduct a series of interviews with relevant personnel. In addition, time spent in these cities was used to gather primary and secondary data, including: IDB official annual and sectoral reports; IDB sectoral, policy and programming assessments; IDB official regional and country reports and statistical data; IMF and World Bank official reports and assessments; think-tank investigations, papers and reports; press briefings, financial-specific information, and secondary material drawn from newspapers, books and academic journals.

Complementing this material, a sample of qualitative interviews based on a predefined list of subjects was also conducted during the fieldwork. Their purpose was to gain more first-hand insights into the IDB and the Argentine political economy of the 1990s in order to provide a degree of confirmation of some of the broader theoretical and substantive claims advanced in the thesis. The selection of individuals to interview was based on the criteria that they should be connected to the IDB and Argentina's government and have directly participated in these relations during the 1990s. The guarantee of anonymity was offered to all interviewees, and an important number of them considered it as a requirement, given that some opinions could affect their position in the IDB, the Argentine government and other international institutions.

Appendix B

Stages of the Americas' PE and governments

Year	Hemispheric PE stage	Argentine PE stage	United States administrations	Argentine administrations
1920s–1940	Transition from Pan American Union towards the inter-American system	Conservative hegemony		
1943				Pedro Ramirez
1944				Edelmiro Farrell
1945	Cold War and internationalisation of the state	Criollo development	Harry Truman	
1946				Juan Doming Peron
1952				Juan Domingo
1953			Dwight Eisenhower	Peron
1955		Democracy for minorities and dictatorship for majorities		José Molina Gómez Eduardo Lonardi Pedro Eugenio Aramburu
1958 May				Arturo Frondizi
1959 May				

(Continued)

(*Continued*)

Year	Hemispheric PE stage	Argentine PE stage	United States administrations	Argentine administrations
1961 April			John Kennedy	
1962 January March April May December				Jose Guido
1963 May October December			Lyndon Johnson	Arturo Illia
1964				Juan Carlos Ongania
1966 June				
1967 January				
1969 June	US hegemonic decline and rise of global governance		Richard Nixon	
1970 June October				Roberto Levingston
1971 March June October				Alejandro Lanusse
1972 October				
1973 May July October		Dictatorship: final solution and new beginning		Hector Campora Raúl Lastiri Juan Domingo Perón
1974 July October			Gerald Ford	Isabel Peron

(*Continued*)

(*Continued*)

Year	Hemispheric PE stage	Argentine PE stage	United States administrations	Argentine administrations
1975 June July August				
1976 February March				Jorge Videla
1977			Jimmy Carter	
1981 March November December			Ronald Reagan	Roberto Viola Carlos Lacoste Leopoldo Galtieri
1982 July August				Reynaldo Bignone
1983 December		Neoliberal–conservative emergence and democratic transition		Raul Alfonsin
1985 February				
1989				
March May July	Financial globalisation, new regionalism, and Washington consensus	Argentine *transformismo*: rise, apogee and decline	George Bush Sr.	Carlos Menem
December				
1991 January				
1993			William Clinton	
1995				Carlos Menem
1996 July				
1999 October				Fernando De La Rua
2001 March			George Bush Jr.	

Based on various sources.

Appendix C

The IDB's financial interventions by political economic stage

Table C.1 IDB investment projects to Argentina, 1991–2001

Loan number	Date of approval	Project name	Project area	(*a*)	Amount disbursed as of December 2002
618/OC-AR	6/3/1991	Agricultural Service Project	Production sector	×	41,127.38
619/OC-AR	6/3/1991	Provinces Development Program	State reform	×	198,664.52
621/OC-AR	28/03/1991	National Drinking Water and Sewerage Program	Production sector		98,668.99
862/OC/AR	31/07/1991	Cardiovascular and Transplant Surgery	Welfare organisation		2,700.00
863/SF-AR	25/09/1991	Provincial Electric Power Program	Production sector		0,806.29
	30/10/1991	Global Credit for Small Business and Microenterprise	Production sector		44,110.26
740/OC-AR	13/01/1993	Multisectoral Preinvestment Program	Estate reform		20,683.02
768/OC-AR	22/09/1993	Environmental Institutional Development	Estate reform		29,600.99
795/OC-AR	1/12/1993	National Highway Corridors	Production sector		243,147.89
797/OC-AR	8/12/1993	Rio Reconquista Clean-up	Welfare organisation		136,065.72
798/OC-AR	8/12/1993	Multisectoral Credit Program	Production sector		40,502.93
802/OC-AR	16/12/1993	Technological Modernisation Program	Production sector		81,705.21
816/OC-AR	29/06/1994	Support for Productive Restructuring	Production sector		144,073.21
826/OC-AR	9/11/1994	Administrative and Financial Reform of the Public Sector	Estate reform		46,466.06
830/OC-AR	16/11/1994	Municipal Social Investment	Welfare organisation	×	166,119.94

(Continued)

Table C.1 (Continued)

Loan number	Date of approval	Project name	Project area	(*a*)	Amount disbursed as of December 2002
845/OC-AR	7/12/1994	Reform and Investment in Education Sector	Welfare organisation		298,619.79
857/OC-AR	11/1/1995	Drinking Water and Sanitation: Stage VI	Production sector		180,020.91
899/OC-AR	8/11/1995	Provincial Agricultural Service I	Production sector	×	91,098.32
925/OC-AR	17/04/1996	TC Loan Preinvestment	Estate reform		13,240.32
940/OC-AR	17/07/1996	Neighbourhood Improvement and Lots with Services	Welfare organisation		35,008.24
962/OC-AR	30/10/1996	Port Modernisation	Production sector		28,484.38
979/OC-AR	11/12/1996	Province of Buenos Aires Support Program	Estate reform	×	336,024.37
989/OC-AR	15/01/1997	Support for Business Restructuring	Production sector		21,429.39
1021/OC-AR	9/7/1997	Care for Vulnerable Groups	Welfare organisation		20,993.11
1031/OC-AR	1/8/1997	Support for Youth Productivity and Employability	Production sector		244,081.79
1034/OC-AR	17/09/1997	Support for AFIP Institutionalisation	Estate reform		79,720.01
1059/OC-AR	25/11/1997	Ecological Recovery Matanza-Riachuelo	Welfare organisation		30,262.79
1060/OC-AR	25/11/1997	Reform of Non-University Higher Education	Production sector		19,382.54
1068/OC-AR	3/12/1998	Investment in Large Cities	Estate reform	×	20,675.35
1082/OC-AR	28/01/1998	Support for Justice System Reform	Estate reform		1,760.14
1107/OC-AR	10/6/1998	Support for GCBA Fiscal Reform	Estate reform	×	57,900.78
1111/OC-AR	29/01/1998	Care for Children and Adolescents at Risk	Welfare organisation		8,677.05
1118/OC-AR	5/8/1998	Food Emergency Loan	Welfare organisation		205,830.17
1134/OC-AR	28/11/1998	Program to Support Reform of Drinking Water	Welfare organisation		8,401.50
1133/OC-AR	28/11/1998	Federal Program for Women	Welfare organisation		1,615.33
1164/OC-AR	16/12/1998	Reform and Development of Argentine Municipios	Welfare organisation	×	18,828.50
1192/OC-AR	4/8/1999	Credit Program Microenterprises II	Production sector		24,272.58

(*Continued*)

Table C.1 (Continued)

Loan number	Date of approval	Project name	Project area	(*a*)	Amount disbursed as of December 2002
1193/OC-AR	11/8/1999	Reform of Primary Healthcare	Welfare organisation		14,974.09
1201/OC-AR	22/09/1999	Technological Modernisation II	Production sector		42,330.63
1206/OC-AR	6/10/1999	Institutional Strengthening for Foreign Trade Policy	Estate reform		205.33
1279/OC-AR	22/10/2000	Institutional Strengthening Ministry of Foreign Affairs	Estate reform		378.00
1287/OC-AR	6/12/2000	State Modernisation in the Province of Cordoba	Estate reform	×	35,835.63
1307/OC-AR	31/01/2001	Neighbourhood Improvement in Rosario	Welfare organisation		2,162.50
1325/OC-AR	13/06/2001	TC Support for Financial Sector Service	Welfare organisation		227.28
TOTAL:					3,136,883.19

Source: Based on IDB/OVE, RE-299 (IDB 2004a).

Note
a   Decentralisation.

Table C.2 IDB investment projects to Argentina, 1991–94: regime consolidation

Loan number	Date of approval	Name of the project	Project area	(*a*)	Amount disbursed as of December 2002
618/OC-AR	6/3/1991	Agricultural Service Project	Production sector	×	41,127.38
621/OC-AR	28/03/1991	National Drinking Water and Sewerage Program	Production sector		98,668.99
863/SF-AR	25/09/1991	Provincial Electric Power Program	Production sector		806.29
643/OC-AR	30/10/1991	Global Credit for Small Business and Microenterprise	Production sector		44,110.26
795/OC-AR	1/12/1993	National Highway Corridor	Production sector		243,147.89
798/OC-AR	8/12/1993	Multisectoral Credit Program	Production sector		40,502.93
802/OC-AR	16/12/1993	Technological Modernisation Program	Production sector		81,705.21
816/OC-AR	29/06/1994	Support for Productive Restructuring	Production sector		144,073.21
					694,142.14
619/OC-AR	6/3/1991	Provinces Development Program	Estate reform	×	198,664.52
740/OC-AR	13/01/1993	Multisectoral Preinvestment Program	Estate reform		20,683.02
768/OC-AR	22/09/1993	Environmental Institutional Development	Estate reform		29,600.99
826/OC-AR	9/11/1994	Administrative and Financial Reform of the Public Sector	Estate reform		46,466.06
					295,414.58
862/OC-AR	31/07/1991	Cardiovascular and Transplant Surgery	Welfare organisation		2,700.00
797/OC-AR	8/12/1993	Rio Reconquista Cleanup	Welfare organisation		136,065.72
830/OC-AR	16/11/1994	Municipal Social Investment	Welfare organisation	×	166,119.94
845/OC-AR	7/12/1994	Reform and Investment in Education Sector	Welfare organisation		298,619.79
TOTAL					*603,505.45*

Source: Based on IDB/OVE, RE-299 (IDB 2004a).

Note
a Decentralisation.

Table C.3 IDB investment projects to Argentina, 1995–98: rising tensions

Loan number	Date of approval	Project name	Project area	(ᵃ)	Amount disbursed as of December 2002
857/OC-AR	11/1/1995	Drinking Water and Sanitation: Stage VI	Production sector		180,020.91
899/OC-AR	8/11/1995	Provincial Agricultural Service I	Production sector	×	91,098.32
962/OC-AR	30/10/1996	Port Modernisation	Production sector		28,484.38
989/OC-AR	15/01/1997	Support for Business Restructuring	Production sector		21,429.39
1031/OC-AR	1/8/1997	Support for Youth Productivity and Employability	Production sector		244,081.79
1060/OC-AR	25/11/1997	Reform of Non-University Higher Education	Production sector		19,382.54
					584,497.33
925/OC-AR	17/04/1996	TC Loan Preinvestment	Estate reform		13,240.32
979/OC-AR	11/12/1996	Province of Buenos Aires Support Program	Estate reform	×	336,024.37
1034/OC-AR	17/09/1997	Support for AFIP Institutionalisation	Estate reform		79,720.01
1068/OC-AR	3/12/1998	Investment in Large Cities	Estate reform	×	20,675.35
1082/OC-AR	28/01/1998	Support for Justice System Reform	Estate reform		1,760.14
1107/OC-AR	10/6/1998	Support for GCBA Fiscal Reform	Estate reform	×	57,900.78
					509,320.97
940/OC-AR	17/07/1996	Neighbourhood Improvement and Lots with Services	Welfare organisation		35,008.24
1021/OC-AR	9/7/1997	Care for Vulnerable Groups	Welfare organisation		20,993.11
1059/OC-AR	25/11/1997	Ecological Recovery Matanza-Riachuelo	Welfare organisation		30,262.79
1111/OC-AR	29/01/1998	Care for Children and Adolescents at Risk	Welfare organisation		8,677.05
1118/OC-AR	5/8/1998	Food Emergency Loan	Welfare organisation		205,830.17
1134/OC-AR	28/11/1998	Program to Support Reform of Drinking Water	Welfare organisation		8,401.50
1133/OC-AR	28/11/1998	Federal Program for Women	Welfare organisation		1,615.33
1164/OC-AR	16/12/1998	Reform and Development of Argentine Municipios	Welfare organisation	×	18,828.50
TOTAL:					*329,616.68*

Source: Based on IDB/OVE, RE-299 (IDB 2004a).

Note
a Decentralisation.

Table C.4 IDB investment projects to Argentina, 1999–2001: regime decline and crisis

Loan number	Date of approval	Project name	Project area	([a])	Amount disbursed as of December 2002
1192/OC-AR	4/8/1999	Credit Program Microenterprises II	Production sector		24,272.58
1201/OC-AR	22/09/1999	Technological Modernisation II	Production sector		42,330.63
1206/OC-AR	6/10/1999	Institutional Strengthening for Foreign Trade Policy	Estate reform		205.33
1279/OC-AR	22/10/2000	Institutional Strengthening Ministry of Foreign Affairs	Estate reform		378.00
1287/OC-AR	6/12/2000	State Modernisation in the Province of Cordoba	Estate reform	×	35,835.63
1307/OC-AR	31/01/2001	Neighbourhood Improvement in Rosario	Welfare organisation		2,162.50
1325/OC-AR	13/06/2001	TC Support for Financial Sector Service	Welfare organisation		227.28
1193/OC-AR	11/8/1999	Reform of Primary Healthcare	Welfare organisation		14,974.09

Source: Based on IDB/OVE, RE-299 (IDB 2004a).

Note
a   Decentralisation.

Table C.5 IDB summary of sector loans to Argentina, 1991–2001

Loan	Year	Amount (US$ millions)	Number of conditions	Number of reformulations	Areas of activity
Public sector reform (633/OC-AR)	1991	325	49	0	Fiscal management and policy, federal civil service reform, Central Bank
Reform of national electric power utilities (682/OC-AR)	1992	300	71	0	Electric power sector
Sector investment loan (733/OC-AR)	1992	350	60	1	Private sector participation and provincial treasury
Debt reduction and service (734/OC-AR)	1992	400	4	0	External debt
Privatisation of provincial banks (865/OC-AR)	1995	750	19	0	Provincial banks
Fiscal adjustment and social reforms (871/OC-AR)	1995	450	14	0	Social and labour sectors
Reform of provincial pension funds (961/OC-AR)	1996	320	40	0	Fiscal sector and provincial pension system
Structural adjustment and security of the banking system (1163/OC-AR) ('Emergency loan')	1998	2,500	112	2	Fiscal relations with provinces and financial monetary, social and infrastructure sectors
Fiscal balance and social management (1295/OC-AR)	2000	400	20	3	Social security, federal civil service, labour market, social development
Financial services (1324/OC-AR)	2001	500	23–27	4	Retirement and pensions, insurance, capital market
Federal commitment to growth and fiscal discipline (1341/OC-AR)	2001	500	22–24	4	Fiscal relations with provinces, fiscal management
TOTAL		*6,795*	*434–440*		

Source: Based on IDB/OVE, RE-299 (IDB 2004a: 31).

Table C.6 IDB summary of sector loans to Argentina, 1991–94: regime consolidation

Loan	Year	Amount (US$ millions)	Number of conditions	Number of reformulations	Areas of activity
Public sector reform (633/ OC-AR)	1991	325	49	0	Fiscal management and policy, federal civil service reform, Central Bank
Reform of national electric power utilities (682/OC-AR)	1992	300	71	0	Electric power sector
Sector investment loan (733/ OC-AR)	1992	350	60	1	Private sector participation and provincial treasury
Debt reduction and service (734/OC-AR)	1992	400	4	0	External debt
TOTAL:		*1375*	*184*		

Source: Based on IDB/OVE, RE-299 (IDB 2004a: 31).

Table C.7 IDB summary of sector loans to Argentina, 1995–98: rising tensions

	Year	Amount (US$ millions)	Number of conditions	Number of reformulations	Areas of activity
Privatisation of provincial banks (865/ OC-AR)	1995	750	19	0	Provincial banks
Fiscal adjustment and social reforms (871/ OC-AR)	1995	450	14	0	Social and labour sectors
Reform of provincial pension funds (961/OC-AR)	1996	320	40	0	Fiscal sector and provincial pension system
TOTAL:		*1520*	*73*		

Source: Based on IDB/OVE, RE-299 (2004a: 31).

Table C.8 IDB summary of sector loans to Argentina 1998–2001: regime decline and crisis

	Year	Amount (US$ millions)	Number of conditions	Number of reformulations	Areas of activity
Structural adjustment and security of the banking system (1163/OC-AR) ('Emergency loan')	1998	2,500	112	2	Fiscal relations with provinces and financial monetary, social and infrastructure sectors
Fiscal balance and social management (1295/OC-AR)	2000	400	20	3	Social security, federal civil service, labour market, social development
Financial services (1324/OC-AR)	2001	500	23–27	4	Retirement and pensions, insurance, capital market
Federal commitment to growth and fiscal discipline (1341/OC-AR)	2001	500	22–24	4	Fiscal relations with provinces, fiscal management
TOTAL:		*3,900*	*132*		

Source: Based on IDB/OVE, RE-299 (IDB 2004a: 31).

Bibliography

Abel, C. and Lewis, C. (eds) (1985) *Latin America, Economic Imperialism and the State: The Political Economy of the External Connection from Independence to the Present*, London: Institute of Latin American Studies, University of London.

—— (2000) *Exclusion and Engagement: Social Policy in Latin America*, London: Institute of Latin American Studies, University of London.

Altimir, O. and Beccaria, L. (2000) 'Distribución del ingreso en la Argentina', in D. Heymann and B. Kosacoff (eds), *La Argentina en los noventa: desempeño económico en un contexto de reformas, Vol. 1*, Buenos Aires: Editorial Universitaria de Buenos Aires and CEPAL Office in Buenos Aires.

Altimir, O., Beccaria, L. and Rozada Gonzalez, M. (2002) 'Income distribution in Argentina, 1974–2000', *CEPAL Review*, 78 (December): 53–82.

APJAE (2006) 'Privatización de la energía en la Republica Argentina: Perdidas y ganancias', Trabajo de investigación realizado por la Asociación del Personal Jerárquico del Agua y Energía, Buenos Aires, Republica Argentina.

Arceo, E. and Basualdo, E. (2002) Las privatizaciones y la consolidación del capital en la economía Argentina, in Azpiazu, D. (ed.) *Privatizaciones y poder económico: La consolidación de una sociedad excluyente,* Buenos Aires: FLACSO and Universidad Nacional de Quilmes.

Arestis, P. (1992) *The Post-Keynesian Approach to Economics*, Aldershot: Edward Elgar.

Argentine Ministry of Economy (2006) 'Economic information', http://www.mecon.gov.ar/peconomica/basehome/infoeco.html.

Arico, J. (1988) *La cola del Diablo,* Buenos Aires: Puntosur.

Artana, D. (1997) 'Los desafíos económicos de la Argentina para el ano 2000', *Revista del Instituto de Capacitación y Formación de Dirigentes Políticos*, no. 1, Buenos Aires: INCAP.

Artana, D. and Dorn, J. (eds) (2003) *Crisis financieras internacionales: Que rol le corresponde al gobierno?,* Buenos Aires: CATO Institute and FIEL.

Astorga, P., Berges, A. and FitzGerald, V. (2002) 'The standard of living in Latin America during the twentieth century', *Discussion Papers in Economic and Social History*, 54 (March).

Azpiazu, D. (ed.) (2002) *Privatizaciones y poder económico: La consolidación de una sociedad excluyente*, Buenos Aires: FLACSO.

Azpiazu, D. and Basualdo, E. (2002) *El Proceso de Privatización en la Argentina: La renegociación con las empresas privatizadas. Revisión contractual y supresión de privilegios y de rentas extraordinarias.* Área de Economía y Tecnología de la FLACSO, Sede Argentina.

Azpiazu, D., Basualdo, E. and Khavisse, M. (1989) *El nuevo poder económico en la Argentina de los años 80*, Buenos Aires: Legasa.

Baker, S. and Weiner, E. (1992) 'Latin America', *Business Week*, 15 June, http://www.businessweek.com/.

Balassa, B. (1980) *Tie Process of International Development and Alternative Development Strategies*, Princeton, NJ: Princeton University Press.

Barrientos, A. (2004) 'Latin America: Towards a liberal-informal welfare regime', in I. Gough and G. Wood (eds), *Insecurity and Welfare Regimes in Asia, Africa and Latin America: Social Policy in Development Contexts*, Cambridge University Press, pp. 121–168.

Basualdo, E. (2001) *Modelo de Acumulación y Sistema Político en Argentina: Notas sobre el transformismo argentino durante la valorización financiera (1976–2001)*, Argentina: Universidad Nacional de Quilmes.

——— (2003) 'Las reformas estructurales y el Plan de Convertibilidad durante la década de los noventa: El auge y la crisis de la valorización financiera', *Revista Realidad Económica*, 200 (December).

Beccaria, L. and López, N. (1996) 'El debilitamiento de los mecanismos de integración social', *Sin Trabajo: Las características del desempleo y sus efectos en la sociedad argentina*, Buenos Aires: Unicef/Losada.

Ben-Artzi, R. (2005) 'Political aid: Is multilateral lending strategic?', unpublished paper, Browne Center for International Politics, University of Pennsylvania.

Benavides, J. (2003) '¿Es posible hacer reformas sostenibles? Consideraciones de análisis y diseño para el sector eléctrico', *Serie de informes técnicos del Departamento de Desarrollo Sostenible*, Washington, DC: Banco Interamericano de Desarrollo.

Bennett, A. and George, A. (1997) 'Research design tasks in case study methods', paper presented at the MacArthur Foundation Workshop on Case Study Methods, Belfer Center for Science and International Affairs (BCSIA), Harvard University, 17–19 October.

Bergsten, F. (1997) 'Open regionalism', *World Economy*, 20: 91–123.

Bezanson, K. *et al.* (2000) 'A foresight and policy study of the multilateral development banks', prepared for the Institute of Development Studies at the University of Sussex, UK, and the Ministry of Foreign Relations of Sweden.

Bielschowsky, R. (1998) 'CEPAL cincuenta años: reflexiones sobre América Latina y el Caribe', *Revista CEPAL*, numero extraordinario, October, Santiago de Chile: CEPAL.

Birdsall, N. (2003) 'Why it matters who runs the IMF and the World Bank', Working Paper no. 22, Washington, DC: Center for Global Development.

Birdsall, N. and Rojas-Suarez, L. (2004) *Financing Development: The Power of Regionalism*, Washington, DC: Center for Global Development.

Bøås, M. and McNeill, D. (eds) (2004) *Global Institutions and Development: Framing the World*, New York: Routledge.

Bonilla, A. and Long, G. (2010) 'Un nuevo regionalismo sudamericano', *ICONOS* 38, pp. 23–104.

Bouille, D., Dubrovsky, H. and Maurer, C. (2001) 'Reform of the electric power sector in developing countries: Case study of Argentina', paper, Institute of Energy Economics, Bariloche Foundation, World Resources Institute.

Bouzas, R. and Keifman, S. (1990) 'Deuda externa y negociaciones financieras en la década de los ochenta: una evaluación de la experiencia argentina', *FLACSO Documentos e Informes de Investigación*, 98.

Brennan, J. (1995) 'Industrial sectors and union politics in Latin American labor movement: Light and power workers in Argentina and Mexico', *Latin American Research Review*, 30 (1): 39–68.

Bronstein, A. (1995) 'Societal change and industrial relations in Latin America: Trends and prospects', *International Labour Review*, 134 (2): 163–187.

Bulmer-Thomas, V. (ed.) (1996) *The New Economic Model in Latin America and Its Impact on Income Distribution and Poverty*, London: Macmillan.

—— (ed.) (2001) *Regional Integration in Latin America and the Caribbean: The Political Economy of Open Regionalism*, London: Institute of Latin American Studies, University of London.

—— (2003) *The Economic History of Latin America Since Independence*, 2nd edn, Cambridge University Press.

Burgess, R. (ed.) (1982a) *Field Research: A Sourcebook and Field Manual*, London: Routledge.

—— (1982b) 'The role of theory in field research', in R. Burgess (ed.), *Field Research: A Sourcebook and Field Manual*, London: Routledge, pp. 209–212.

Burgos, R. and Perez, C. (2002) 'The Gramscian intervention in the theoretical and political production of the Latin American Left', *Latin American Perspectives*, 29 (1): pp. 9–37.

Buxton, J. and Phillips, N. (eds) (1999) *Development in Latin American Political Economy: States, Markets and Actors*, New York: Manchester University Press.

Caballero, R. (2000) 'Macroeconomic volatility in Latin America: A conceptual framework and three case studies', *Economía,* pp. 31–88.

Caballero, R. and Dornbusch, R. (2002) 'The battle for Argentina', paper, Massachusetts Institute of Technology.

Calderon, C. and Serven, L. (2004) 'Trends in Infrastructure in Latin America, 1980–2001', World Bank Policy Research Working Paper, no. 3401.

Calvo, G. (1996) *Capital Flows, and Macroeconomic Management: Tequila Lessons*, mimeo, Center for International Economics (CIE), University of Maryland.

—— (2000a) 'The case for hard pegs in the brave new world of global finance', mimeo, University of Maryland.

—— (2000b) 'Capital market and the exchange rate: with special reference to the dollarization debate in Latin America', mimeo, Center for International Economics (CIE), University of Maryland.

Calvo, G. and Mendoza, E. (1996) 'Mexico's balance-of-payment crisis: a chronicle of a death foretold', *Journal of International Economics,* 41 (3–4), pp. 235–264.

Calvo, G. and Reinhart C. (1999) 'Fear of floating: theory and evidence', mimeo, University of Maryland.

Calvo, G., Leiderman, L. and Reinhart, C. (1993) 'Capital inflows and real exchange appreciation in Latin America: The role of external factors', *IMF Staff Papers*, 40 (1): 108–151.

—— (1996) 'Inflows of capital to developing countries in the 1990s', *Journal of Economic Perspectives*, 10 (2) (Spring): 123–139.

Castells, M. (1996) *The Rise of the Network Society*, Oxford: Blackwell.

Cavallo, D. (2004a) 'America Latina y el Consenso de Washington', Module no. 1, Department of Economics, Harvard University.

—— (2004b) 'Argentina and the IMF during the two Bush Administrations', *International Finance*, 7 (1): 137–150.

CEPAL (UN Economic Commission for Latin America and the Caribbean) (1983) *Latin America*, Report, Santiago de Chile: CEPAL.

—— (1990) *Transformación Productiva con Equidad: la tarea prioritaria del desarrollo de América Latina y el Caribe en los años noventa* (LC/G.1601-P). Santiago de Chile, Marzo de 1990. Publicación de las Naciones Unidas, no. de venta: S.90.II.G.6.

—— (1994) *Open Regionalism in Latin America and the Caribbean: Economic Integration as a Contribution to Changing Production Patterns with Social Equity*, LC.G.1801, SES 25.

—— (2000) *Globalization and Regionalization: A View from Latin America and Caribbean*. Accessible at http://www.eclac.org/.

Chudnovsky, D. and Lopez, A. (2000) 'El boom de inversion extranjera directa en Argentina en los años 1990: Caracteristicas, determinantes e impactos', paper presented at the Regional Conference 'What future for Mercosur?, Buenos Aires, 20–30 November.

Clarín newspaper, several articles available at http://www.clarin.com/.

Cline, W. (2002) 'Financial Crisis and Poverty in Emerging Market Economies', Working Paper No. 8, Center for Global Development, June.

Cohen, B. (2008) *International Political Economy. An Intellectual History*. Princeton, NJ: Princeton University Press, pp. 1–66.

Cox, R. (1981) 'Social forces, states and world orders: Beyond international relations theory', *Millennium Journal of International Studies*, 10 (2): 126–155.

—— (1987) *Production, Power, and World Order: Social Forces in the Making of History*, New York: Columbia University Press.

—— (1989) 'Middlepowermanship: Japan and the future world order', *International Journal*, 44 (Autumn): 826–827.

—— (1992) 'Multilateralism and world order', *Review of International Studies*, 18 (2): 161–180.

—— (1996a) 'Social forces, states, and world orders: Beyond international relations theory', in R. Cox and T. Sinclair, *Approaches to World Order*, Cambridge: Cambridge University Press, pp. 85–123.

—— (1996b) 'Gramsci, hegemony, and international relations. An essay in method', in R. Cox and T. Sinclair, *Approaches to World Order*, Cambridge: Cambridge University Press, pp. 124–143.

—— (1997) 'Democracy in hard times: Economic globalisation and the limits to liberal democracy', In A. McGrew (ed.), *The Transformation of Democracy? Globalisation and Territorial Democracy*, Cambridge: Polity Press.

—— (2000) 'Political economy and world order: Problems of power and knowledge at the turn of the millennium', in R. Stubbs and G. Underhill (eds), *Political Economy and the Changing Global Order*, Toronto: Oxford University Press, pp. 25–37.

—— (2009) 'The "British School" in the global context', *The New Political Economy*, 14(3): 316–328.

Cox, R. and Schechter, M. (2002) *The Political Economy of a Plural World: Critical Reflections on Power, Morals and Civilization*, London: Routledge.

Cox, R. and Sinclair, T. (1996) *Approaches to World Order*, Cambridge: Cambridge University Press.

Culpeper, R. (1993) *The Regional Development Banks, vol. 5, Titans or Behemoths?*, Boulder, CO: Rienner.

—— (1999) 'Long-Term Financing for Development in the Presence of Market Instability', paper at Annual Meeting of the Central American Bank for Economic Integration, 28 October.

—— (2000) 'Systemic reform at a standstill: a flock of "Gs" in search of global financial stability', prepared for Commonwealth Secretariat/World Bank Conference on 'Developing Countries and Global Financial Architecture', Marlborough House, London, 22–23 June.

Dal Din, C. (2000) 'La Apertura Financiera Argentina de los '90. Una visión complementaria de la balanza de pagos', *FIEL Documento de Trabajo*, no. 64.

Damill, M. (2002) 'El balance de pagos y la deuda externa publica bajo la convertibilidad', paper, Cedes, Centre of Studies of State and Society.

Damill, M., Frenkel, R. and Rapetti, M. (2005) 'La deuda Argentina: historia, default y *reestructuración'*, paper, Cedes, Centre of Studies of State and Society.

Dasgupta, D. and Ratha, D. (2000) 'The role of short-term debt in recent crisis', *Finance and Development*, 37 (December): 54–57.

Deacon, B., Hulse, M. and Stubbs, P. (1997) *Global Social Policy: International Organizations and the Future of Welfare*, London: Sage.

DeLong, B. (2004) Website, available at http://www.j-bradford-delong.net/.

Devlin, R. and Castro, L. (2004) 'Regional banks and regionalism: A new frontier for development financing', in N. Birdsall and L. Rojas-Suarez, *Financing Development: The Power of Regionalism*, Washington, DC: Center for Global Development, pp. 41–82.

Diaz Alejandro, C. (1970) *Essays on the Economic History of the Argentine Republic*, London: Yale University Press.

—— (1989) 'Comment on two (or more) Peronisms', in G. Di Tella and R. Dornbusch (eds), *The Political Economy of Argentina, 1946–83*, London: Macmillan and Saint Antony's College, Oxford, pp. 86–88.

—— (2000) 'Latin America in the 1930s', in R. Thorp (ed.), *An Economic History of Twentieth-Century Latin America, Vol. 2: Latin America in the 1930s: The Role of the Periphery in World Crisis*, London: Palgrave, pp. 15–42.

Diaz-Bonilla, E. and Schamis, H. (2001) 'From redistribution to stability: The evolution of exchange rate policies in Argentina 1950–98', in J. Frieden and E. Stein (eds), *The Currency Game: Exchange Rate Politics in Latin America*, Washington, DC: Inter-American Development Bank, pp. 65–118.

Di Tella, T. (1998) 'El futuro de los partidos políticos en la Argentina', *Revista de la CEPAL*, Numero Extraordinario, pp. 343–350.

Di Tella, G. and Dornbusch, R. (eds) (1989) *The Political Economy of Argentina, 1946–83*, London: Macmillan and Saint Antony's College, Oxford.

Dornbusch, R. (1996) *Currency Crises in the Aftermath of Reform*, Cambridge, MA: Massachusetts Institute of Technology.

—— (1999) *The Brazil Problem: V-Shaped Recovery and Beyond*, Cambridge, MA: Massachusetts Institute of Technology.

Dornbusch, R. and Edwards, S. (1991) The *Macroeconomic of Populism in Latin America*, Chicago: Chicago University Press.

Downward, P. and Mearman, A. (2006) 'Retroduction as mixed-methods triangulation in economic research reorienting economics into social science', *Cambridge Journal of Economics*, April: 1–23.

Drucker, P. (1976) *Unseen Revolution: How Pension Fund Socialism Came to America*, New York: Harper and Row.

Eaton, K. (2005) 'Menem and the Governors: Intergovernmental relations in the 1990s', in S. Levitsky and M. Murillo (eds), *The Politics of Institutional Weakness: Argentine Democracy*, University Park, PA: Pennsylvania State University Press, pp. 88–114.

Eatwell, J. (1996) *International Financial Liberation: The Impact on World Development*, New York: United Nations Development Programme.

Eatwell, J. and Taylor, L. (1999) 'Towards an effective regulation of international capital markets', *Politic and Gesellschaft, International Politics and Society*, 3: 279–286.

Edwards, S. (1998) 'Openness, productivity and growth: What do we really know', *Economic Journal*, 108 (44) (March): 383–398.

—— (2000) *Twenty-Five Years of Stabilization Programs in Latin America: The Exchange Rate Connection*, paper of National Bureau of Economic Research, Anderson Graduate School of Management, University of California and Universidad Austral.

Eichengreen, B. and Hausman, R. (2004) 'The mystery of original sin', in B. Eichengreen and R. Hausmann (eds), *Other People's Money*, University of Chicago Press.

Energy Information Administration (EIA) (1997) *Electricity Reform Abroad and US Investment*, Washington, DC: US Department of Energy, available at http://www.eia.doe.gov/.

Epstein, G. (2006) *Financialization of the World Economy*, Aldershot: Edward Elgar.

Escude, C. and Cisneros, A. (2000) *Historia de las Relaciones Exteriores Argentinas*, Buenos Aires: Consejo Argentino para las Relaciones Exteriores; Centro de Estudios de Política Exterior.

Espinosa Carranza, J. (2002) 'Enrique Iglesias: reto y respuesta', in IDB Mas, *Que un Banco: Banco interamericano de Desarrollo, 40 Anos*, Washington, DC: Banco interamericano de Desarrollo, pp. 129–192.

Etchemendy, S. (2005) 'Old actors in new markets: Transforming the populist/industrial coalition in Argentina, 1989–2001', in S. Levitsky and M. Murillo (eds), *The Politics of Institutional Weakness: Argentine Democracy*, Pennsylvania: Pennsylvania University Press, pp. 62–87.

Fanelli, J. and Machinea, J. (1994) 'Capital Movements in Argentina', *Documento CEDES, Serie Economia,* available at: http://www.cedes.org/.

Farnsworth, C. (1988) 'Restructuring planned by Latin Aid Bank', *New York Times*, 20 December, p. D20.

Fawcett, L. and Hurrel, A. (eds) (1995) *Regionalism in World Politics*, Oxford: Oxford University Press.

Ffrench-Davis, R. (2002) 'Financial crises and national policy issues: An overview', *WIDER Discussion Paper*, no. 81, August.

Ffrench-Davis, R. and Larrain, G. (2002) 'How optimal are the extremes? Latin American exchange rate policies during the Asian crises', *WIDER Discussion Paper*, no. 18, January.

FitzGerald, V. (2002) 'The instability of the emerging market assets demand schedule', WIDER *Discussion Paper*, no. 80, August.

FMI (2001) 'Emerging market debt: Quarterly report on development and prospects', Washington, DC: FMI, August.

Foley, D. (2002) 'The strange history of the economic agent', paper, Department of Economics, New School University, New York.

—— (2003) 'Rationality and ideology in economics', paper prepared for the Department of Economics, Graduate Faculty, New School University, New York.

FONDAD (2003) *The Crisis That Was Not Prevented: Argentina, the IMF, and Globalisation*, available at: www.fondad.org.

Franco, M. (2002) *Fases y momento actual de la estructura social Argentina*, Mendoza: Universidad Nacional de Cuyo.

Frenkel, J. and Schmukler, S. (1998) 'Crises, contagion, and country funds: Effects on East Asia and Latin America', in G. Reuven (ed.), *Managing Capital Flows and Exchange Rates: Perspectives from Pacific Basin*, New York: Cambridge University Press, pp. 232–266.

Frenkel, R. (1998) 'Capital market liberalization and economic performance in Latin America', in *SCEPA Working Papers 1998–06*, New York: The New School, Schwartz Center for Economic Policy Analysis (SCEPA).

—— (2003) 'Gobalization and financial crises in Latin America', *Iktisat Isletme ve Finans, Bilgesel Yayincilik*, 18 (207): 41–56.

—— (2004) 'Real exchange rate and employment in Argentina, Brazil, Chile and Mexico', paper prepared for the G24 meeting, draft.

Frenkel, R. and González Rozada, M. (2002) 'Tendencias de la distribución de ingresos en los años noventa', *Nuevos Documentos CEDES*, Área económica.

Frenkel, R. and Ros, J. (2004) 'Unemployment, macroeconomic policy and labour market: Argentina', Working Paper no. 309, February, Kellogg Institute.

Frieden, J. and Stein, E. (eds) (2001) *The Currency Game: Exchange Rate Politics in Latin America*, Washington: Inter-American Bank, Latin American Research Network.

Gamble, A. (2001) 'Regional blocs, world order and the new medievalism', in M. Telo (ed.), *European Union and New Regionalism*, Aldershot: Ashgate, pp. 21–38.

—— (2003) 'States and world order', in J. Busumtwi-Sam and G. Kelly (eds), *Turbulence and New Direction in Global Political Economy*, London: Palgrave Macmillan, pp. 49–66.

Gamble, A. and Payne, T. (eds) (1996) *Regionalism and World Order*, London: Palgrave Macmillan.

—— (2003) 'The world order approach', in F. Söderbaum and T. Shaw, *Theories of New Regionalism*, Houndmills: Palgrave Macmillan, pp. 43–62.

García Delgado, D. (1994) *Estado y Sociedad. La nueva relación a partir del cambio estructural*, Buenos Aires: FLACSO/Grupo Editor de America Latina.

Garret, G. and Mitchell, D. (1999) 'Globalisation and the welfare state', mimeo.

General Accounting Office, United States, GAO (1996) 'Budget Issues: Privatization Practices in Argentina', Report to the Honourable Scott Klug, House of Representatives. Washington, DC: General Accounting Office.

Gerchunoff, P. and Canovas, G. (1996) 'Privatization: the Argentine experience', in G. William (ed.), *Bigger Economies, Smaller Governments. Privatization in Latin America*, Boulder, CO: Westview Press.

Gerchunoff, P. and Llach, L. (2005) *El ciclo de la illusion y el desencanto. Un siglo de políticas económicas argentinas*, Buenos Aires: Ariel.

Germain, R. (1997) *The International Organization of Credit: States and Global Finance in the World-Economy*, Cambridge: Cambridge University Press.

—— (2002) 'Reforming the International Financial Architecture: The New Political Agenda', paper prepared for the Department of International Politics, University of Wales, Aberystwyth.

Giddens, A. (1996) 'Globalization: A keynote address', *UNRISD News*, 15.

Gill, S. (1993) Epistemology, ontology, and the 'Italian school, in S. Gill (ed.) *Gramsci, Historical Materialism and International Relations*, New York: Cambridge University Press, pp. 21–48.

—— (2000a) Knowledge, Politics, and Neo-Liberal Political Economy, in R. Stubbs and R. Underhill (eds) *Political Economy and the Changing Global Order*, 2nd edn, Canada: Oxford University Press, pp. 48–59.

—— (2000b) 'The constitution of global capitalism', paper presented to a panel: The Capitalist World, Past and Present at the International Studies Association Annual Convention, Los Angeles, available at http://www.theglobalsite.ac.uk.

Glaser, B. (1982) 'Generating formal theory', in R. Burgess (ed.), *Field Research: A sourcebook and field manual*, London: Routledge, pp. 225–232.

Glick, R., Moreno, R. and Spiegel, M. (2001) *Financial Crisis in Emerging Markets*, Cambridge: Cambridge University Press.

Goldstein, M. and Turner, P. (1996) 'Banking crises in emerging economies: Origins and policy options', *BIS Economic Papers*, 46.

González, E. (2006) 'La verdad sobre Endesa', *Libertad digital*, http://www.libertaddigital.com, accessed 19 September 2006.

Gough, I. and Wood, G. (eds) (2004) *Insecurity and Welfare Regimes in Asia, Africa and Latin America: Social Policy in Development Contexts*, Cambridge: Cambridge University Press.

Gramsci, A. (1971) *Selections from the Prison Notebooks of Antonio Gramsci*, ed. and trans. Q. Hoare and G. Nowell Smith, London: Lawrence and Wishart.

Gray, J. (1998) *The False Dawn*, London: Granta.

Griffith-Jones, S. (1984) *International Finance and Latin America*, New York: St. Martin's Press.

—— (ed.) (1988) *Managing World Debt*, London: Harvester Wheatsheaf.

—— (1994) *Assessment of the IDB Lending Programme, 1979–92*, Sussex: Institute of Development Studies.

—— (2002a) 'Capital flows to developing countries', *WIDER Discussion Papers*, available at http://www.stephanygj.com/papers.

—— (2002b) 'Governance of the World Bank', paper prepared for DFID, available at http://www.stephanygj.com/papers.

—— (2003) 'The context for capital account liberalisation; Where Goes the International Financial System?', Institute of Development Studies, University of Sussex, available at http://www.stephanygj.com/papers.

Griffith-Jones, S. and Ffrench-Davis, R. (eds) (1995) *Coping with Capital Surges. The Return of Finance to Latin America*, Boulder, CO: Lynne Rienner Publishers.

Grugel, J. (1996) 'Latin America and the remaking of the Americas', in A. Gamble and A. Payne (eds), *Regionalism and World Order*, London: Macmillan, pp. 131–167.

—— (ed.) (1999) *Democracy Without Borders. Transnationalisation and Conditionality in New Democracies*, London: Routledge.

—— (2001) *Democratization: A Critical Introduction*. Basingstoke: Palgrave.

Gurria, J. and Volcker, P. (2001) 'The role of the multilateral development banks in emerging market economies', Findings of the Commission on the Role of the MDBs in Emerging Markets, Washington, DC: Inter-American Dialogue.

Haagh, L. and Helgo, C. (eds) (2002) *Social Policy Reform and Market Governance in Latin America*, New York: Palgrave Macmillan.

Haber, S. (ed.) (2002) *Crony Capitalism and Economic Growth in Latin America: Theory and Evidence*, Stanford, CA: Hoover Institution Press.

Hall, D. (2004) 'Electricity in Latin America 2004', Public Services International Research Unit (PSIRU), http://www.psiru.org.

—— (2005) 'Electricity privatisation and restructuring in Latin America and the impact on workers', Public Services International Research Unit (PSIRU), http://www.psiru.org.

Hall, S. (1982) 'The rediscovery of ideology', in M. Gurevitch *et al.* (eds) *Culture, Society and the Media*, London: Methuen.

Halperin Donghi, T. (1993) *The Contemporary History of Latin America*, 3rd edn, Durham, NC: Duke University Press.

Hanke, S. (2002) 'Currency boards', *Paper Cato Institute,* no. 579, January, available at http://www.elcato.org/.

Hartwell, C. (2001) 'The case against capital controls: Financial flows, crises, and the flip side of the free trade argument', *Policy Analysis*, 14 June: 403.

Hausmann, R. (1999) 'Should there be five currencies or one hundred and five?', *Foreign Policy*, 116: 65–79.

Hay, C. (2002) *Political Analysis: A Critical Introduction*, Houndmills: Palgrave.

Held, D., McGrew, A., Goldblatt, D. and Perraton, J. (1999) *Global Transformations: Politics and Culture*, Cambridge: Polity Press.

Helleiner, E. (1994) *States and the Reemergence of Global Finance*, Ithaca, NY: Cornell University Press.

Hernández, D. (2003) 'Political process and the outcome of structural reforms in pension systems', Seminario de Evaluación de las Reformas de la Seguridad Social, Montevideo *CLAEH*, 27–28 April.

Herrera, F. (1970) 'A decade of achievements', address by Mr. Felipe Herrera, President of the Inter-American Development Bank, at the Eleventh Annual Meeting of the Board of Governors of the Bank in Punta del Este, Uruguay, 20–24 April, Washington, DC.

Herring, H. (1955) *History of Latin America from the Beginnings to the Present*, New York: Alfred Knopf.

Herz, R., Kappen, J. and Monari, L. (2005) 'Study on investment and private sector participation in power distribution in Latin America and the Caribbean Region', *ESMA Technical Paper* no. 089, World Bank Group.

Hettne, B. (2003) 'The new regionalism revisited', in F. Söderbaum and T. Shaw (eds), *Theories of New Regionalism*, Houndmills: Palgrave Macmillan, pp. 22–42.

Hettne, B. and Inotai, A. (1994) *The New Regionalism: Implications for Global Development and International Security,* Helsinki: United Nations University World Institute for Development and Economic Research.

Hettne, B. and Söderbaum, F. (1999) 'Rethinking development theory: Guest Editor's Introduction', *Journal of International Relations and Development*, 2 (4): 354–357.

Higgott, B. (1994) 'International political economy', in A. Groom and M. Light (eds), *Contemporary International Relations: A Guide to Theory*, London: Pinter, pp. 69–114.

Hirst, P. and Thompson, G. (1996) *Globalization in Question: The International Economy and the Possibilities of Governance*, Cambridge: Polity Press.

Hobson, J. (2003) 'Disappearing taxes or the 'race to the middle'? Fiscal policy in the OECD, in L. Weiss (ed.) *States in the Global Economy: Bringing Domestic Institutions Back in*, Cambridge: Cambridge University Press.

Hobson, J. and Ramesh, M. (2002) 'Globalisation makes of states what states make of it: Between agency and structure in the state/globalisation debate', *New Political Economy*, 7 (1): 5–22.

Hobson, J. and Seabrooke, L. (2006) *Everyday International Political Economy: Non-Elite Agency in the Transformations of the World Economy*, Cambridge: Cambridge University Press.

Huber, E. and Stephens, J. (2001) *Development and Crisis of the Welfare State: Parties and Policies in Global Markets*, Chicago: University of Chicago Press.

Huntington, S. (1993) 'The clash of civilizations', *Foreign Affairs*, 72 (3) (Summer): 22–28.

Iglesias, E. (2004) 'Comments', in N. Birdsall and L. Rojas-Suarez (eds), *Financing Development: The Power of Regionalism*, Washington, DC: Center for Global Development, pp. 83–86.

Inter-American Development Bank (IDB) (1991a) GN-1686–7: 'Debt and debt service reduction facility: Operational guidelines', 22 March, Washington, DC: IDB.

—— (1991b) 863/SF-AR: 'Provincial electric power program', Washington, DC: IDB.

—— (1991c) 633/OC-AR: 'Public sector reform', Washington, DC: IDB.

—— (1991d) 619/OC-AR: 'Provinces development program', Washington, DC: IDB.

—— (1992) 682/OC-AR: 'Reform of national electric power utilities', Washington, DC: IDB.

—— (1994) AB-1704: 'Informe sobre la octaba reposicion de capital del Banco Interamericano de Desarrollo', Washington, DC: IDB.

—— (1995a) 'Amendment relating to the eighth general increase in the resources of the Bank', Washington, DC: IDB.

—— (1995b) 865/OC-AR: 'Provincial banks privatization sector loan', Washington, DC: IDB.

—— (1995c) 871/OC-AR: 'Sector program in support of fiscal adjustment and social reform', Washington, DC: IDB.

—— (1996) 961/OC-AR: 'Provincial social security sector reform program', Washington, DC: IDB.

—— (1997a) GN-1894–5: 'Strategy for poverty reduction', IDB Board, Washington, DC: IDB.

—— (1997b) 1021/OC-AR: 'Care for vulnerable groups', Washington, DC: IDB

—— (1997c) 1031/OC-AR: 'Support for youth productivity and employability', Washington, DC: IDB.

—— (1998a) OA-330: 'Sector loans-specific rules: Bank operations administration manual', February, Washington, DC: IDB.

—— (1998b) 'Elementos estratégicos para el sector energía en América Latina y el Caribe', SDS/ENV, Washington, DC: IDB.

—— (1998c) 1111/OC-AR: 'Care for children and adolescents at risk', Washington, DC: IDB.

—— (1998d) 1118/OC-AR, 'Emergency flood rehabilitation program', Washington, DC: IDB.

—— (1998d) 1163/OC-AR: ''Structural adjustment and security of the banking system', Washington, DC: IDB.

—— (1998e) 1164/OC-AR, 'Municipal reform and development program', Washington, DC: IDB.

—— (1999a) OVE, RE-239: 'Summary report: Evaluation of the policy-based loan portfolio-phase III', Washington, DC: IDB.

—— (1999b) OVE, RE-242: 'Evaluation report: Action plan for Group C and D countries', Washington, DC: IDB.

—— (2000a) CS-3292–5: 'Report of an independent consultant on the development impact and credit quality of the private sector department portfolio', presented at an informal meeting of the Board of Executive Directors, Washington, DC: IDB.

—— (2000b) 1295/OC-AR: 'Fiscal balance and social management', Washington, DC: IDB.

—— (2001a) 'Energy sector strategy', Sustainable Development Department (SDS), Washington, DC: IDB.

—— (2001b) OVE, RE-246: 'Nota de evaluación del programa con Argentina – período 1996–1999', Washington, DC: IDB.

—— (2001b) OVE, RE-250: 'Summary of findings – decentralization and effective citizen participation: Six cautionary tales', Washington, DC: IDB.

—— (2001c) OVE, RE-251: 'Evaluation report: Emergency loans', Washington, DC: IDB.

—— (2001d) 1324/OC-AR: 'Financial services', Washington, DC: IDB.

—— (2001e) 1341/OC-AR: 'Federal commitment to growth and fiscal discipline', Washington, DC: IDB.

—— (2002a) OVE, RE-273: 'Evaluation of bank action and strategy for small and medium enterprise (1990–2000)', Washington, DC: IDB.

—— (2002b) 'Competitiveness: The business of growth: Report economic and social progress in Latin America', Research Department (RS), Washington, DC: IDB.

—— (2002c) OVE, RE-258: 'Reseña del trabajo del OVE relativa a la eficacia en función del desarrollo', Washington, DC: IDB.

—— (2002d) OVE, RE-260: 'Development effectiveness report', Washington, DC: IDB.

—— (2003a) OVE, RE-287: 'Synthesis of OVE evaluations of bank action for private sector department', Washington, DC: IDB.

—— (2003b) OVE, RE-288: 'Poverty reduction and the IDB: An evaluation of the bank's strategy and efforts', Washington, DC: IDB.

—— (2003c) 'Modernization of the state: Strategy document', IDB Board, Washington, DC: IDB.

—— (2003d) 'Modernization of the state: Strategy document', Sustainable Development Department (SDS), Washington, DC: IDB.

—— (2003e) OVE, RE-279: 'Oversight note on the performance criteria for allocating concessional resources', Washington, DC: IDB.

—— (2003f, 2004) 'Evaluation of MIF projects', Multilateral Investment Fund, Washington, DC: IDB.

—— (2003g) OVE, MIF/GN-78–3: 'Evaluation of microfinance', Washington, DC: IDB.

—— (2003h) OVE, MIF/GN-78–4: 'Financial reform and capital markets', Washington, DC: IDB.

—— (2003i) OVE, MIF/GN-78–8: 'Human resources and labor market projects', Washington, DC: IDB.

—— (2004a) OVE, RE-299: 'Country program evaluation (CPE) Argentina 1990–2002', Washington, DC: IDB.

—— (2004b) OVE, RE-300: 'Instruments and development: An evaluation of IDB lending modalities', Washington, DC: IDB.

—— (2004c) OVE, RE-303: 'Evaluation of the bank's direct private sector lending program 1995–2003', Office of Evaluation and Oversight, Washington, DC: IDB.

—— (2004c) 'Independent evaluation report to the IIC Board of Executive Directors CII/RE-1, CII/RE-2, and CII/RE-3 (2001–2003)', Washington, DC: IDB.

—— (2004d) 'A decade of development thinking' RES, Washington, DC: IDB.

—— (2004e) OVE, MIF/GN-79–9: 'Private participation in infrastructure', Washington, DC: IDB.

International Financial Institutions Commission (2000) Meltzer Report, March, Washington, DC.

Jones, C. (1991) 'Qualitative interviewing', in A. Graham (ed.), *Handbook for Research Students in the Social Sciences*, London: Falmer Press, pp. 203–212.

Kaminsky, G. and Reinhart, C. (1999) *Financial Crises in Asia and Latin America: Then and Now*, Washington, DC: Board of Governors of the Federal Reserve System.
—— (2000) 'On crises, contagion, and confusion', *Journal of International Economics*, 51 (1) (June): 145–168.
—— (2002) 'The center and the periphery: the globalization of financial turmoil', mimeo, Washington, DC: George Washington University.
Kaminsky, G., Lyons, R. and Schmukler, S. (2001) 'Managers, investors, and crises: Mutual fund strategies in emerging markets', *The World Bank Economic Review*, 15 (2): 315–382.
Kennedy, J. F. (1962) News Conference, Historical Resources, John F. Kennedy Presidential Library, available at http://www.jfklibrary.org/Historical+Resources/Archives/Reference+Desk/Press+Conferences/003POF05Pressconference38_07051962.htm.
Keynes, J. (1936) *The General Theory of Employment, Interest and Money*, London: Macmillan.
Kosacoff, B. (1999) 'Las multinacionales argentinas', *Boletín Informativo Techint*, no. 300, available at: http://www.boletintechint.com/boin/index.asp.
—— (ed.) (2000) *Corporate Strategies Under Structural Adjustment in Argentina*, London: Macmillan.
Krueger, A. (2002) 'Why crony capitalism is bad for economic growth', in S. Haber (ed.), *Crony Capitalism and Economic Growth in Latin America: Theory and Evidence*, Stanford, CA: Hoover Institution Press, pp. 1–24.
Krugman, P. (1991) 'Regional blocs: The good, the bad and the ugly', *International Economy*, November/December: 54.
—— (1995) 'Dutch tulips and emerging markets', *Foreign Affairs*, 74 (July): 28–38.
Kulfas, M. (1999) *Características de la inversión extranjera en Argentina en la década del noventa*, Buenos Aires: CEP.
—— (2001) *El impacto del proceso de fusiones y adquisiciones en la Argentina sobre el mapa de grandes empresas*, Santiago de Chile: CEPAL.
Kulfas, M. and Schorr, M. (2003) 'Deuda externa y valorización financiera en la Argentina actual: Factores explicativos del crecimiento del endeudamiento externo y perspectivas ante el proceso de renegociación', *Revista Realidad Económica*, 198 (August–September): 1–21.
Kuwayama, M. (1993) 'Regionalización abierta de America Latina para su adecuada inserción Internacional', *Documento de Trabajo*, 20 (September), CEPAL.
—— (1999) 'Open regionalism in Asia Pacific and Latin America: A survey of the literature', *Series comercio internacional CEPAL*, December.
La Nación newspaper, several articles available at http://www.lanacion.com.ar/.
Lanata, J. (2003) *Argentinos, Vol. 2: Desde Yrigoyen hasta la caída de De la Rua*, Buenos Aires: Ediciones B.
Larrain, J. (1983) *Marxist Theories of Ideology*, London: Hutchinson.
Lawson, T. (2003) *Reorienting Economics*, London: Routledge.
Levine, R. and Zervos, S. (1996) 'Stock market development and long-run growth', *The World Bank Economic Review*, 10 (2): 323–339.
Levinson, J. and de Onis, J. (1970) *The Alliance That Lost Its Way: A Critical Report on the Alliance for Progress*, Chicago: Quadrangle.
Levitsky, S. (2003) *Transforming Labor-Based Parties in Latin America: Argentina Peronism in Comparative Perspective*, Cambridge: Cambridge University Press.

Levitsky, S. and Murillo, M. (2003) 'Argentina weathers the storm', *Journal of Democracy*, 14 (October): 152–166.

—— (eds) (2005) *The Politics of Institutional Weakness: Argentine Democracy*, Pennsylvania: Pennsylvania University Press.

Lewis, C. (2000) 'The political economy of macroeconomic stability: History, democracy and the rule of the economic game in the Argentina', unpublished.

—— (2003) 'Estado, Mercado y Sociedad: políticas e instituciones de acción económica y social en América Latina desde 1900', unpublished.

Lewis, P. (1988) 'Latins fighting US bid for veto power at bank', *New York Times*, 12 January, p. D3.

Leys, C. (1996a), *The Rise and Fall of Development Theory*, Bloomington: Indiana University Press.

—— (1996b) 'The crisis in "development theory"', *New Political Economy*, 1 (1): 41–58.

Littlechild, S. and Skerk, C. (2004) 'Regulation of transmission expansion in Argentina Part 1: State ownership, reform and the Fourth Line', *Cambridge Working Papers in Economics*, CWPE 0464.

Llach, J. (1997) *Otro siglo, otra Argentina*, Buenos Aires: Ariel.

Lora, E., Pages-Serra, C., Panizza, U. and Stein, E. (2004) *A Decade of Development Thinking*, Washington, DC: Research Department, Inter-American Development Bank.

Loser, C. (2006) 'Argentina's turnaround', on NPR's 'Kojo Nnamdi Show', Washington, DC.

Lousteau, M. (2003) *Hacia un federalismo solidario*, Buenos Aires: Temas Grupo Editorial.

Lozano, C. (2001) *Remarcas del mercado laboral en Argentina*, Buenos Aires: Instituto de Estudios y Formación.

Lucioni, L. (2003) 'Orientación del financiamiento de organismos internacionales a provincias', *Revista CEPAL*, serie estudios y perspectivas, no. 17.

MacDonald, C. (1980) 'The Politics of Intervention: The United States in Argentina, 1941–1946', *Journal of Latin American Studies* 12 (2): 365–396.

—— (1985) 'The US, the Cold War and Peron', in C. Abel and C. Lewis (eds), *Latin America, Economic Imperialism and the State: The Political Economy of the External Connection from Independence to the Present*, London: Institute of Latin American Studies, University of London, pp. 405–414.

McGrew, A. (ed.) (1997) *The Transformation of Democracy?*, Cambridge: Polity Press.

Mainwaring, S. and Sully, T. (1995) *Building Democratic Institutions. Party Systems in Latin América*, Stanford, CA: Stanford University Press.

Maldonado, P. and Palma, R. (2004) 'Seguridad y calidad del abastecimiento eléctrico a mas de 10 anos de la reforma de la industria eléctrica en países de América del Sur', *Series recursos naturales e infraestructura*, 72, Santiago de Chile: CEPAL.

Mann, M. (1997) 'Has globalization ended the rise and rise of the nation-state?', *Review of International Political Economy*, 4 (3): 497–513.

May, T. (2001) *Social Research: Issues, Methods and Process*, 3rd edn, Open University Press.

Meltzer, A. (1998) 'Financial structure, saving and growth: Safety nets, regulation, and risk reduction in global financial markets', prepared for the First International Monetary Conference of the Bank of Korea, Seoul, Korea, 22 June.

—— (2001) 'Reforming the international financial institutions: A plan for financial stability and economic development', paper, Carnegie Mellon University.

—— (2002) 'Argentina and the IMF', Testimony before the Committee on Financial Structure Subcommittee on International Monetary Policy and Trade, U.S. House of Representatives, 5 March.

—— (2004) 'Comments', in N. Birdsall and L. Rojas-Suarez (eds), *Financing Development: The Power of Regionalism*, Washington, DC: Center for Global Development, pp. 216–220.

Menem, C. (2000) 'Dollarization: A common currency for the Americas?', paper, Federal Reserve Bank of Dallas.

Merton, R. (1957) *Social Theory and Social Structure*, New York: Free Press.

Mesa-Lago, C. (1996) 'Pension system reforms in Latin America: The position of the international organizations', *Revista CEPAL*, 60: 73–98.

—— (2004) 'Experiences in the Americas with social security pensions and their reform: Lessons for workers and unions', *Social Protection: What Workers and Trade Unions should know, Labour Education*, 121 (April), ILO.

Mesa-Lago, C. and Muller, K. (2004) *La política de las reformas de pensión en América Latina después de dos décadas*, Caracas: Nueva Sociedad.

Millan, J. (1999) *Elementos estratégicos para el sector energía en América Latina y el Caribe*, Washington, DC: Inter-American Development Bank.

—— (2006) *Entre el mercado y el Estado: Tres décadas de reformas en el sector eléctrico de América Latina*, Washington, DC: Banco interamericano de Desarrollo.

Millan, J. and von der Fehr, N. (eds) (2003) *Keeping the Lights on: Power Sector Reform in Latin America*, Washington, DC: Inter-American Development Bank.

Millan, J., Lora, E. and Micco, A. (2001) 'Sustainability of the Electricity Sector Reforms in Latin America', paper prepared for the Seminar Toward Competitiveness: The Institutional Path, Annual Meetings of the Board of Governors, Inter-American Development Bank and Inter-American Investment Corporation, Santiago de Chile, 16 March.

Mistry, P. (1995) *Multilateral Development Banks*, FONDAD.

Morton, A. (2007) *Unravelling Gramsci: Hegemony and Passive Revolution in the Global Political Economy,* London: Pluto Press.

Murillo, V. (2001) 'Conviction versus necessity: Public utility Privatization in Argentina, Chile and Mexico', paper prepared for the 97th Annual Meeting of the American Political Science Association, San Francisco, 30 August–2 September.

—— (2002) 'Political bias in policy convergence: Privatization choices in Latin America', *World Politics*, 54 (July): 462–493.

Murillo, V. and Finchelstein, D. (2004) 'Privatización y poder de Mercado: el caso de la generación de energía eléctrica en la Argentina', *Desarrollo Económico*, 44 (173) (April–June): 131–144.

Murmis, M. and Portantiero, J. (1971) *Estudios sobre los orígenes del Peronismo*, Buenos Aires: Siglo XXI.

Murphy, C. and Tooze, R. (eds) (1991a) *The New International Political Economy*, Boulder, CO: Lynne Rienner.

—— (1991b) 'Introduction', in C. Murphy and R. Tooze (eds), *The New International Political Economy*, Boulder, CO: Lynne Rienner, pp. 1–7.

—— (1991c) 'Getting beyond the "common sense" of the IPE orthodoxy', in C. Murphy and R. Tooze (eds), *The New International Political Economy*, Boulder, CO: Lynne Rienner, pp. 11–31.

Murphy, R., Artana, D. and Navajas, F. (2003) 'La crisis económica argentina', in Artana, D. and Dorn, J. (eds) *Crisis financieras internacionales: Que rol le corresponde al gobierno?,* Buenos Aires: CATO Institute and FIEL.

Mussa, M. (2002) 'Argentina and the Fund: From triumph to tragedy', Working Paper, Washington, DC: Institute for International Economics.

Naim, M. (1999) 'Washington consensus or Washington confusion?', working draft of a paper prepared for the IMF Conference on Second Generation Reforms, Washington, DC.

Nef, L. (1994) 'The political economy of inter-American relations: A structural and historical overview', in R. Stubbs and G. Underhill (eds), *Political Economy and the Changing Global Order*, New York: Oxford University Press, pp. 404–418.

Nochteff, H. (1998) 'Neoconservadorismo y subdesarrollo. Una mirada a la economía Argentina', in H. Nochteff (ed.), *La Economía argentina a fin de siglo*, Buenos Aires: Eudeba.

—— (2001) *La experiencia argentina de los 90 desde el enfoque de la competitividad sistémica*, Flacso Área de Economía y Tecnología.

O'Brien, T. and Rother, L. (2004) 'The Pinochet money trial', *New York Times*, December.

Ocampo, J. (2000) 'Recasting the International Agenda', *CEPA Working Paper Series III*, no. 19.

—— (2002) 'Capital account, and counter-cyclical prudential regulations in developing countries', *WIDER Discussion Papers*, no. 2002/82, August.

O'Donnell, G. (1973) *Modernization and Bureaucratic-Authoritarianism: Studies in South America Politics*, Berkeley, CA: Institute for International Studies.

—— (1997) *Estado y alianzas en Argentina, 1956–1976, in Contrapunto: Ensayos escogidos sobre autoritarismo y democratización*, Buenos Aires: Paidós.

—— (2001) 'Comentarios', in E. Basualdo, *Modelo de Acumulación y Sistema Político en Argentina: Notas sobre el transformismo argentino durante la valorización financiera (1976–2001)*, Bernal, Argentina: Universidad Nacional de Quilmes, pp. 57–73.

Overbeek, H. (1993) *Restructuring Hegemony in the Global Political Economy: The Rise of Transnational Neo-Liberalism in the 1980s*, New York: Routledge.

Página 12, different articles available at http://www.pagina12.com.ar.

Palermo, V. (1994) 'El Menemismo, Perdurara?', in A. Iturrieta (ed.), *El Pensamiento Político Argentino Contemporáneo*, Buenos Aires: Grupo Editor Latinoamericano, pp. 309–345.

Palma, G. (1998) 'Three and a half cycles of "mania, panic, and [asymmetric] crash": East Asia and Latin America compared', *Cambridge Journal of Economics*, 22: 789–808.

Palumbo, A. and Scott, A. (2003) 'Weber, Durkheim and the sociology of the modern state', in T. Ball and R. Bellamy (eds), *The Cambridge History of Twentieth-Century Political Thought*, Cambridge: Cambridge University Press, pp. 368–391.

Payne, A. (1996) 'The United States and its enterprise for the Americas', in A. Gamble and A. Payne (eds), *Regionalism and World Order*, London: Macmillan, pp. 93–129.

—— (2000) 'Reframing the global politics of development', *Journal of International Relations and Development*, 2 (4): 369–379.

—— (2001) 'The global politics of development: Towards a new research agenda', *Progress in Development Studies*, 1 (1): 5–19.

—— (2004) *The New Regional Politics of Development*, New York: Palgrave.

—— (2005) *The Global Politics of Unequal Development*, London: Palgrave.

Payne, A. and Phillips, N. (2010) *Development*, Cambridge: Polity.

Phillips, N. (1999) 'Global and regional links', in J. Buxton and N. Phillips (eds), *Development in Latin American Political Economy: States, Markets and Actors*, Manchester: Manchester University Press, pp. 72–92.

Platt, D. (1985) 'Dependency and the historian: further objections', in C. Abel and C. Lewis (eds), *Latin America, Economic Imperialism and the State: The Political Economy of the External Connection from Independence to the Present*, London: Institute of Latin American Studies, University of London, pp. 29–39.

Polanyi, K. (1975) *The Great Transformation*, New York: Octagon.

—— (1977) 'The economistic fallacy', *Review (Fernand Braudel Center)*, 1 (1), (Summer): pp. 9–18.

Pollitt, M. (2004) 'Electricity reform in Argentina: Lessons for developing countries', *Cambridge Working Papers in Economics*, CM 52.

Portantiero, J. (1973) 'Clases dominantes y crisis política', *Pasado y Presente*, 1 (April–June).

—— (1989) 'Political and economic crises in Argentina', in G. Di Tella and R. Dornbusch (eds), *The Political Economy of Argentina, 1946–83*, London: Macmillan and Saint Antony's College, Oxford, pp. 16–26.

Pou, P. (2000) 'La reforma estructural Argentina en la década de 1990', *Finanzas y Desarrollo*, 37 (1): 13–15.

Poulantzas, N. (1975) *Classes in Contemporary Capitalism*, London: NLB.

Powell, W. and DiMaggio, W. (eds) (1991) *The New Institutionalism in Organizational Analysis*, Chicago: University of Chicago.

Prebisch, R. (1971) *Change and Development – Latin America's Great Task: Report Submitted to the Inter-American Development Bank*, New York: Praeger.

Quijano, J. (2004) 'La *cabaña* del tío Tom', Entrevista, *Pagina 12*, 21 August.

Radelet, S. and Sachs, J. (1988) 'The East Asian financial crisis: Diagnosis, remedies, prospects', paper prepared for the Brookings Panel, Washington, DC.

Ramos, J. (1983) *La Era del Peronismo: 1947–1976*, Buenos Aires: Ediciones del Mar Dulce.

Rapoport, M. (1988) 'El modelo agroexportador argentino', in M. Rapoport (ed.), *Economía e historia. Contribuciones a la historia económica argentina*, Buenos Aires: Tesis.

—— (2002) 'El plan de convertibilidad y la economía Argentina: 1991–1999', available at: http://www.historiared.com/Articles.

Rapoport, M. and Cervo, A. (eds) (2002) *El Cono Sur: Una historia común*, Buenos Aires: Fondo de Cultura Económica.

Rapoport, M. and Madrid, E. (2002) 'Los países del Cono Sur y las grandes potencias', in M. Rapoport and A. Cervo (eds), *El Cono Sur: Una historia común*, Buenos Aires: Fondo de Cultura Económica, pp. 225–280.

Ratha, D. (2001) 'Complementary between multilateral lending and private flows to developing countries', *Policy Research* Working Paper no. 2746, World Bank.

Repetto, F. and Alonso, G. (2004) 'La economía política de la política social argentina: una mirada desde la desregulación y la descentralización', *Series políticas sociales*, no. 97, CEPAL.

Rock, D. (1987) *Argentina, 1516–1987: From Spanish Colonization to the Falklands War and Alfonsin*, London: Tauris.

—— (2002) 'Racking Argentina', *New Left Review*, 17 (September-October): 56–86.

Rodriguez-Rozic, O. (1999) 'Antonio Ortiz-Mena: continuidad y cambio', in IDB Mas, *Que un Banco: Banco Interamericano de Desarrollo, 40 Anos*, Washington, DC: Banco interamericano de Desarrollo, pp. 59–129.

Rodrik, D. (1995) 'Why is there multilateral lending?' Working Paper no. 5160, National Bureau of Economic Research, June.

—— (1997) 'Has globalization gone too far?', mimeo, Washington, DC: Institute for International Economics.

—— (2002) 'Reform in Argentina, take two. Trade rout', *New Republic*, 2 January.

—— (2003) 'Argentina: A case of globalisation gone too far or not far enough?', in FONDAD, *The Crisis That Was Not Prevented: Argentina, the IMF, and Globalisation*, at http://www.fondad.org.

Rodrik, D. and Velazco, A. (1999) 'Short-term capital flows', paper prepared for the 1999 ABCDE Conference at the World Bank.

Rofman, R. (2004) 'The economic crisis in Argentina and its impacts on the pension system', Working Paper, IMF.

Rojas-Suarez, L. (2005) 'Domestic financial regulation in developing countries: Can they effectively limit the impact of capital account volatility?', Center for Global Development, Working Paper no. 59, May.

Ros, J. (2004) 'Latin America's unemployment experience in 1990', mimeo.

Rosenau, J. (1997) *Along the Domestic–Foreign Frontier: Exploring Governance in a Turbulent World*, Cambridge: Cambridge University Press.

Rostow, W. (1960) *The Stages of Economic Growth: a Non-Communist Manifesto*, London: Cambridge University Press.

Sachs, J. and Larrain, F. (1999) 'Why dollarization is more straitjacket than salvation', *Foreign Policy*, 116: 80–92.

Sagasti, F. (2002) 'La banca multilateral de desarrollo en América Latina', *Series Financiamiento del Desarrollo*, no. 119, Santiago de Chile: CEPAL Unidad de Estudios Especiales.

Sagasti, F. and Alcalde, G. (1999) *Development Cooperation in a Fractured Global Order: An Arduous Transition*, Ottawa: International Development Research Centre.

Sagasti, F., Bezanson, K. and Prada, F. (2001) *The Future of Development Financing: Challenges, Scenarios and Strategic Choices*, Institute of Development Studies (IDS), University of Sussex.

Sally, R. (2000) 'Developing country trade policy reform and the WTO', *CATO Journal*, 19 (3): 403–423.

Salomon Smith Barney (1998) *Private Pension Funds in Latin America: 1998 Update. Latin America Equity Research. Industry Report*, New York: Salomon Smith Barney.

—— (2001) *Private Pension Funds in Latin America: 2001 Update. Latin America Equity Research. Industry Report*, New York: Salomon Smith Barney.

Sánchez, A. (2006) 'América Latina y la búsqueda de un nuevo paradigma energético Mundial', *Nueva Sociedad*, July-August, pp. 39–49.

Scalabrini Ortiz, R. (1998) 'La Republica de Otaria, in Bases para la Reconstrucción Nacional, Tomo 2, Editorial Plus Ultra', at http://ar.geocities.com/raulscalabriniortiz/esc08.htm, accessed 27 January 2006.

Schamis, H. E. (1998) 'The politics of economic reform: Distributional Coalitions and policy change in Latin America', Working Paper no. 150, February, available at http://kellogg.nd.edu/publications/workingpapers/WPS/250.pdf.

Scheman, R. (1997) 'Banking on growth: The role of the Inter-American Development Bank', *Journal of Interamerican Studies and World Affairs*, Spring, available at http://www.jstor.org/journals/00221937.html.

Schuler, K. (2002) 'Fixing Argentina', *CATO Policy Analysis*, 445.

Schvarzer, J. (1998) *Implantación de un modelo económico. La experiencia argentina entre 1975 y el 2000*, Buenos Aires: Editora.

—— (2003) 'La crisis en Argentina: el fracaso historico de un sistema perverso', *European Review of Latin American and Caribbean Studies* (CIEDLA, Amsterdam), 74 (4): 85–92.

Schwartz, A. (1998) 'International financial crises: Myths and realities', *CATO Journal*, 17 (3).

Sinclair, T. (1996) 'Beyond international relations theory: Robert W. Cox and approaches to world order', in R. Cox and T. Sinclair, *Approaches to World Order*, Cambridge: Cambridge University Press, pp. 3–18.

Söderbaum, F. (2003) 'Introduction: Theories of new regionalism', in F. Söderbaum and T. Shaw (eds), *Theories of New Regionalism*, Houndmills: Palgrave Macmillan, pp. 1–21.

Söderbaum, F. and Shaw, T. (eds) (2003) Theories of New Regionalism. Houndmills: Palgrave Macmillan.

Stalling, B. (1992) 'International influence on economic policy: Debt, stabilization, and structural reform', in S. Haggard and R. Kaufman (eds), *The Politics of Economic Adjustment*, Princeton, NJ: Princeton University Press.

—— (ed.) (1997a) *Global Change, Regional Response: The New International Context of Development*, New York: Cambridge University Press.

—— (1997b) 'The new international context of development', in B. Stalling (ed.) *Global Change, Regional Response: The New International Context of Development*, New York: Cambridge University Press, pp. 349–387.

Stalling, B. and Streeck, W. (1997) 'Capitalism in conflict? The United States, Europe, and Japan in the post-cold war world', in B. Stalling (ed.), *Global Change, Regional Response: The New International Context of Development*, New York: Cambridge University Press, pp. 67–99.

Stiglitz, J. (2002) *Globalization and Its Discontents*, London: Penguin Books.

Strange, S. (1970) 'International economics and international relations: a case of mutual neglect', *International Affairs*, 46 (2), pp. 304–315.

—— (1971) 'Sterling and British policy: A political view', *International Affairs* 47 (2): 302–315.

—— (1982) 'Cave! Hic Dragons: A critique of regime analysis', *International Organization*, 36 (2): 479–496.

—— (1987) 'The persistent myth of lost hegemony', *International Organization*, 41 (4): 551–574.

—— (1988) *Estates and Markets*, 2nd edn, London: Pinter.

Stubbs, R. and Underhill, R. (eds) (2005) *Political Economy and the Changing Global Order*, 2nd edn, Toronto: Oxford University Press.

Swank, D. (2003) 'Withering welfare? Globalisation, political economic institutions, and contemporary welfare states', in L. Weiss (ed.), *States in the Global Economy: Bringing Domestic Institutions Back in*, New York: Cambridge University Press, pp. 58–82.

Szusterman, C. (1989) 'The "Revolución libertadora"', in G. Di Tella and R. Dornbusch (eds), *The Political Economy of Argentina, 1946–83*, London: Macmillan and Saint Antony's College, Oxford, pp. 89–103.

Taylor, I. (2001) 'Multilateralism, neo-liberalism and security in Asia: The role of the Asia Pacific Economic Co-operation Forum', Working Paper no. 19, Singapore: Institute of Defence and Strategic Studies, December.

—— (2005) 'Hegemony, neoliberal "good governance" and the International Monetary Fund', in M. Bøås and D. McNeill (eds), *Global Institutions and Development: Framing the world?*, New York: Routledge, pp. 124–136.

Taylor, L. (ed.) (2001) *External Liberalization, Economic Performance, and Social Policy*, New York: Oxford University Press.

——— (2004) *Reconstructing Macroeconomics: Structuralist Proposals and Critiques of the Mainstream*, Cambridge, MA: Harvard University Press.

Taylor, L. and Ros, R. (2000) *Balance of Payments Liberalization in Latin America: Effects on Growth, Distribution and Poverty*, New School University.

The Economist (2002) 'Argentina's crisis: Floating into the unknown', 7 February.

Thelen, K. (1999) 'Historical institutionalism in comparative politics', *Annual Review of Political Science*, 2.

Thompson, E. (1963) *The Making of the English Working Class*, London: Gollancz.

Thorp, R. (1985) 'Introduction', in C. Abel and C. Lewis (eds), *Latin America, Economic Imperialism and the State: The Political Economy of the External Connection from Independence to the Present*, London: Institute of Latin American Studies, University of London, pp. 397–404.

——— (ed.) (2000) *An Economic History of Twentieth-Century Latin America, Vol. 2: Latin America in the 1930s: The Role of the Periphery in World Crisis*, Houndmills: Palgrave.

Thorp, R., Ocampo, J. and Cardenas, E. (eds) (2000) *An Economic History of Twentieth-Century Latin America, Vol. 3: Industrialization and the State in Latin America*, Houndmills: Palgrave.

Titelman, D. (2002) 'Multilateral banking and development financing in a context of financial volatility', *Series Financing of Development*, no. 121, Special Studies Unit, Executive Secretariat Office, CEPAL.

Tomassini, L. (1999) 'La visión de Felipe Herrera: mas que un banco', in IDB Mas, *Que un Banco: Banco Interamericano de Desarrollo, 40 Anos*, Washington, DC: Banco interamericano de Desarrollo, pp. 1–58.

Torres, J. and Gerchunoff, P. (1999) 'La economía política de las reformas institucionales en Argentina. Los casos de la política de privatización de Entel, la reforma de la seguridad social y la reforma laboral', Working Paper R-349, Office of the Chief Economist, Inter-American Development Bank.

Tussie, D. (1994) 'Argentine case study', in S. Griffith-Jones, *Assessment of the IDB Lending Programme, 1979–92*, Brighton, Sussex: Institute of Development Studies, pp. 118–141.

——— (1995) *The Inter-American Development Bank*, in series The Multilateral Development Banks, Ottawa: North-South Institute.

——— (2003) 'Regionalism: Providing a substance to multilateralism?', in F. Söderbaum and T. Shaw (eds), *Theories of New Regionalism*, Houndmills: Palgrave Macmillan, pp. 99–116.

Underhill, G. (2000) 'State, market, and global political economy: Genealogy of an (inter?) discipline', *International Affairs*, 76: 805–824.

Underhill, G. and Zhang, X. (2001) 'Global structures and national imperatives: In search of normative underpinnings for international financial order', paper prepared for 'From Naples to Genoa: A New World of Finance and Development', Italian Treasury, Rome, 31 May–1 June.

UNDP (UN Development Programme) (2001) United Nations Human Development Report, http://www.imf.org/external/pubs/ft/seminar/1999/reforms/Naim.HTM, 26 April.

Uthoff, A. (2006) 'Bienestar y reformas a los sistemas de pensiones en América Latina', *Revista de la CEPAL*, no. 89, August, pp. 9–29.

Vaca, A. and Cao, H. (2001) 'Gasto publico. Es la solución un ajuste en la administración publica nacional?', *Revista Realidad Económica* (Buenos Aires), 180 (May-June): 33–39.

van der Pijl, K. (1993) 'Soviet Socialism and passive revolution', in S. Gill (ed.) *Gramsci, Historical Materialism and International Relations,* New York: Cambridge University Press, pp. 237–258.

Varas, A. (1992) 'From coercion to partnership: A new paradigm for security in the Western hemisphere?', in H. Schoultz and A. Varas (eds), *The United States and Latin America in the 1990s,* London and Chapel Hill: University of North Carolina Press, pp. 46–65.

—— (1995) 'Latin America: Toward a new reliance on the market', in B. Stalling (ed.), *Global Change, Regional Response: The new international context of development,* New York: Cambridge University Press, pp. 273–308.

Vásquez, I. (2003) 'Reparación de la relación acreedor-deudor en el mercado financiero International', in D. Artana and J. Dorn (eds), *Crisis financieras internacionales: Que rol le corresponde al gobierno,* Argentina: CATO Institute.

Verbitsky, H. (1993a) De eso no se habla, *Pagina 12,* 5 December.

—— (1993b) *Hacer la Corte. La construcción de un poder absoluto sin justicia ni control,* Buenos Aires: Planeta.

—— (2003) 'Los primeros dos meses de Kirchner', *Pagina 12,* 27 July, available at http://www.pagina12.com.ar.

Villanueva, J. (1972) 'El origen de la industrialización argentina', *Desarrollo Económico,* 12 (47), Buenos Aires: Institución de Desarrollo Económico y Social.

Vitelli, G. (2001) 'Los Resultados de la Convertibilidad', *Realidad Económica,* 181 (August), IADE, Buenos Aires.

Volcker Report: 'Findings commission on the role of the MDBs in emerging markets: The role of the multilateral development banks in emerging market economies', Jose Angel Gurria and Paul Volcker, Carnegie Endowment for International Peace; EMP Financial Advisors, LLC, The Inter-American Dialogue, available at http://www.thedialogue.org.

Wallerstein, I. (1979) *The Capitalist World Economy,* Cambridge: Cambridge University Press.

—— (1993) *Historical Capitalism,* London: Verso.

Walter, A. (2002) 'Understanding financial globalisation', paper for the Institute of Defense and Strategic Studies, Singapore.

Waltz, K. (1979) *Theory of International Politics.* New York: McGraw Hill.

Weaver, F. (2000) *Latin America in the World Economy: Mercantile Colonialism to GlobalCapitalism,* Boulder, CO: Westview Press.

Weisbrot, M. and Baker, D. (2002) 'What happened to Argentina?' *Briefing Papers,*Washington, DC: Center for Economic and Policy Research.

Weiss, L. (2003a) 'Is the state being "transformed" by globalisation?', in L. Weiss (ed.), *States in the Global Economy: Bringing Domestic Institutions Back in,* Cambridge: Cambridge University Press, pp. 293–317.

—— (ed.) (2003b) *States in the Global Economy: Bringing Domestic Institutions Back in,* Cambridge: Cambridge University Press.

Welch, C. and Oringer, J. (1998) 'Structural adjustment programs', *Infocus Foreign Policy,* 2 (3), April.

Williamson, J. (2000) 'What should the World Bank think about the Washington Consensus', *The World Bank Research Observer,* 15 (2) (August): 251–264.

—— (2004) 'The Washington consensus as policy prescription for development', Practitioners in Development Lecture, World Bank, 13 January, available at http://www.worldbank.org/.

Willis, E., Garman, C. and Haggard, S. (1999) 'Decentralization in Latin America', *Latin American Review*, 34 (1): 7–56.

Wood, A. (1997) 'The IMF's final frontier? Assessing "second generation" reforms', Bretton Woods Project, June.

World Bank (1993) *Argentina's Privatization Program: Experience, Issues, and Lessons*, Washington, DC: World Bank.

—— (1998) Global development finance, Washington DC.: World Bank.

Wyplosz, C. (1999) 'International financial instability', in I. Kaul, I. Grunberg and M. Stern (eds), *Global Public Goods: International Cooperation in the 21st Century*, New York: United Nations Development Programme, pp. 152–189.

Yeager, L. (2001) 'How to avoid international financial crises', *CATO Journal*, 17 (3).

Yeates, N. (2005) '"Globalization" and social policy in a development context: regional responses', Social Policy and Development Programme, UNRISD, Paper no. 18, April.

Yermo, J. (2000) 'Pension funds in Latin America: Recent trends and regulatory challenges', in *Insurance and Private Pensions Compendium for Emerging Economies*, Book 2, Par 2:2.

Index

Note: page numbers in **bold** refer to illustrations